COHERENT VARIETY

Recent Titles in Contributions in Political Science
Series Editor: Bernard K. Johnpoll

Governor Rockefeller in New York: The Apex of Pragmatic Liberalism in the United States
James E. Underwood and William J. Daniels

Neo-Marxism: The Meanings of Modern Radicalism
Robert A. Gorman

The Politics of Pressure: American Arms and Israeli Policy Since the Six Day War
David Pollock

Congress, the Executive Branch, and Special Interests: The American Response to the Arab Boycott of Israel
Kennan Lee Teslik

Third World Policies of Industrialized Nations
Phillip Taylor and Gregory A. Raymond, editors

"For Immediate Release": Candidate Press Releases in American Political Campaigns
Jan Pons Vermeer

The Vice President as Policy Maker: Rockefeller in the Ford White House
Michael Turner

A Contemporary Crisis: Political Hostage-Taking and the Experience of Western Europe
Clive C. Aston

Socialism of a Different Kind: Reshaping the Left in France
Bernard E. Brown

Aging and Public Policy: The Politics of Growing Old in America
Edited by William P. Browne and Laura Katz Olson

Influence, Change, and the Legislative Process
Janet Miller Grenzke

COHERENT VARIETY

The Idea of Diversity in British and American Conservative Thought

MICHAEL D. CLARK

CONTRIBUTIONS IN POLITICAL SCIENCE, NUMBER 86

GREENWOOD PRESS
WESTPORT, CONNECTICUT • LONDON, ENGLAND

Library of Congress Cataloging in Publication Data

Clark, Michael D. (Michael Dorsey), 1937-
  Coherent variety.

  (Contributions in political science, ISSN 0147-1066:
no. 86)
  Bibliography: p.
  Includes index.
  1. Pluralism. 2. Difference (Philosophy) 3. Con-
servatism—Great Britain.   4. Conservatism—United
States.   I. Title.   II. Series.
BD394.C57 1983   320'.01'1   82-9228
ISBN 0-313-23284-9 (lib. bdg.)   AACR2

Library of Congress Catalog Card Number: 82-9228
ISBN: 0-313-23284-9
ISSN: 0147-1066

First published in 1983

Greenwood Press
A division of Congressional Information Service, Inc.
88 Post Road West
Westport, Connecticut 06881

Printed in the United States of America

10 9 8 7 6 5 4 3 2 1

For my parents,
Helen Gambrill Clark
and
Louis Dorsey Clark

Contents

Acknowledgments   ix

   Introduction   3

Part One: The Conservative Stake in a Diverse World   19

  1. "Abundant Virtue": The Religious Vision   21

  2. Tradition and the Dimension of Time   36

  3. G. K. Chesterton and the Scale of Existence   51

Part Two: British and American Patterns   61

  4. Law, Science, Romance   63

  5. The "English Garden of Politics"   85

  6. Federalism and Diversity in the United States   104

  7. Southern Demons   125

Part Three: Conservatism, Diversity, and Modernity   139

  8. Several Turn-of-the Century Voices   141

  9. The Specter of Uniformity   159

 10. Modern Multiplicity and Diverse Conservatism   177

11. Conservatives and Others   195
    Conclusion   208
Selected Bibliography   215
Index   223

Acknowledgments

I am indebted to many for their help in the writing of this book. The University of New Orleans granted me the leave during which I did much of the basic work on it. Members of the staff of the Earl K. Long Library provided assistance in obtaining materials. Dr. Thomas Schlunz and other colleagues in the History Department at U.N.O. offered useful comments and suggestions. Mrs. Darlene Clark as departmental secretary typed the preliminary draft of my manuscript.

A brief early version of this study was published as an article in *Modern Age.** I am grateful particularly to that publication's editor, Dr. David S. Collier, for his advice and encouragement.

I am especially indebted to my wife, Mary Dugan Clark, who worked long and hard to prepare the final copy of this work for publication. Thomas and Laura Clark have lent to the enterprise that note of confidence which comes best from the younger members of the partnership of generations.

M.D.C.

*Michael D. Clark, "The Idea of Diversity in Conservative Thought," *Modern Age* 22 (Fall 1978): 358-370.

COHERENT VARIETY

Introduction

The modern world offers, in many respects, a spectacle of extraordinary diversity. Technological complexity, the proliferation and specialization of occupations, the enormous variety of manufactured products available in advanced capitalist nations, the range of accessible amusements and diversions—all contribute to the impression of a world diverse as never before. If Herbert Spencer and John Fiske charted the course of civilization toward "definite coherent heterogeneity," then surely, it seems, they were right at least about the heterogeneity. Granted that mass production has necessarily standardized certain aspects of economic life, has not this been more than offset by the greater range of choices open to the individual, and above all by the array of *ideas*—ethical and aesthetical, physical and metaphysical—which solicit his attention from the crowded paperback shelves of bookstores and the increasingly thick catalogues of the universities? The modern world is nothing, it seems, if not a world of variety.

Yet the idea has been abroad in the West, for perhaps two hundred years, that precisely the opposite is the case. Apparent in Edmund Burke's animadversions upon the French Revolution, assuming something like definitive shape in Alexis de Tocqueville's *Democracy in America* almost half a century later, and elaborated by a multitude of critics and commentators since, is the theme that modernity means uniformity, leveling, and standardization: that we grow more alike, and that the pleasing and interesting differences of traditional life are fated to shrink, and perhaps altogether to disappear. Contemporary observers lament that regional custom succumbs to the euthanasia of the automobile, the supermarket, and the television, or in certain parts of the world is reduced to a rearguard action as Scottish, Quebecois, or Basque nationalism. Prevailing secular creeds seem to push for a world uniformly metric, classless, and unisex. Even the very complexity of a technically advanced civilization has appeared to some to present only a final bland face of sameness. Thus Henry Adams described the modern world precisely in the two terms of multiplicity and monotone—or more dramatically, of chaos and entropy.

Of course Adams was a notorious prophet of doom, and the invocation of his name will raise doubts in some minds about the seriousness of this modern specter of uniformity. Is this merely one of those fashionable and perennial notions with which those of sufficient leisure worry themselves? Does it arise perhaps from upper-class dismay at assaults on privilege and the attendant damage to the colorful plumage of an aristocratic society, lodging among the unexamined critical stock of elitist-minded intellectuals? Is the plea for diversity, that is to say, simply a disguised attack on equality? Or, more subtly, is the modern impression of uniformity a kind of historical illusion? We think of the past in terms of discrete and diverse orders and events: the Middle Ages become a pageant of ranks and corporations, of stained glass and Crusades, popes and kings. Surely to the peasant, at least, ordinary life was not this at all, but a monotony as unrelieved as that of any twentieth-century assembly line. The growing historical consciousness of modern man, from a similar stance, would feed an appetite for novelty, for *making history,* for perceiving significance and contrast in a way that the daily routine cannot satisfy. Or perhaps this yearning is only a symptom of the jaded and restless modern temperament, seduced early by the Romantic spirit to demand intense and extreme experience, and kept in a state of perpetual excitement subsequently by the accelerated pace of technological change and by communications which make any sensation instantaneously accessible to anyone within the range of radio or television. Not even these media, it would follow, can sate the appetite for novelty thus aroused;

as with the drug addict, larger doses are required as the accustomed becomes tame.

Although I think overdrawn, this last argument has at least the merit of suggesting the distinction between diversity objectively considered and diversity subjectively perceived. An objective view, if such is possible, would surely confirm that the world becomes both more uniform and more diverse: that certain possibilities multiply while others are cut off, and that a more standardized mode of existence is the very product of those innovations which make it possible to do different things and live in different ways. Perhaps the apparent paradox could be unraveled. Emile Durkheim argued, for example, that the lessening of collective diversity in modern times—as between regions, nations, and classes—was compensated for by the increase of individual diversity,[1] and this analysis has been echoed by a number of later commentators.

The objective aspect of the problem, however, seems the less important. The world has always offered a host of variegated phenomena to those prepared to mark them. In the more decisive sense, diversity is a matter of psychology. A garden containing several different kinds of flowers may give a stronger impression of diversity than the boardwalk at a garish seaside resort, lined with every possible amusement and souvenir. The few necessities of an old-fashioned farmhouse may suggest a more interesting variety than its appliance-stocked suburban counterpart. What counts in such cases is not the quantity of different articles, or even the measurable variations among them, but the perception of discrete qualities or objects of definite value and relationship, in such numbers as the mind can readily grasp. Sheer multiplicity overwhelms; it comes in time to seem mere cacophony, and finally chaos, that undifferentiated whirl which was supposed to antedate history, and not to be its dizzying culmination.

This is not to say that diversity is all in the mind, for the configurations of the physical and social environment, as well as the ideas and beliefs which the mind entertains, will sway one's perception of it. The significance of the many critiques of modern "uniformity" lies in the light they shed on both the inner and the external world, and especially in the evidence they offer as to why unprecedented complexity of life should leave for so many so bland a taste of sameness, why "progress," "liberation," and "personal fulfillment" should so often end in ennui.

The conservative answer to this question, as we shall see, has been found largely in the loss of a moral and intellectual order sufficient persuasively to establish place and value in life—to define the standards and rules by which diversity is measured. Without such rules, on the artificial scale of play, the diversity of the pieces in the game of chess is trivialized to that between bits of wood or ivory of differing size and shape. To add, still in the absence of rules, fifteen new pieces to the game, each of different configuration, would not add to one's impression of diversity, but on the contrary, simply enlarge a collection of random figures. The real diversity of the pieces arises from their variety of clearly defined powers of movement. Life is not a game, but as Johan Huizinga pointed out, it has gamelike aspects and involves an analogous consciousness of rule and standard. The conditions of modernity, of course, have worked against clear and differentiated assessments of value. The relatively definite and coherent social hierarchy of traditional life has long since given way to the uncertainties of class and competition in democratic, industrial society. More decisive has been the erosion of clear moral standards and of any generally accepted hierarchy of values. The point here is not to join the chorus of lamentation for such issue of a decadent civilization, but to note its effect on the sense of diversity. According to a long line of conservative thinkers, the effect has been to attenuate the sense of difference and distinction. Obvious and great social and economic differences may persist, but they are decreasingly viewed as necessary to a diverse social order; rather they seem the product of injustice or merely accidental: in either case illegitimate. The blurring of moral distinctions tends to make one course of conduct, within broad limits, seem as good as another. Traditional canons of loyalty and duty were very far from being consistently observed. But they did draw reasonably clear distinctions and thus preserve, even in their violation, a sense of genuine diversity in human behavior—a diversity which mattered morally, rather than being simply a trivial matter of personal taste or self-expression. Where nothing much matters, distinctions are superfluous.

Any set of rules, any value-setting scheme, represents of course a principle of unity. Ideally, *one* code, *one* scale of values governs.

The tendency of conservative thought, therefore, has been to conclude that authentic diversity depends precisely on unity. The two are mutually dependent. Any principle of unity must encompass the actual variety of experience, else it is no true unity. Without the unifying principle, on the other hand, diversity collapses into mere randomness. Henry Adams was more than half right, it may be, in thinking that the loss of the unity offered by the Christian faith entailed the weakening intensity of felt experience in all areas of life, and that twentieth-century multiplicity inclined toward entropy, the ultimate sameness.

Conservative diagnoses of this modern malaise rest, as this study will attempt to show, on a substantial tradition of thought which, over the last two hundred years or more, has concerned itself with what its exemplars have viewed as pervasive threats to a properly diversified social order, and, indeed, to a properly diversified cosmos. Conservatism as a modern, self-conscious school of political philosophy is generally conceded to have taken its rise from the period of the French Revolution, although its roots lie far deeper. If the revolution be regarded as our initial landmark, we find modern conservatism at its very inception confronting the prospect of uniformity. Edmund Burke's complaint that the revolutionaries were attempting to "confound all sorts of citizens . . . into one homogeneous mass,"[2] reverberated in many later conservative indictments of radicals who in the name of freedom created national states of such weight as to crush the diverse environments in which freedom could flourish. Accompanying the protest against the reduction of society to detached individuals in the social mass has been another against the reduction of a variegated Creation to atoms-and-the-void, or whatever fashionable determinism stands at a given moment in its stead. Conservatism at its best has sought to marshal the riches of experience against the poverty of ideological and theoretical monomania.

This aspect of conservative thought is apparent enough to anyone who does much reading among Burke and his successors of the last two centuries, and has been noted by some historians of the school. Russell Kirk, for example, listed as one of his "six canons of conservative thought": "affection for the proliferating variety and mystery of traditional life, as distinguished from the narrowing uniformity and equalitarianism and utilitarian aims of most radical systems,''[3] and he has enlarged on the theme elsewhere. Nevertheless, this "canon" has remained relatively inconspicuous. Asked what basic ideas he associates with conservatism, the average educated person might suggest authority, tradition, resistance to innovation; he would surely be far less likely to suggest a devotion to diversity.

There are clear reasons for this. Diversity seems, in the first place, ill to comport with other conservative values. Allegiance to authority and tradition suggests, as readily as superficially, an uncomplicated ideal of unity. Diversity, on the other hand, suggests presumably liberal values: freedom, toleration, and openness to experimentation and change. Such associations obscure an entire facet of conservative sensibility. Secondly, it must be acknowledged that conservatism is compromised by its own checkered history. Heirs of a body of thought deeply committed to those arrangements which make for a diverse social order, conservatives have not always remained true to this program. They have frequently been tempted to the support of overweening national power, especially in Europe, but also in the United States when it seemed to serve internal security or economic convenience. Especially in the United States, conservatives have also often gone to what is superficially the opposite extreme of championing an almost unlimited "individualism," with little heed to the sorts of social groupings which nurture liberty, diversity, and mature individuality alike. A conservatism distorted in the direction of mass regimentation or in that of social atomism has little affinity with the idea of diversity.

Yet, as with apparent paradox, individual "liberation" and the power of government, disorder and standardization, have grown apace, there has been a kindling recognition that the most tolerable solutions to social problems define themselves by neither the atom nor the mass. And in an age when liberals have very largely thrown their weight on the side of the concentration and centralization of power, and of the efforts of bureaucracy to achieve standardization and uniformity in national life, it may be that the aspect of conservative thought which gives support to diversity has become its most distinctive and constructive aspect. The proper contribution of the conservative spirit, I believe, is to keep alive in human life those ideas and qualities of permanent value which successive generations have accumulated, and, more, to make accessible to the present the rich diversity of past experience. An imposed or evolved uniformity can only impoverish that society which should attain it, not more in its inheritance than in the resources with which it can contend with the future.

Diversity in the simplest definition means variety: a multiplicity of different creatures, qualities, or objects. Considered as a conservative value, it connotes as well, however, a felicitous relationship among the entities concerned, rather than mere unlikeness or detachment. The relationship must be to a degree harmonious, although "harmony" is an inadequate term to convey the conservative insistence on private, unregulated, and frequently competitive spheres of life. The ancillary term "plenitude" suggests the fullness and abundance with which the quality of diversity has usually been associated, in contrast to the barrenness of unrelieved homogeneity. The antithesis of diversity, strictly speaking, is not unity but uniformity. "Unity" may consist in a joining of entities which retain their different qualities (as in the concept of "unity-in-diversity"); "uniformity" clearly means sameness. In practice, however, those who have dealt with the issues under discussion have employed both terms in opposition to diversity, and usage must therefore depend largely on context.

Under the abstract general definition, several primary kinds of diversity, relevant to the problem at hand, can be discerned. There is first what we may term "cosmic" diversity, the diversity of the natural world. Men have long drawn inspiration from the multifariousness of nature, have identified it with the greatness of its Creator, and until recently, at least, have perceived in it an analogue to the diversity of society. Second, to jump from the primal to the most characteristically modern, we can isolate as a type the diversity of individuals. This constitutes the essentially liberal ideal of a society of men and women unconstrained by customary or arbitrary authority, and free to express themselves, so long as they do not injure others, as they will. Modern liberals have generally supposed that a society of healthy individual diversities will follow as a natural consequence of such freedom. Yet conservatives, at least of the traditionalist school, have been inclined to doubt that much real diversity can be sustained on a purely individual basis.

A society characterized only by individual freedom, they have felt, would be atomistic rather than diverse, with little sustenance for a more than trivial diversity among the social atoms. While not necessarily denigrating individual diversity, therefore, conservatives have argued that it must be supported by a third basic type: the diversity of groups—of nationalities, states, regions, communities, orders, ranks, corporate bodies, families. Such groupings, in this view, nurture individuality even while they shape it; at the same time, they serve as barriers against the pressures for uniformity emanating from central authority.

We must now attempt to relate "diversity" to certain other terms, more explicitly to "freedom," in particular, and to "equality." Freedom, in a sense, is a procedural quality, whereas diversity is substantive. A certain minimum of freedom is necessary for diversity to exist. But freedom does not logically guarantee diversity, and even in practice does not foster it in any direct proportion. Unless cultural pressures for conformity are overwhelming, certainly, a formal freedom to differ will result in some degree of difference. But in a day when personal liberation and freedom from social constraint (in other than the economic sphere) are touted as the way to happiness and "fulfillment," even as life becomes in many respects more uniform, the distinction between freedom and diversity becomes a crucial one. Largely complementary, the two qualities may in some situations be independent, or even opposed. To be brought into their proper relationship, in the conservative view, freedom and diversity require order, rules, and delimitations. Each, to have much meaning, requires the other.

Equality is complementary to diversity only in a more limited way. Logically the terms are entirely compatible. Apples and oranges can be different without being unequal, as can black and white people, and men and women—a point that would be too obvious to need stating were it not so often lost sight of. The relationship can be more positive. Equality before the law, and certain applications of that tricky formulation "equality of opportunity," may help a diversified society to flourish. But beyond these levels, conflict is apt to arise. This is particularly the case where the effort to ensure equality of rights or of opportunity graduates into an effort to secure equality of condition. A society composed of individuals of equal wealth, power, and status is unlikely to be a diverse society. Class differences have such pervasive effect on manners, values, and outlook that to eliminate them, assuming this to be possible, would be to cut off a taproot of social variety. This is not to justify all diversities or inequalities of condition. But the tendency of conservative thought in Great Britain and America has been to conceive of diversity as a primary social good, to be balanced against other goods. To the often-noted antithesis of liberty and equality, diversity adds a third factor, which properly mediates between the other two. Where the principle of equality works to impose uniformity, a perceived need for diversity reinforces the claims of liberty. Where a too narrowly conceived liberty operates to bury manifold individual and local possibilities in an unrestrained competitive struggle, on the other hand, the requirements of diversity give weight to the assumption of an equal natural dignity among human beings.

Unfortunately, efforts to secure a greater measure of justice have lately tended to minimize or denigrate legitimate diversities. Where differences are acknowledged, as between ethnic groups or the sexes, it is often with the reassurance that they are really of no account. (In a less bland and timid society, they might be considered as not only of account, but of positive and precious value.) Thus the fashionable term "pluralism" seems now to imply not only equality, but indifference—a condition that ends up not being very pluralistic at all. For this reason, despite the honorable associations of "pluralism" with William James and others, I have chosen in preference to it the term "diversity," which suggests elements of comity and genuine distinction far more in keeping with the tenor of conservative thought.

Conservatism, no less than other broad social and political philosophies, must grapple with the tangled counterpoint of unity and multiplicity. The riddle of the One and the Many constitutes as inescapably perennial a polarity in human thought as there can be. It is not so much a problem to be solved as the expression of complementary aspects of human perception of reality. Philosophical and religious formulations must take both sides of experience into account, if only to deny the "ultimate reality" of one or the other.

The mainstream of Western thought has denied the reality of neither unity nor multiplicity, although radical monisms and, to a much lesser extent, radical pluralisms, have flourished at the fringes. In general, the bias of the Western mind has been toward unity. Polytheism was supplanted by the great monotheistic systems, thus placing on the principle of unity the stamp of deity. The Platonic and Neoplatonic schools of thought most prominently showed a yearning for a transcendent and eternal unity which strongly tinctured subsequent religious and philosophical conceptions.[4]

There have always been, of course, countervailing tendencies. If God was One, He was also, for Christians, Three, and His companies of angels and saints assuaged the believer's need for multiple approaches to the Godhead. Furthermore, God was believed to express His greatness through the plenitude and diversity of His creation—a fecundity long schematized as the "Great Chain of Being." Scientific thought was dominated for centuries by the Aristotelian world of qualities and correspondences, which emphasized as much the diversity as the unity of nature. This diverse cosmos was supplanted in the seventeenth century by the mechanical scheme of Galileo and others, describing a world of atoms in motion from which all "secondary qualities" were banished to the limbo of the subjective. But scientific monism was offset—compensated for, perhaps—by a new aesthetic, arising in early modern times and reaching its apogee in the Romantic Movement, which took deliberate delight in diversity. Never, after the Romantics, could uniformity enjoy such unquestioned aesthetic appeal as it once had had, when mountains were considered blemishes upon the originally smooth surface of the earth.

Delight in diversity, as the Romantic consciousness indicated, draws sustenance from levels of temperament, emotion, and memory perhaps as profound as those which issue in the ordering, unifying drive of the intellect. If the adult feels nostalgia for the safe wholeness of infancy, there is nostalgia too for the fresh joy of discovery in differentiation. The child learns to distinguish himself from his environment, from mother and father; he learns to distinguish between increasingly refined categories and becomes acquainted with an ever-increasing variety of objects, qualities, and ideas. Adam naming the animals furnishes an obvious analogue to this normal process, representing in highly compressed form the long childhood experience of the race. The child's sense of the sharp contrasts of the world can take on the fairy-tale lineaments of fearsome monsters and valiant heroes. Yet even in the daylight world, the objects of perception—the house, the streetcar, the oak tree—have the vivid and portentous quality of the freshly seen. Later experience almost inevitably brings a sad fading of this "splendour in the objects of sense," as Wordsworth called it.[5] To reconstitute it more than fleetingly on an adult level requires heavy resources of faith and imagination—those of the artist or the saint. But in at least two ways the lengthening experience of life should keep alive the feeling for diversity. The spirit of play which Huizinga found to be a perennial element of civilization is inseparable from a delight in "variation," whether manifested in sartorial fashions, the high reaches of art and philosophy, or sport itself.[6] And the process of maturation should continue to refine the intellectual grasp of diversities, sharpening one's ability to draw and define distinctions.

Such considerations help suggest answers to a larger question: Why, after all, should diversity be accounted one of the world's goods? From a conservative point of view, it must be underscored, it is so only in relation to other goods. Conservatives have emphatically refused to embrace diversity for diversity's sake. None would question that particular diversities—such as those established by systems of caste or slavery—may be utterly pernicious. Within the bounds set by this qualification, the reasons for the conservative esteem of diversity should emerge in the course of this study; a few points, however, might tentatively be suggested at the outset.

It is not merely sentimental, first, to suggest that diversity makes life more interesting. And surely the society with clear distinctions of value and a wide range of possibilities surpasses in interest and vitality the society in which such diversities are lacking, as a game of chess surpasses in fascination a game of checkers. Society need not comprise a hierarchy from pawn to king. But traditional or other forms and distinctions seem to bring to life at large what explicit play provides in microcosm: a counterpoint of order and variety which gives meaning and absorbs energies and talents. Second, in rough analogy to the principle of natural selection, it can be argued that diversity is essential to a high level of creativity:

that without the existence of different social groups experimenting along different lines, human possibilities are limited and human development in consequence is apt to be stultified. Third—an argument suggested by Robert Nozick[7]—if we grant that individual preferences will and ought to persist, it follows that no society lacking in significant differences between goups, no matter how thoroughly libertarian and egalitarian, can possibly offer the range of choices to satisfy such preferences. Equality of opportunity means little where there is no diversity of opportunity.

Above all, conservatives have historically contended that diversity, whether perceived in society or in the natural world, is to be cherished as a reality principle, even a basis of sanity. As G. K. Chesterton pointed out, it is the madman who is the prisoner of one idea.[8] The conservative feeling has been that any doctrine or course of action which slights the rich and various accretion of human experience, or seeks to subordinate this experience to a vision of future perfection, represents an insane and dangerous simplicity. On another plane, conservatives have associated diversity with the actual fullness and creativity that dwells in the universe, agreeing again with Chesterton that "the highest thing does not tend to union only; the highest thing tends also to differentiation."[9] Chesterton cited the Trinity as the supreme expression of this maxim; it could apply as well to the "Great Chain of Being." Formulations have varied. But to cherish the coherent variety of the world, according to a venerable line of conservative thought, is incomparably more generous in spirit, and more alive to manifold actuality, than the opposite urge to uniformity and standardization.

The limitation of this study to British and American conservatism does not imply the irrelevance of conservative (and much nonconservative) thought elsewhere, especially on the European continent. Figures like the Baron de Montesquieu, Joseph de Maistre, and Wilhelm von Humboldt defended the diversity of the world in ways often quite similar to those of their counterparts across the Atlantic and the English Channel. Indeed, I have made use of Continental figures where they can most effectively represent common conservative themes, and especially when, as with Alexis de Tocqueville, they were influential in the English-speaking countries. My grouping together of British and American traditions, on the other hand, does not imply their identity; on the contrary, their historical differences illuminate certain aspects of the subject. British and American conservatives have alike tended toward an empiricism which sets them somewhat apart from the "rationalist" conservatives more heavily represented on the Continent, however. The empirical approach, as Robert Schuettinger points out, has inclined the British and Americans more wholeheartedly to the defense of liberty and diversity.[10]

Within its appointed geographical scope, this is intended as a study of the idea of diversity in relation to conservative thought. It is not of course maintained that conservatism is entirely defined by the defense of diversity, or that diversity has not been at times strongly defended by liberals or radicals. Certainly it is not contended that conservatives have always been on the side of diversity; there have always been strong countercurrents within the (itself very diverse) body of conservative thought. It is contended that the defense of diversity is an important element within the conservative tradition.

But what is the "conservative tradition"? The problem of definition must plague anyone who tries to write seriously about conservatives—or liberals. Distinctions that intuitively seem obvious become less so under close analysis, as an apparently keen edge is reduced to raggedness under the microscope. Even if we are content not to peer too closely, the problem is complicated by the existence of a number of different schools of conservative thought, including the Burkean or traditionalist, the libertarian and free-market varieties, and an American probusiness type not completely in accord with any of the others.

I shall explore later some of the differences among conservatives as they relate to the idea of diversity. It may be helpful here, however, to say something of the distinctions between conservatives and liberals. Those of most fundamental importance for Britain and America were articulated in the generation of Edmund Burke and Thomas Paine: conservatives relying more on experience and tradition in social and political matters, friendly to the just exercise of public and private authority, and believing in the cohesion of society and of social groups, not only in the present, but through the course of time; liberals more eager to rationalize politics, allowing a greater degree of individual autonomy, and more comfortable with Paine's notion of the sovereignty of each generation, unbeholden to the past. With traditionalists and libertarians now at odds over such questions as the draft, censorship, and legalization of marijuana, clearly eighteenth- and nineteenth-century distinctions no longer so neatly separate "conservatives" from "liberals." Yet not all the lines are so blurred. Contemporary conservatives join in opposition to most of the centralizing and collectivizing policies of the national state. It is probably safe to say that conservatives of all types now give greater weight to the rights of private property than do their opponents, and are correspondingly more suspicious of the public regulation of economic relationships. (Even here, we must assume that the conservative businessman who favors that governmental regulation in which he perceives an advantage to himself is "rising above principle," not acting on it.) Let us reserve for later consideration the suggestion that attitudes toward diversity provide another test.

In all, the "conservative tradition" is a rambling thing, more like a house to which rooms and wings have been added haphazardly by successive generations than a mansion built by blueprint. This is entirely appropriate for a school of thought which disdains the obsessively rational. But it also makes it difficult to find a point of unity. If there is one, it is probably psychological—involving perhaps a temperamental preference in human affairs for the private, the nonuniversal, the idiosyncratically diverse. The lack of more precise canons, however, renders the conventional labels very inadequate, especially when one seeks to apply them across decades and centuries. One may join a Conservative or a Liberal Party, where such exist, but conservatism and liberalism themselves are not parties or clubs. They are patterns of thought shared in varying proportions by all individuals, who to complicate matters further are apt to appear quite different to posterity than they did to themselves or their contemporaries. The eighteenth century was hardly conscious of the liberal-conservative scale which we assume. In the nineteenth, thinkers like Tocqueville and Acton, who appear conservative from the present vantage point, were apt to think of themselves as liberals. My intention has been simply to draw on figures who are relevant in a positive way to the past and present concerns of conservative thought, a criterion which has permitted me even to cite, in certain aspects of his thinking, William James, whom no one would label a conservative. Although this procedure may strike some as insufficiently exclusive, I am persuaded that the currents which nurture conservative thinking are too widely and deeply abroad for a useful discussion of the subject to be limited to those whose conservatism might be certified as pure.

At the same time, this study makes no pretense of all-inclusiveness on what is, after all, a very broad subject. It will be enough if it can establish the historical legitimacy of the conservative espousal of diversity and pursue some of its more important implications. Intended as an essay in intellectual history, it cannot claim to be entirely dispassionate; it is only hoped that the author's analysis of and general sympathy for the aspect of conservatism described will fairly inform each other.

NOTES

1. Emile Durkheim, *The Division of Labor in Society,* trans. George Simpson (New York: Macmillan Co., 1933), 135-138.

2. Edmund Burke, "Reflections on the Revolution in France," *The Works of the Right Honourable Edmund Burke* (London: George Bell & Sons, 1892), II, 455.

3. Russell Kirk, *The Conservative Mind* (Chicago: Henry Regnery, 1960), 7.

4. On the superior attraction of unity to western mystics and rationalists alike, see Robert A. Nisbet, *The Quest for Community* (New York: Oxford University Press, 1953), 172.

5. Ernest de Selincourt, ed., *The Letters of William and Dorothy Wordsworth* (Oxford: Clarendon Press, 1970), II, 189 (Wordsworth to Catherine Clarkson, January 1815).

6. Johan Huizinga, *Homo Ludens: a Study of the Play Element in Culture* (Boston: Beacon Press, 1959), 10 and passim. Huizinga clearly regarded modern trends toward uniformity as inimical to the play spirit and hence to civilization itself (e.g., pp. 193, 197).

7. Robert Nozick, *Anarchy, State, and Utopia* (New York: Basic Books, 1974), 297-334.

8. Gilbert K. Chesterton, *Orthodoxy* (New York: John Lane Company, 1909), 38-39.

9. Gilbert K. Chesterton, *Heretics* (New York: John Lane Company, 1909), 80.

10. Robert Lindsay Schuettinger, ed., *The Conservative Tradition in European Thought* (New York: G. P. Putnam's Sons, 1970), 22-23. Montesquieu, with his affinity with British empiricism, is an exception to this characterization.

Part One

The Conservative Stake in a Diverse World

1 "Abundant Virtue": The Religious Vision

God, of course, is the paramount unifying principle in traditional thought. He is also, as we have reason to appreciate now, the paramount diversifying principle. It seems easier for Western man to perceive a diverse world when that world is understood as the product of the bounty and manifold potentiality of God than when it is regarded as the fortuitous concourse of matter and energy. The divine principle maintains the value and relationship of each part and marks each as a distinct manifestation of the myriad possibilities contained within the Godhead. With the fading from consciousness of this principle, all tends finally to appear the undifferentiated stuff of Whirl, wherein even consciousness itself sinks after the brief life of an epiphenomenon to dissolution.

Acceptance of a divinely created and sanctioned order establishes place and value—which is to say, diversity—far more satisfactorily than any political, scientific, or other partial order can do. For anything less than divinity in its lineaments of infinity and mystery is ultimately reductionist in effect. The members of an exclusively political order are reduced to political ciphers not differing significantly from their fellows. Inhabitants of a world understood exclusively on scientific lines are inevitably reduced to the common level of scientific data. A divine cosmology, at least in the Christian tradition, can escape these limitations, however. God is prolific enough to create a diverse world and big enough to encompass it.

He imparts an autonomy to the creature that not even Calvinist predestination dared obviate. And unlike the politician or the scientist, He measures ultimate value, and the creature's place in the scheme of things. To be sure, the logic of divine omnipotence can push the scheme over the edge into pantheism, in which all differences are illusory, just as an opposite, nominalist logic can break the world into unconnected and undifferentiated atoms. In practice, the Christian cosmos has rested on a fine and indeed mysterious balance, which can be provisionally described as that of unity-in-diversity.

On a more practical plane, the acceptance of the overarching unity provided by the divine order can make subordinate diversities less threatening and more acceptable. It is not always remembered how essential the binding force of religion was to the system not only of conservatives, but of many liberals, as late as the nineteenth century. For the Jacksonian Democratic historian George Bancroft, democracy was workable because every person had access to universal truth: God spoke through the people, and although the individual might err, the mass in the long run could not deviate from the plan of Providence. Without such divine guidance, Bancroft suggested, democracy would break up in unmanageable conflicts.

From a Roman Catholic position, and one certainly more conservative than that of Bancroft, Lord Acton could reach a similar conclusion, citing with approval late in his career "the conviction, which Tocqueville made a cornerstone, that nations that have not the self-governing force of religion within them are unprepared for freedom."[1] Characteristically for an Englishman, Acton was particularly aware of the relevance to this principle of diverse groups and orders. Some years earlier he had written of the universalizing tendencies of Christianity, which provided a common basis of life for nations otherwise sharply disparate. Yet the role of Christianity, as Acton saw it, was not to erase all differences, as of law and custom, but to make room for them within a framework of spiritual and ecclesiastical unity. Further, if only from self-interest, the Church was disposed to defend

> national liberty against uniformity and centralisation with an energy inspired by perfect community of interests. For

the same enemy threatens both; and the State which is reluctant to tolerate differences, and to do justice to the peculiar character of various races, must from the same cause interfere in the internal government of religion.[2]

A more recent comment, in an exposition of British conservatism by Reginald J. White, emphasizes that religious order makes possible a measure of group autonomy and diversity. "Conservatism," White points out, "sees men not under a political but under a cosmological order." Indeed, he argues, only religion is properly concerned with men in their ultimate individuality, while the state should regard groups and classes. Thus, on the one hand, private life is protected as "a sphere of moral free-agency," while the diverse orders and ranks of society are recognized and regulated. Leaving the soul to God, conservatives can insist "that society is not a collection of 'universalized individuals', nor the sum of individuals statistically aggregated, but the product of a system of real relationships *between* individuals, classes, groups and interests."[3]

That God as an ordering principle could effectively maintain diversity against theological or scientific determinism, and against physical or social atomism, owed much to the nature of the Christian deity. Christianity was monotheistic, but not monistic in temper and import. It distinguished sharply between Creator and Creation, as compared to its animistic and polytheistic predecessors. God's creatures, if endowed with souls, maintained their autonomous identities eternally, whether in heaven or hell; they were never absorbed into Emerson's Oversoul or achieved Nirvana. Pantheism, which renders all diversity illusory, was always heretical. Indeed, while avoiding outright polytheism, Christianity sanctioned the proliferation of spiritual entities of diverse dignities and functions: saints, angels, archangels, the Virgin Mary. The principle of variety encompassed even God Himself, as G. K. Chesterton perceived. The triune God was no despot, but a being involved by His nature in the diversities of life itself.

The god who is a mere awful unity is not only a king but an Eastern king. The *heart* of humanity, especially of European humanity, is certainly much more satisfied by the strange hints and symbols that gather round the Trinitarian idea, the image of a council at which mercy pleads as well as justice, the conception of a sort of liberty and variety existing even in the inmost chamber of the world. . . . If this love of a living complexity be our test, it is certainly healthier to have the Trinitarian religion than the Unitarian. For to us Trinitarians (if I may say it with reverence)—to us God Himself is a society.[4]

In a quite different way, Chesterton's American contemporary, the philosopher Josiah Royce, conceived of God as literally a community of individual wills through which the "Absolute" realized His manifold being. From standpoints of varying orthodoxy, the Christian conception of divinity lent itself to images of community and diversity.

God was, moreover, in an ancient and rich tradition, an abundant, fertile, creative being, Who delighted in the very diversity of His creation. "The general end of God's external working," as Richard Hooker put it in the seventeenth century, "is the exercise of his most glorious and most abundant virtue. Which abundance doth shew itself in variety, and for that cause this variety is oftentimes in Scripture exprest by the name of *riches*."[5] This divine principle—"the wisdom of God, which shineth in the beautiful variety of all things"— was reflected in the ranks and orders of society, each part of the social order manifesting its particular abilities and shouldering its particular duties. Less standard a Christian argument was Hooker's application of the principle of diversity to the degree of latitude and toleration within the Church, although he was able to quote St. Augustine in support of the contention that the "unity of belief" was compatible with the "variety of certain ordinances." God's wisdom showed most clearly in "the manifold and yet harmonious dissimilitude of those ways, whereby his Church upon earth is guided from age to age, throughout all generations of men."[6]

Although the logic of the seventeenth-century scientific revolution worked ultimately against this sense of "beautiful variety," there was a time when science seemed to confirm and augment the vision of plentitude entertained by churchmen like Hooker. The school of "natural theology," which arose in the seventeenth century and remained a potent force into the nineteenth, assumed that divine fullness could be read in the scientific study of creation. Representative of this approach was *The Wisdom of God Manifested in the Works of the Creation* (1690) by the English naturalist John Ray. Ray used the idea of diversity as a part of what became known as the argument from design: that the intricacy and pattern to be found in nature demonstrated the existence of God, even as the existence of a watch implied a watchmaker, in William Paley's later and famous analogy.

Ray drew upon the still relatively new inventions of the telescope and microscope to support a paean to the stupendous diversity of the universe. The number of fixed stars, he pointed out, was acknowledged to be "next to infinite." He conjectured that every one of these suns was circled by planets, each of these planets "in all likelihood furnished with a great variety of corporeal Creatures animate and inanimate as the Earth is, and all as different in Nature as they are in Place from the terrestrial, and from each other."[7] On earth alone, Ray estimated, there were ten thousand or more distinct species of insects, and perhaps millions of cunningly designed microscopic organisms in a single drop of water. Who could believe that such a universe could be produced "by the fortuitous concourse of Atomes?"[8]

Diversity for Ray consisted not merely in sheer numbers of different organisms; it was inherent in the very design of the universe. The earth itself, with its varying environments, and especially in its fertile mixtures of water and dry land, was constructed to support a wide array of life forms. More than this, Ray was impressed by the intricacy of design by which a diversity of means could be made to serve the same end. He noted in studying the eye, for example, the "great variety of Parts all conspiring to the Use of Vision." God showed too that He could "perform the same thing by divers means." Thus not only feathered creatures could fly, but bats, insects, even some fish. "Cetaceous fishes" swam as well as the genuinely piscene varieties. So in innumerable ways the creatures partook of the "overflowing Goodness of the Creator."[9]

The school of natural theology to which Ray belonged was especially inclined to the celebration of diversity as a manifestation of God's glory in nature and as a way of showing design. But the root concept of the manifold nature of divine goodness was too deeply a part of Christianity to be attributed exclusively to particular groups or tendencies. Even the austerities of the Puritans made room for it. In America Jonathan Edwards attempted to relate the unity of God to the diversity of His creation. For the Calvinist, the overwhelming power and majesty of the one threatened to negate the beauties of the other. Since God possessed "infinitely the greatest share of existence," Edwards was obliged to stipulate, "all other being, even the whole universe, is as nothing in comparison of the divine Being." The entire beauty of creation was then simply a reflection of the infinite beauty of God—yet reflected it was, and in manifold ways. Consequently, in Edwards's theology, true virtue consisted essentially in benevolence to being in general, yet benevolence to being in general would lead as an ancillary movement to benevolence to the particular, which might be enjoyed so far as consistent with the "highest good of being in general." So might the diversities of the world be celebrated.[10]

There is, to be sure, a discernible difference of emphasis between Ray and Edwards. The American is more constrained, more parsimonious, in his praise of diversity. Diversity is relegated to a secondary order of beauty and virtue; the first consists in a principle of unity: "the union of heart to being in general, or to God, the being of beings." And even on this secondary level, the virtue lay not in the diversity itself, but in its ordering to one unified design or purpose. It was especially the cunning of God to order the natural world so that diverse things should be brought into a "uniformity," as seen in the proportions of the human body. Man could imitate this faculty: "such is the agreement of the colors, figures, dimensions, and distances of the different spots on a chess board. Such is the beauty of the figures on a piece of chintz or brocade." The greater the variety, the greater the beauty—but only if it could be brought into a pattern of "uniformity."[11]

The power and clarity of Edwards's thought itself labored always to bring matters to uniformity. This is evident in his well-known use of Newtonian science and Lockean psychology to refurbish Calvinist doctrine. His adaptation of "sensationalist" precepts showed a man's salvation to be determined by his spiritual experience no less than, according to Locke, his mundane ideas stemmed from the impressions of the five senses. He dematerialized Newtonian atomism to depict God acting in the universe at every point, each "atom" a locus of attraction simply because God so willed it. Such ideas were monistic in tendency. Had Edwards been a scientist, his patterns of thought might well have earned for him the charge of being a reductionist; as a minister and theologian, he skirted a pantheist position which threatened to submerge all distinctions. If Edwards was neither reductionist nor pantheist, it was because his fundamental religious orthodoxy preserved in him a sense of God's fullness diffused in the world. Though God's ultimate end was one, he wrote, it was expressed in a variety of ways. God's external glory was the "emanation" of His internal glory, and the diversity of the world necessarily followed.[12] Edwards found a striking metaphor for this emanation, one clearly derived from the Newtonian work in optics which so captured the imagination of the eighteenth century:

> There is a variety in light. One and the same white light, though it seems to be an exceeding simple thing, yet contains a very great variety of kinds of rays, all of . . . excellent and lovely appearance. So the same simple spirit of God seems to contain a great variety, and therefore He is in Revelation called seven spirits. There is one body, one spirit, and yet a vast variety of gifts, I. Cor. 12.4: Now there are diversities of gifts, but the same spirit, and verse 11: All these worketh that one and self-same spirit.[13]

The association of divine creativity with diversity of being, depicted by Ray in the mode of natural theology and by Edwards in a Puritan vein, was most lavishly developed in the master idea of the "Great Chain of Being," which Arthur O. Lovejoy, in a classic of intellectual history, traced from its ancient origins to its denouement amid the romantic and evolutionary currents of the nineteenth century. The term denominated a stupendous hierarchy of creaturehood, extending without gap or break from inanimate matter through progressively higher forms of life to man, and, in its traditional religious formulation, through the ranks of angels and other heavenly spirits to God Himself. Originally the scheme was innocent of evolutionary connotation, representing simply the "Self-Transcending Fecundity" of the Creator, Who was not content to abide in His changeless perfection, but was impelled to express His goodness in the creation of "a temporal and material and extremely multiple and variegated universe." According to this "principle of plenitude," the "Absolute" could not exist alone, but had in its perfection to realize the manifold possibilities of creation. The idea, as Lovejoy explains, contained an inherent tension which could never be quite eliminated, and which became obvious in Neoplatonic and some medieval representations: the unity and self-sufficiency of God viewed as the Idea of the Good was hardly compatible with the self-transcendence, fecundity, and diversity attributed to a God Who was also the Idea of Goodness.[14] But whether in strict logic or not, the plan seemed satisfactorily to reconcile the observable multiplicity and tumult of the world with the presumed unity of the Creator and of His order.

Most widely diffused during the eighteenth century, the Chain-of-Being idea became part of the mental furniture of the age. The well-known lines of Alexander Pope furnished the keynote:

> Vast chain of Being! which from God began,
> Natures ethereal, human, angel, man,
> Beast, bird, fish, insect, what no eye can see,
> No glass can reach; from Infinite to thee,
> From thee to Nothing.—On superior powers
> Were we to press, inferior might on ours:
> Or in the full creation leave a void,
> Where, one step broken, the great scale's destroyed:
> From Nature's chain whatever link you strike,
> Tenth or ten thousandth, breaks the chain alike.[15]

It was not merely the conceit of poets. The practical and more prosaic intelligence of John Adams could casually invoke the principle, for example, in support of the idea of natural inequalities among human beings. "Nature," he pointed out, "which has established in the universe a chain of being and universal order, descending from Arch Angels to microscopic animalcules, has ordained that no two objects shall be perfectly alike, and no two creatures perfectly equal."[16] The reference to "Arch Angels" may have been hyperbolic, but Adams did not doubt the basic scheme.

The full development of the "Great-Chain-of-Being" idea helped to give to the principle of variety a religious and intellectual sanction which it had never so clearly enjoyed in the Western tradition.

Leibniz, in whose philosophy the idea played the most pervasive role among major systems of thought, in particular accorded to variety a new "sort of cosmic dignity," Lovejoy points out, "by attributing it to God himself" in a thoroughly rational scheme. Conceiving of the principle of plenitude as realizable fully only in time, Leibniz also helped to turn the Chain of Being from a purely static conception toward notions of change and progress.[17]

Leibniz argued that the diversity of the Creation increased the total amount of good in the world, that even the highest good, if repeated endlessly, "would be superfluity, and poverty too." Anticipating the objection that a uniform system would be free from irregularities, he answered that "it would be an irregularity to be too uniform, that would offend against the rules of harmony." Variety, indeed, opened the door to a host of evils, but apparent flaws contributed to the beauty of the whole.[18] God combined the greatest possible variety with the greatest possible order to arrive as near to perfection as possible; thus, in the real world, things "which are uniform and contain no variety are never anything but abstractions, like time, space, and the other entities of pure mathematics."[19]

The Chain-of-Being idea had certain rather obvious affinities with conservatism. The principle of hierarchy was easily transferred. There is, to be sure, a qualitative difference between a hierarchy of species, ranging from single-celled life forms to human beings, and a hierarchy of social ranks. But they seemed to offer analogous spectacles of progression and subordination, plenitude, and order-in-diversity. An eighteenth-century American, William Livingston, gave stock expression to the notion of the social chain, noting that

> the great Variety of Powers, Characters and Conditions, obvious in Human Life, is an illustrious Proof of the benignity and Wisdom of the Supreme Governor of the Universe. From this vast Diversity naturally result Superiority and Pre-eminence in some, and Dependence and subjection in others. To this *natural* Difference of Character, Society has introduced the additional Distinction of a political Disparity, by conferring on various of its Members, a Variety of Honours and Privileges in a gradual Subordination from the chief Magistrate, to the least dignified of his Subjects.[20]

Such attitudes clearly lent themselves to smugness on the part of the higher links in the social chain, who could view their position in the world as part of the divine scheme. An idea is not refuted by the self-interest of those who advance it, but the persuasiveness of this "Cosmic Toryism" (in Basil Willey's phrase) was eventually offset by its clearly self-serving aspects. In its most complete expression it justified without qualification the status quo, which had to be recognized as the inevitable and benign result of providential bounty. Thus, in Pope's watchcry, "WHATEVER IS, IS RIGHT."[21] Plenitude and diversity were identified too closely not only with hierarchy and inequality—possibly encouraging later radicals and democrats to associate equality with uniformity—but also with the defects of the social order. The principle of plenitude was partly a way of solving the problem of evil, by making it a necessary part of the benevolent whole. "Thus," wrote Leibniz, "the apparent deformities of our little worlds combine to become beauties in the great world, and have nothing in them which is opposed to the oneness of an infinitely perfect universal principle: on the contrary, they increase our wonder at the wisdom of him who makes evil serve the greater good."[22]

In less philosophical minds, at least, there was here a clear invitation to moral callousness. Willey remarked of eighteenth-century optimism, drawing heavily as it did on the Chain of Being, that it was

> in essence an apologia for the status quo, presenting you with a God who loved abundance and variety better than happiness or progress, and a universe whose "goodness" consisted in its containing the greatest possible range of phenomena, many of which seem evil to all but the philosophers.[23]

There was even a foreshadowing of that later aberration of conservative (and liberal) thought which sought to make conflict the mainspring of existence, for preoccupation with the organic plenitude of the world could lead optimists "to draw an almost Darwinian or Malthusian picture of a Nature overcrowded with aspirants for life and consequently given over to a ubiquitous struggle for existence."[24]

From the standpoint of diversity itself, if not from that of conservatism, there was a more subtle pitfall. Paeans to the variety of creaturehood were sometimes overshadowed by a more solid commitment to uniformity. The Great Chain of Being sanctioned the plenitude and diversity of the universe, but only of course within the providential scheme. The monistic, determined aspect of this scheme could make it an example of what William James called the "block universe," into which neither contingency, nor moral significance, nor even, consequently, genuine variety truly entered. And in the Enlightenment version of the Chain of Being, as Lovejoy noted, there was a tendency to standardize and to simplify; and to account for diversity through a standardized and simplified plan of nature was to minimize diversity. The accepted notion that there could be no breach of continuity in the Chain of Being, furthermore, was at odds with any real quality of differentness, which could only be manifest by an object or creature being clearly set apart from its closest relations. Diversity maximized as limitless plenitude turned back against itself.[25]

Although the Chain of Being contributed to early evolutionary thought, the thoroughgoing temporalizing of the idea changed it beyond recognition. In its classic form it was linked closely to the doctrine of special creations in biology, just as its social application was plausible primarily in a stable aristocratic society. Despite its serious fallacies—even, as may be said, its ultimate intellectual failure—it was probably the most thoroughly developed explication of the diversity of the universe ever expounded in Western thought. And the diversity, within the ultimate unity of God's creation, such a concept, pushed to a "logical conclusion," can cancel itself out. The most fundamental precepts of the Chain-of-Being idea, that divine creativity has been expressed through the diversity of creation and that this diversity represents ranks of relatively higher and lower creatures, have hardly been refuted, however modern science and philosophy may judge them irrelevant to their concerns. There has been too much of the reductionist spirit in the modern temper for "plenitude" and "diversity" to be entertained as favored cosmological terms. But on an everyday level of experience, the Chain of Being may still seem more to comport with reality than those systems which reduce the multifariousness of experience to one bleak monism or another.

For early conservative thought, the Chain of Being provided strong supports for rank, order, and hierarchy, and argued the essential benevolence of the existing society and cosmos; more than that, it served as the emblem of a loving and ordering Providence. It suggested powerfully the richness of just what it was which was to be conserved against the "terrible simplifiers" of the eighteenth century. It posed, however, serious questions: Was diversity merely a function of inequality? And is diversity contained within a unitary scheme a genuine diversity, or simply, as William James would later suggest, a sham? These questions, however, could not obscure a deeply engrained conservative commitment to the diversified order which the individual confronted whether he dealt with God or man.

The religious nexus joined conservatism to diversity in other ways. Not only could Being be classified in terms which expressed the diversity and plenitude of divine creation, but God could be seen to work in a cunning variety of ways to achieve his object, ways which shamed and often negated the simple efforts of man. Joseph de Maistre well expressed this sense of divine subtlety in working toward a design:

> In the works of man, everything is as poor as its author; vision is confined, means are limited, scope is restricted, movements are labored, and results are humdrum. In divine works, boundless riches reveal themselves even in the smallest component; its power operates effortlessly: in its hands . . . everything is a means, nothing an obstacle: and the irregularities produced by the work of free agents come to fall into place in the general order.[26]

For Maistre, this plenitude of method taught a lesson of reverence. "The omnipotent wisdom governing all things," he thought, "has means at its disposal so numerous, so diversified, so wonderful that the part we can comprehend should well teach us to revere the other."[27]

Maistre's countryman, Alexis de Tocqueville, wrote in very similar tones. Although Tocqueville made the opposition between egalitarian uniformity and traditional diversity a major theme of his *Democracy in America,* one of his more profound comments on the subject of variety associated it simply with the ways of God.

Men place the greatness of their idea of unity in the means, God in the ends; hence this idea of greatness, as men conceive it, leads us to infinite littleness. To compel all men to follow the same course towards the same object is a human conception; to introduce infinite variety of action, but so combined that all these acts lead in a thousand different ways to the accomplishment of one great design, is a divine conception.

Human efforts to attain unity through simplicity of means, Tocqueville added, were generally barren; God's use of endlessly varied means to accomplish His unitary purpose, on the other hand, was "infinitely fruitful."[28]

The implications of these formulations for conservative thought are clear. Human efforts are limited by the very simplicity of their means; the hubris of attempting to substitute a political or social program for the design of Providence can only reduce human stature. It would be out of keeping with the tenor of Tocqueville's work, at least, to read into this a disavowal of all attempts to ameliorate the conditions of life. But to overstep the bounds, to reach for some final consummation of history through the simplicity of a leader principle or an ideology, leads in this view only to the radical reduction of human possibilities—"infinite littleness." Something—very much, in fact—must be left outside of human plans, if not with faith in God's wisdom, at least in acknowledgment of man's ignorance.

It ought to be underscored too that in the view of Maistre and Tocqueville, divine means in all their diversity work toward a unity of ultimate design. Since basic themes in conservative thinking are joined to conceptions of unity—authority, prescription, monotheism itself—it is important to find ways to relate such unity to the diversity which is inherent not only in much of the tradition that conservatives defend, but in much of their opposition to centralization and concentration of power. The French thinkers (different from each other as they were in important respects) combine to argue the reductive nature of human attempts at unity, in contrast to the divine unity of purpose encompassing all the diversities of the world.

The conservative stake in a divinely ordained plenitude and diversity was, then, very great. The Chain of Being offered an analogue for a social order based on place and rank, while the infinite subtlety of divine purpose militated against human efforts too quickly to break down natural and social distinctions—the actual variety of existence—in the name of equality or of uniformity. From a more positive standpoint, the celebration of diversity and plenitude provided a warrant for the present enjoyment of the world; smugly and self-righteously often enough, no doubt, but without yielding to despair at incomprehensible multiplicity or sacrificing all immediate and partial hopes to Utopia, which is no place at all.

NOTES

1. John Emerich Edward Dalberg-Acton, *Essays on Freedom and Power* (Glencoe, Ill.: The Free Press, 1949), 256.
2. Ibid., 186-188.
3. Reginald J. White, ed., *The Conservative Tradition* (New York: New York University Press, 1957), 4-8.
4. Gilbert K. Chesterton, *Orthodoxy* (New York: John Lane Company, 1909), 250-251. See also Chesterton, *Heretics* (New York: John Lane Company, 1909), 80.
5. Richard Hooker, *Of the Laws of Ecclesiastical Polity* (London: J. M. Dent & Sons, Ltd., 1954), I, 152-153.
6. Ibid., I, 341, 415; II, 338, 354.
7. John Ray, *The Wisdom of God Manifested in the Works of the Creation* (London: Samuel Smith, 1691), 1-2.
8. Ibid., 7, 119, 18.
9. Ibid., 149, 182, 9-10, 129.
10. Jonathan Edwards, *The Nature of True Virtue* (Ann Arbor: University of Michigan Press, 1960), 14-15, 3-5, 8.
11. Ibid., 37-38, 27-28.
12. Jonathan Edwards, "Dissertation Concerning the End for Which God Created the World," *The Works of President Edwards* (New York: Leavitt and Company, 1851), II, 253-254. For Edwards's use of Locke and Newton, see Perry Miller, *Jonathan Edwards* (New York: Delta, 1967), 52-68, 82-96.
13. Jonathan Edwards, *Images or Shadows of Divine Things* (New Haven: Yale University Press, 1948), 62-63. See also "The Beauty of the World," in ibid., 135-137, wherein Edwards explicitly cites Newton; and

Edwards, "Dissertation," 250, on light: "What can be thought of, that so naturally and aptly represents the emanation of the internal glory of God; or the flowing forth, and abundant communication of that infinite fulness of good that is in God?"

14. Arthur O. Lovejoy, *The Great Chain of Being* (New York: Harper & Row, 1960), 49, 82-83.

15. Alexander Pope, "Essay on Man," I, *Selected Poetry & Prose,* ed. William K. Wimsatt, Jr. (New York: Rinehart & Co., 1958), 136.

16. John Adams, *Discourses on Davila* (New York: Da Capo Press, 1973), 20.

17. Lovejoy, *Chain of Being,* 224, 244.

18. Gottfried Wilhelm Leibniz, *Theodicy* (London: Routledge & Kegan Paul, Ltd., 1951), 198, 260, 216.

19. Gottfried Wilhelm Leibniz, "The Monadology," *Philosophical Writings,* trans. Mary Morris (London: J. M. Dent & Sons, Ltd., 1956), 13; Leibniz, "New Essays on the Human Understanding," ibid., 172.

20. Quoted by Henry F. May, *The Enlightenment in America* (New York: Oxford University Press, 1976), 27.

21. Pope, "Essay on Man," I, *Selected Poetry & Prose,* 137.

22. Leibniz, *Theodicy,* 216.

23. Basil Willey, *The Eighteenth Century Background* (New York: Columbia University Press, 1940), 48.

24. Lovejoy, *Chain of Being,* 218.

25. Ibid., 293, 332.

26. Joseph de Maistre, "Considerations on France," *The Works of Joseph de Maistre* (New York: Macmillan, 1965), 47.

27. Joseph de Maistre, "The Saint Petersburg Dialogues," *Works,* 220.

28. Alexis de Tocqueville, *Democracy in America* (New York: Vintage Books, 1959), II, 386-387.

2 Tradition and the Dimension of Time

To a certain way of thinking, conservative reliance on traditional standards and patterns of life is at the opposite pole from the acceptance of diversity. There is a part of modern mythology which operates to associate tradition with a stuffy, repressive conformity, with a "Main Street" atmosphere that the brave and talented escape by fleeing to New York—or, more recently, to California. What is the liberated woman or man liberated from, in the imaginations of those devoted to that particular cliché? In part, certainly, from "tradition," regarded as monolithic, destructive archaism, a legacy of ancient fear and ignorance.

Such attitudes can easily enough be marked as superficial at the outset: as unity can contain diversity, tradition can encompass a variety of traditions and a diversity of people who observe them. And realizing something of this perhaps, even sensing a corrective to present abominations, not even society's rebels have been wont to reject tradition in any consistent fashion. There were clearly aspects of the counterculture of the nineteen-sixties which appealed to traditionalist yearnings for a way of life at once less cluttered and less standardized. The reaction against "technocracy" had perforce a traditionalist ingredient, however untraditional its devotees might be in other respects. Bohemians have always had a warm spot for the traditional life of other peoples, if sufficiently primitive or quaint. And why should they not?

Americans (to cite another suspect group) have as a people remained highly ambivalent on the subject of tradition. In some ways they do resemble their European caricature as acolytes of novelty, lacking a past and ever eager to replace a building which has stood on its foundations for more than twenty years with a gleaming new supermarket or car wash. Yet there is too a real thirst for a sense of the traditional, as every antique hunter and a good many tourists can attest. New colleges and societies are pathetically eager to "start" traditions, undeterred by any Burkean superstition that tradition evolves in a long and gradual process of experience and accretion. On a more substantial plane, political and institutional traditions, many of which, like trial by jury, long antedate the United States of America, still command a certain respect. Allegations of being soft on slavery or capitalism have not quite destroyed the hallowing aura of tradition which gathered around the founding fathers, and even the Supreme Court finds it politic to pay some lip service to constitutional lore and precedent.

Such evidences do not, of course, demonstrate any substantial commitment to traditional modes of public or private life. They indicate certainly, on the one hand, a nostalgia for what is perceived as a simpler and purer way of life, and, on the other, the lingering notion that even the most sweeping institutional changes are fittingly accomplished by some gesture of obeisance to long-established principles. Tradition, of course, means something much more. Beyond the dictionary definitions, it connotes a life lived in the consciousness of its continuity with past and future; reliance on time-tested personal and vicarious experience, not necessarily to dictate the course of one's life, but to furnish the forms which give it meaning; and a preference for custom rather than either law or fashion as a source of the authoritative. The traditionalist need not exclude the new out of hand, for tradition itself consists in the accumulation of once-novel practices; the presumption, however, lies with experience, and innovation is required to prove its necessity or superiority. Needless to say, all of these precepts are at odds with the distinctive features of modernity.

Accepting the traditionalist approach to life, the conservative has been called an "optimist about the past." He need not be. Indeed, his sense of the limitations and corruptions of human nature should permit him to look the past full in the face, without illusion. One need not be oblivious to the wars, the famines, the oppressions, the sheer monotonous drudgery of life during the Middle Ages, for example—not even Henry Adams was unaware of these melancholy aspects—to find in the stained glass of Chartres cathedral, or in medieval ideals of faith and loyalty, values of enduring significance. The past cannot and should not be recaptured, but it can furnish paradigms for the construction of the future. One need not, moreover, embrace any particular tradition—which may be good or bad—in order to regard a sense of the traditional as a necessary component of the full experience of human life.

The appeal to tradition, then, is not without complication. And to see in tradition an unqualified principle of unity, a simple prescription for a homogeneous pattern of life, is to entertain illusions. The value of tradition lies in the interplay of the qualities of unity and diversity with which it impresses the receptive imagination. The very homogeneous, unitary quality of tradition serves in the first place as a standard of measurement and judgment. Diversity most comfortably subsists within a definite tradition and in relation to an explicit or implicit norm. As an architectural "tradition"— Gothic, for obvious example—can encompass considerable diversity of style, so can such a less tangible tradition as that of the "gentleman." The Western tradition of the gentleman, remarkably coherent from the late Middle Ages down at least to the early twentieth century, left room for individual variation, indeed for eccentricity, while retaining accepted standards of judgment. Again the principle applies that without such unifying elements, diversity collapses into meaninglessness.

There is, furthermore, a strong affinity between diversity and continuity in time. Tradition sorts out social phenomena and accords them discrete values. To the extent that they may be regarded as permanent, the qualities of life can be seen as distinct. Where nothing is permanent, on the other hand, everything floats on the surface of experience; one phenomenon merges with another; there are no clear grounds for ranking one quality above another. Contemporary American life tends toward this situation: fad succeeds fad; more and more is made to be disposable; even the loftiest ideals drift on the flux of vocal interests and movements. Some of the most fashionable ideas draw toward a spurious Nirvana of value-free, relative, "polymorphous perversity," in which all distinctions and barriers are to be eliminated; no one is to win or lose, no one to succeed or fail; nothing is to be regarded as of intrinsically more worth than something else. The effect may be homogeneity; it may be chaos; it is probably both. It is not diversity.

Tradition ascribes *significance* to difference. G. K. Chesterton cited the simple case of apparel. The modern world, he pointed out, does not offer less varied or colorful clothing than did the more tradition-minded Middle Ages; medieval clothing, indeed, could be drab as well as colorful. But colors were worn for a reason, to signify a trade, or a particular family, or religious status. The trouble, Chesterton thought, was not that modern people saw no "splendid colours or striking effects," but that they saw them too much, and divorced from meaning.[1] Diversity, it follows, inheres not in surface differences of a physical or sensory nature, but in the significance ascribed to them. Clothing may seem a superficial matter, especially to the modern mind, but the principle can be extended into deeper regions. Diversity, as of manners, "life-style," or occupation, is as real as the meaning found in the particular variations. If differences make no difference, diversity is an illusion.

In strict logic, significant differences need not arise from tradition. However, in the Western world, diversity has been nurtured by the endurance of traditional patterns of life. This has not of course been the result of any deliberate design; political and religious authorities, even in the most tradition-bound ages, have been characteristically eager to centralize and to standardize. But where, in circumstances of poor communication or limited political control, differences between groups have been deep and significant, their perpetuation has assumed the aspect of tradition, whereas it has been distinctively modern methods, policies, and technology which have been most successful in breaking them down. Few regional cultures are able to withstand the standardizing blandishments of the radio, the television, and the automobile, for obvious examples. The introduction of these wonders is not without estimable benefits, and it may be rationalized alternatively as inevitable or as the result of free choice; however regarded, it tends to uniformity. Revolutionary and totalitarian regimes, on the other hand, set out deliberately to destroy cultural diversity. The genesis of "totalitarian democracy," in J. L. Talmon's interpretation, drew on a profound hostility to it. "Men were gripped by the idea that the conditions, a product of faith, time and custom, in which they and their forefathers had been living, were unnatural and had all to be replaced by deliberately planned uniform patterns, which would be natural and rational."[2]

These observations simply begin to establish that diversity is traditionally preserved and that that which is hostile to tradition is apt in effect, if not in intent, to be hostile to diversity. Regarded explicitly in the dimension of time, the connection appears more clearly. Any great tradition must be, in a sense, the result of variety in time; it accretes through time, takes on new meanings, adapts, if successful, to changing and sometimes widely varying circumstances. This was Edmund Burke's point about the British constitution:

> A nation is not an idea only of local extent, and individual momentary aggregation; but it is an idea of continuity, which extends in time as well as in numbers and in space. And this is a choice not of one day, or one set of people, not a tumultuary and giddy choice; it is a deliberate election of ages and of generations; it is a constitution made by what is ten thousand times better than choice, it is made by the peculiar circumstances, occasions, tempers, dispositions, and moral, civil, and social habitudes of the people, which disclose themselves only in a long space of time.[3]

The new is simple—even if represented by a machine of the most intricate complexity. (Modern technology embodies this apparent paradox: it uses the most complicated means in order to simplify, and often to attenuate.) In terms of human purpose and accommodation, it is the ancient which is complex, and which, being complex, is most likely to make room for diversity.

Diversity is itself a complex and frequently elusive quality, and can hardly be ascribed to traditional life without complication. There is ample literature, fictional as well as historical, attesting to that life as dull, conformist, and narrow—something from which to escape. One thinks, in America, of the bleak physical and social scenes of Ellen Glasgow and O. E. Rölvaag. How do such representations square with traditional diversity as conservatives have been wont to defend it from modern uniformity and standardization? To some extent, we may be dealing with different things: relative homogeneity within the traditional group, yet a heterogeneity among the groups themselves, depending on such differences as those of locality, status, family, or religion. In traditional Europe, national and regional differences—even differences between neighboring counties or villages—were often far greater than those one finds today in traveling from one end of the United States to the other. Localities were divided by language or dialect, architecture, clothing styles, custom in all its manifestations. Yet within one's immediate group, we might suppose, life was vastly simpler and more homogeneous than it would be now, with the range of available occupations, amusements, and general modes of subsistence far more limited.

Yet even this explanation is unsatisfactory. The figures portrayed by writers like Glasgow and Rölvaag may have been oppressed by their common environments, but they were not lacking in variety of character, and such fictional representations tend to be supported by personal experience. Not without some basis in fact is the village "character" a stock figure. More traditional societies may contain a lesser range of beliefs, ideas, and values—those things to which intellectuals are partial—and less practical wherewithal than their modern urban counterparts; whether they display a less varied range of personality is more doubtful. Then too, there are degrees of traditionalism. Neither the American small town nor the English village of recent history was a medieval manor; each fell somewhere between the complex communications of modern urban life and the confined relationships of the thoroughly traditional society, possibly nurturing a sturdier sense of diversity than either extreme.

Even disregarding such distinctions, however, it can be maintained that the smaller scale of more traditional ways of life makes diversity more visible. It seems paradoxical that the older world characterized by general deprivation and want was able to view itself to the extent that it did in terms of bounty, plenitude, and teeming life, as represented in the tenacious idea of the "Great Chain of Being." Today, in contrast, those groups most benefited by the affluence of advanced industrial societies are most obsessed with the paucity of the world's resources and most likely to draw their intellectual sustenance from philosophies which argue the essential poverty of existence. The ascetic, whether voluntary or not, may have a livelier sense of the distinct goods of creation than the glutton.

At the same time, it is less a question of the number of alternatives available in any given society than of the variety which actually enters one's everyday life. Chesterton, ever alive to the positive value of limitation, saw this quite clearly. Despite the modern penchant for "large empires and large ideas," there was a sense, he thought, in which the member of a small community inhabited a much larger world than his less provincial fellow.

> He knows much more of the fierce varieties and uncompromising divergences of men. The reason is obvious. In a large community we can choose our companions. In a small community our companions are chosen for us. Thus in all extensive and highly civilized societies groups come into existence founded upon what is called sympathy, and shut out the real world more sharply than the gates of a monastery. There is nothing really narrow about the clan; the thing which is really narrow is the clique. The men of the clan live together because they all wear the same tartan or are all descended from the same sacred cow; but in their souls, by the divine luck of things, there will always be more colours than in any tartan. But the men of the clique live together because they have the same kind of soul, and their narrowness is a narrowness of spiritual coherence and contentment, like that which exists in hell. A big society is a society for the promotion of narrowness. It is a machinery for the purpose of guarding the solitary and sensitive individual from all experience of the bitter and bracing human compromises. It is, in the most literal sense of the words, a society for the prevention of Christian knowledge.[4]

The principle applied particularly to the family, that preeminent object of modern abuse and fascination. To be born, it seemed to Chesterton, was the "supreme adventure": it was to enter a fairy tale, not because the family was necessarily happy, but because of its strange and even alarming "divergencies and varieties." The family was paramount among those "great limitations and frameworks which fashion and create the poetry and variety of life," and those who rebelled against the family, Chesterton thought, were simply rebels against humanity.[5]

Diversity, in this line of thought, was at bottom largely psychological—depending, no doubt, on an irreducible multiplicity of phenomena and personalities, but no less on one's interest in and willingness to perceive them in terms of variety. A certain type at least of modern man drew back from such perception, Chesterton noted, and shrank from "the brutal vivacity and brutal variety of common men."[6] Modern life may contain a raw multiplicity which surpasses that of any previous society, but it seems also to be true that modern people tend to insulate themselves from this teeming and often disturbing multiplicity. Philippe Ariès thought it characteristic of the Middle Ages that "people lived in a state of contrast; high birth or great wealth rubbed shoulders with poverty, vice with virtue, scandal with devotion." Eventually, however, the middle class "seceded; it withdrew from the vast polymorphous society to organize itself separately, in a homogeneous environment," and substituted a "conventional model" of individual behavior for the "bizarre juxtaposition" of medieval classes. Ariès attributed modern conceptions of family and class (and, tentatively, of race) to this "same intolerance towards variety, the same insistence on uniformity."[7] Although family life and related matters of social history are the subjects of much present controversy, this specimen at least serves to suggest the paramount importance for our thesis, not of the objective or abstract multiplicity of a given society, but of the subjective experience of diversity within it.

Even when modern man does not insulate himself from the objective multiplicity of his environment, psychological factors may operate to minimize its diverse quality. Multiplicity can overwhelm, especially when it lacks order and relation. Where everything is "different," there is no difference that really matters. If no deeper explanation applies, certainly it can be said that such endless nominalism sates and cloys, paralyzing the ability to draw significant distinctions. It does so most effectively, it seems, where the natural

environment has been supplanted by the artificial. As superficially more complex as is the artificial world, John Crowe Ransom
suggested, it substitutes the abstract for the concrete, and the
abstract tends toward simplicity, whereas the concrete must embrace
variety.[8] Thus the May garden delights the eye with its diversity,
while the roadside clutter and daily outpouring of television entertainment conceal with difficulty the guiding genius of monotony.

The distinction between abstract simplicity and concrete variety
brings us close to the center of the conservative vision of social
existence. From at least Burke's time onward, whatever the vagaries
of conservative thought, one of its constant themes has been the
belief that the actual reality of experience is too complex and diverse
to yield to any monistic, abstract plan, even if intended with the
utmost sincerity for human improvement, without the onset of
tyranny and the systematic impoverishment of life. Abstraction,
in this view, may aid in explaining aspects of reality; it is insufferable
when it attempts to govern reality. This acceptance of the variety of
experience is not incompatible with an emphasis on the unity of the
moral law. Allowance for diversity is not relativism. The same
fundamental precepts of right and wrong may apply to the most
various conditions of life. The task of the statesman, in a venerable
line of conservative thought, is to adhere to the moral standard
without violating the diversity of circumstance in which it is to find
expression. Analogously, the historian, even if he emphasizes
general principles, must recognize the extreme diversity of their
manifestations.

> By contemplating the vast variety of particular characters and
> events; by examining the strange combination of causes, dif-
> ferent, remote, and seemingly opposite, that often concur in
> producing one effect; and the surprising fertility of one single
> and uniform cause in the producing of a multitude of effects,
> as different, as remote, and seemingly as opposite; by tracing
> carefully . . . all the minute and sometimes scarce conceivable
> circumstances, either in the characters of actors, or in the
> course of actions, that history enables him to trace,

one may, thought Lord Bolingbroke, sharpen one's judgment and
powers of penetration.[9]

Burke shows basically the same sense of human variety expressed through time. But whereas Bolingbroke, in the passage quoted above, was primarily interested in deriving a limited number of consistent principles from multifarious experience, Burke was driven to a practical and intellectual defense of multifarious experience itself. Life had to be defended, he found, from those who were not content to distill general principles from it, but who wished to reduce it to conformity with abstractions removed from it. The value accorded to diversity is fundamental to Burke's thought, as much so as his closely related precepts of authority, prescription, and continuity, to which more attention has been paid. Diversity was for Burke, in the first place, a reality principle: life and society *were* limitlessly varied, especially as seen in the dimension of time; traditions, including the British constitutional tradition, were simply accretions of the immensely varied experiences of men and women through the centuries. Diversity, further, was in accord with nature and with the divinely ordained principles of order and subordination which nature embodied. Finally, one glimpses in Burke something of the aesthetic preference for variety of the Romantic, and a corresponding revulsion at standardization. (In his early writings on aesthetics, Burke showed an awareness of the role of variation in the effect of beauty; on the other hand, "sublimity," to which he certainly never thought social arrangements could aspire, was characterized by "perfect simplicity" and "absolute uniformity.")[10]

Temperamentally as well as politically, Burke reacted strongly, as Russell Kirk put it, to the "infatuation with simplicity" which he recognized in the revolutionaries of his time, and "loathed the barren monotony of any society stripped of diversity and individuality." Any such Procrustean effort, he perceived, must lead to "the crowning simplicity of despotism."[11] Human experience was far too complex to be encompassed by a simple formula. A professor might at his pleasure reduce it to a set of abstractions; the statesman must deal with diverse reality. "Circumstances," thought Burke, "are infinite, are infinitely combined; are variable and transient; he who does not take them into consideration is not erroneous, but stark mad." Any theory purporting to secure general happiness or universal rights, which failed to take into account "the peculiar and characteristic situation of a people, . . . their opinions, prejudices, habits, and all the circumstances that diversify and colour life," was correspondingly suspect.[12]

These metaphysic rights entering into common life, like rays of light which pierce into a dense medium, are, by the laws of nature, refracted from their straight line. Indeed in the gross and complicated mass of human passions and concerns, the primitive rights of men undergo such a variety of refractions and reflections, that it becomes absurd to talk of them as if they continued in the simplicity of their original direction. The nature of man is intricate; the objects of society are of the greatest possible complexity: and therefore no simple disposition or direction of power can be suitable either to man's nature, or to the quality of his affairs.[13]

With rights, so also with policy. Great Britain, like other modern nations, embraced interests which were *"various, multiform, and intricate."* Therefore its constitution, if it was to be the constitution of a free people, must remain similarly complex, embracing objects "of the greatest possible variety."[14] The principle had obvious application to Anglo-American difficulties. Burke, as he wrote to the sheriffs of the City of Bristol in 1777, was led early to think that

instead of troubling our understandings with speculations concerning the unity of empire, and the identity or distinction of legislative powers . . . it was our duty, in all soberness, to conform our government to the character and circumstances of the several people who composed this mighty and strangely diversified mass. I never was wild enough to conceive, that one method would serve for the whole; that the natives of Hindostan and those of Virginia could be ordered in the same manner; or that the [Anglo-Indian] Cutchery court and the grand jury of Salem could be regulated on a similar plan. I was persuaded that government was a practical thing, made for the happiness of mankind, and not to furnish a spectacle of uniformity, to gratify the schemes of visionary politicians.

Unlike geometrical or metaphysical propositions of universal validity, Burke added, "social and civil freedom, like all other things in common life, are variously mixed and modified, enjoyed in very different degrees, and shaped into an infinite diversity of forms, according to the temper and circumstances of every community."[15]

With the French Revolution, questions arose which were different from and more basic than those raised by the possession of a heterogeneous empire. The French seemed to Burke to be attacking the very nature of human society. Whereas, he pointed out, classical philosophers had remained conscious that differences of birth, education, property, and many other circumstances rendered men so different as to be, "as it were, so many different species of animals," and therefore to be accorded different privileges and places within the state, the revolutionary legislators were taking

the directly contrary course. They have attempted to confound all sorts of citizens, as well as they could into one homogeneous mass; and then they divided this their amalgama into a number of incoherent republics. They reduce men to loose counters, merely for the sake of simple telling, and not to figures, whose power is to arise from their place in the table.[16]

Repelled by the division of France into departments carried out by the revolutionary votaries of Reason, Burke was driven to articulate his feeling for local and traditional loyalties as necessary parts of national allegiance. No one, he was persuaded, was ever genuinely attached to an arbitrary division imposed from above, or to any neatly and rationally surveyed "Chequer No. 71." Loyalty and love of country were trained in the family, in the neighborhood, in provincial associations, Burke thought, and not in an abstract and unmediated commitment to the nation.[17]

Perhaps enough has been said to suggest that diversity deserves to be ranked as one of the primary values in Burkean thought. Burke clearly viewed diversity as part of the natural and providential order of the world, and forced uniformity as therefore a violation of that order. There is no doubt that he associated diversity as well with social hierarchy and that his use of the term was, in part, a frank defense of a class system. "In all societies consisting of various descriptions of citizens," he was persuaded, "some description must be uppermost. The levelers therefore, only change and pervert the natural order of things." They never really equalized; at most they could shuffle the order of precedence. In particular, Burke singled out the right to own property and to perpetuate it in a family as a differentiating factor essential to the continuity and well-being of society.[18]

Since Burke represents, by general consent, the seminal moment in the genesis of modern conservative thought, we should take care to consider the import of his argument. Conservatism has customarily been viewed by its opponents as a narrow philosophy, narrow in its tolerance and sympathies, and narrow in its defense of privilege and the status quo. To deny that this or any other political philosophy is hedged by limitations of vision and self-interest is both futile and unnecessary. Political word and deed cannot reasonably be judged by purity of motive, as Calvinists judged propensity to salvation. Except in the utterly cynical, self-interest (enlightened or otherwise) is generally inseparable from a certain sense of what is fitting and proper in the political order. The diversities fostered by the local and immediate groupings of people—Burke's celebrated "little platoons"—and by the slow accumulations of time and tradition, represent the real broadness, the authentic liberality, of conservative reliance on experience, in contrast to the dreadful narrowness of revolutionaries who standardize and regiment in the name of equality.

Burke naturally expressed himself in eighteenth-century terms which emphasized rank and station as essential to the well-ordered society. Social uniformity, in this view, was simply the counterfeit of order, an instituted disorder, in fact, as it violated the natural and providential scheme of things. Uniformity was also temperamentally and aesthetically unsatisfactory. The revolutionary disregard of the ancient French provinces in the division of the country into departmental "chequers" is perceived as ugly and as obnoxious to the deepest sensibilities. In twentieth-century parlance, Burke might have said that this action and the spirit that it represented were "alienating" or destructive of "roots." For the most part, this sort of reaction remains implicit. But Burke is a genuine transitional figure in this respect. He represents at the same time an older sense of social hierarchy and a newer diversitarian aesthetic which has been one strain in the modern consciousness (although in constant tension with its polar opposite, the urge to uniformity).

The solvents which combine these two elements in Burke's thought are, from the positive standpoint, the reverence for tradition, in which the social order is established and sanctioned, and which ensures a pleasingly diverse social and political landscape; and from the negative standpoint, an extreme distrust of macroscopic planning fatal to hierarchy and diversity alike. Burke was convinced that the moral as well as the social order must encompass the actual diversity of life, and further that real diversity could not be planned. "The states of the Christian world," he pointed out, "have grown to their present magnitude in a great length of time, and by a great variety of accidents. . . . Not one of them has been formed upon a regular plan or with any unity of design." The British state seemed to him particularly praiseworthy as "that which pursues the greatest variety of ends, and is the least disposed to sacrifice any one of them to another, or to the whole. It aims at taking in the entire circle of human desires, and securing for them their fair enjoyment." The attempt of the French to create a state from abstract design, on the other hand, while achieving "unity and consistency in perfection," attained also a prescription for state power of the sort that a later age would call totalitarian: "dominion over minds by proselytism, over bodies by arms."[19]

Burke imparted to conservative thought, then, the notion that the real diversity of life can only be expressed through tradition, viewed as the product of the constructs and accommodations, the compromises and accidents, which have accumulated almost by a sort of natural selection in the course of time. Over against this accreted richness and variety of experience, in conservative imagery, bent the cruel figure of Procrustes, cutting the long limb short and stretching the short to fit the bed—never, as Burke exclaimed, his "hero of legislation."[20] Impatience with the vagaries of life ended in tyranny compounded of noble ends and ignoble means. Much in this Burkean vein, Samuel Taylor Coleridge remarked that the radical program consisted in the imposition

> of abstract reason, which, belonging only to beings equable and unchanging, are above man; while the materials implements and agency of its realization are found in terror, secrecy, falsehood, cupidity, and all the passions and practices which are, or ought to be, *below* man.[21]

Diversity, then, was human; to violate it in the name of an ideal unity was to evoke moral chaos.

NOTES

1. Gilbert K. Chesterton, *The Uses of Diversity* (London: The Library Press, Ltd., [1920]), 127-129.

2. J. L. Talmon, *The Origins of Totalitarian Democracy* (New York: W. W. Norton & Co., 1970), 3.

3. Edmund Burke, *The Works of the Right Honourable Edmund Burke* (London: George Bell & Sons, 1884-1892), VI, 147.

4. Gilbert K. Chesterton, *Heretics* (New York: John Lane Company, 1909), 180-181.

5. Ibid., 188-195.

6. Ibid., 184.

7. Philippe Ariès, *Centuries of Childhood: A Social History of Family Life,* trans. Robert Baldick (New York: Alfred A. Knopf, 1962), 414-415.

8. John Crowe Ransom, *God Without Thunder* (Hamden, Conn.: Archon Books, 1965), 124-125, 258, 291, 296.

9. Henry Saint John, 1st Viscount Bolingbroke, *Historical Writings* (Chicago: University of Chicago Press, 1972), 28-29.

10. Burke, *Works,* I, 132-133, 141-142, 154.

11. Russell Kirk, *The Conservative Mind* (Chicago: Henry Regnery, 1960), 66, 117.

12. Burke, *Works,* VI, 114, 116.

13. Ibid., II, 334.

14. Ibid., III, 28-29; V, 253-254.

15. Ibid., II, 28-29.

16. Ibid., II, 454-455.

17. Ibid., II, 467.

18. Ibid., II, 322-324.

19. Ibid., V, 253-255.

20. Ibid., I, 258.

21. Samuel Taylor Coleridge, *The Political Thought of Samuel Taylor Coleridge* (London: Jonathan Cape, 1938), 120.

3 G. K. Chesterton and the Scale of Existence

The sense of diversity draws upon a cluster of related qualities which may be summed up as having to do with the magnitude of experience: with the value placed on life itself, with the estimate of man as a creature in the universe, with the range and scale of the possibilities of existence. Conversely, a sense of the largeness of life depends upon perception of the variety and relative magnitude of the objects, qualities, and beings which make it up. There is little of such sense in a monistic or morally flattened world. Nineteenth-century materialistic determinism and such reductionist twentieth-century schools as the behaviorist, because they purport to explain experience in the narrowest possible terms ("atoms in motion" or "stimulus and response") are inimical to this kind of consciousness. As there is no proper scale, no basis for comparisons of value, there is nothing to prevent the life of the individual from swelling subjectively to encompass the universe, while dwindling objectively toward nullity. Indeed, given the inflation of the modern ego, endlessly obsessed with its own practical insignificance, this seems in ponderable measure to have occurred, preparing the mind for a way of life based on private hedonism and bureaucratic omnicompetence.

Perception of diversity and judgment of magnitude, then, are interdependent faculties, requiring a sense of significant place in a world of real differences and distinctions. For long ages this sense was maintained preeminently by religious conceptions. The range between heaven and hell in the Christian cosmos was vast, and the plenitude of creation between was the badge of divine glory. Man, in particular, was a creature of such magnitude as to contain within himself the potential for eternal blissful company with God or eternal damnation. Even the most devout today shrink from the latter in its old and literal sense of endless torture, but for all its harshness on one side of the ledger of judgment, the belief in the eternal consequences of human life undoubtedly preserved a sense of the enormous and diverse possibilities of man's existence. It seems a paradox that this sense of human range and significance depended upon a complementary awareness of man as a severely limited and corrupt being. It was, of course, the possibility of grace (and of its absence) which reconciled the two. In the modern world, on the contrary, where the reigning ideologies have supposed man to be unlimited in his secular possibilities and scientific and technological hubris has swept all before it, man's self-image has shrunk drastically. He appears no longer a noble or tragic creature; if possibly the riddle and the jest, he hardly thinks of himself as the glory of the universe. Such a being is reduced indeed. His possibilities are the external ones of technology, not the internal ones of the soul. And if the existentialism in which he dabbles offers a measure of dignity and freedom, it must also sit him down with Nothingness for company, for Plenitude has departed.

The sense of range and scale has also a close affinity with the sense of tradition. To feel oneself part of a tradition is to draw upon the varied experience of the past; it is also to be assured of the magnitude of one's own existence in relation to other existences in the dimension of time. Nothing so conduces to the counterfeit Nirvana of mass society as Thomas Paine's sovereignty of each generation, while Burke's vision of society as a partnership of the living, the dead, and the yet to be born extends indefinitely the range within which each "partner" understands and judges his own life.

The magnitude of life, as the term is used here, has little to do with physical size. The two may even be opposed, and at best the relationship is problematical. Sheer scale in space, when not simply overwhelming, can make one conscious of the qualitative magnitude of life—"broaden one's horizons" in the cant phrase. Man is a sacramental creature, who looks for the inward and spiritual grace in the outward and visible sign. Men have been known to see the glory of God proclaimed in the vast and cold beauty of the galaxies, and science fiction writers have occasionally achieved a new vision of plenitude and diversity in a universe teeming with life. In an earlier day the transatlantic and transpacific discoveries expanded at least on a secular level the European sense of the world's scope and variety. Yet one cannot blink the fact that the Age of Discovery was accompanied by the shrinkage of the medieval world-picture, which however geographically and astronomically cramped, displayed a cosmos immense and infinitely diversified in moral terms, stretching from God to Satan. Nor can it be maintained that the discovery of the immense physical dimensions of the universe during the last several centuries has been accompanied by a corresponding hypertrophy of the perceived magnitude of individual life. Greater "human possibilities," indeed, have been glimpsed by everyone, but they almost always have to do with more intricate technology and enhanced comfort, offering little analogue to the earlier vision of man struggling between heaven and hell, his eternity in the balance—an infinite being in the plane of his immortality.

Among modern writers who have seen these issues most clearly was G. K. Chesterton. Chesterton perceived that the magnitude, or significance, of life had little to do with physical size, unless to be obscured by it, and everything to do with such qualities as variety, adventure, and mystery. Chesterton blamed Herbert Spencer for popularizing the notion that astronomical dimensions overawed spiritual ideas:

> The size of this scientific universe gave one no novelty, no relief. The cosmos went on for ever, but not in its wildest constellation could there be anything really interesting; anything, for instance, such as forgiveness or free will. . . . So these expanders of the universe had nothing to show us except more and more infinite corridors of space lit by ghastly suns and empty of all that is divine.

Such a universe, it seemed to Chesterton, might as well be regarded as small as to be regarded as large; it was a trivial and suffocating waste in which "one never found the smallest window or a whisper of outer air.''[1] Materialism, in this view, possessed a kind of ''insane simplicity,'' like the madman imprisoned by his obsession with one idea. It rendered the whole of life even less significant than its parts. The Christian universe, in which there were spiritual qualities and beings, even miracles, was a far more diverse and, in the deepest sense, a far larger universe. ''The Christian admits that the universe is manifold and even miscellaneous, just as a sane man knows that he is complex. . . . But the materialist's world is quite simple and solid, just as the madman is quite sure he is sane.''[2]

In Chesterton's world it is the limited which offers the most variety and genuine magnitude of experience, while the purportedly universal is paradoxically cramped and narrow. A walled garden may show more of the multifarious glory of creation than a limitless but vacuous cosmos. Unfortunately, modern thought ''went against the fairy feeling about strict limits and conditions. The one thing it loved to talk about was expansion and largeness.''[3] The surprising result was the declining accessibility of adventure, which required nothing more urgently than a sense of limits, of orthodoxy. The modern impoverishment of adventure has been frequently lamented. Oliver Wendell Holmes, Jr. complained in 1886 that ''the scope for intellectual, as for physical adventure, is narrowing,'' and lately Paul Zweig has written about the depressed condition of adventure as a literary mode.[4] The thirst for adventure evidently persists, as those who set off around the world in sailboats or scale mountains and skyscrapers attest, but for the onlooker, at least, adventure does perhaps lack the cultural and symbolic weight that it once had. Chesterton wrote of the deepest adventure, the adventure of the spirit, and saw far into a modern impoverishment of soul.

Chesterton explicitly associated variety with adventure, and understood them both as aspects of religious orthodoxy. He was impressed by the way that the Catholic Church had made use of different, and even violently conflicting, qualities, of pacifism and bellicosity, of the clashing emotions of rival patriotisms, of celibacy and the family. Of the latter pair, he observed that the Church ''has kept them side by side like two strong colours, red and white, like the red and white upon the shield of St. George. It has always had a healthy hatred of pink.'' Whereas paganism rested on a symmetry, he thought, Christianity achieved a new kind of balance, one of apparent accidents. "In a Gothic cathedral the columns were all different, but they were all necessary."⁵

The balance was a precarious one; an orthodoxy constructed of such diversities was anything but safe and humdrum. Indeed, Chesterton thought, "there never was anything so perilous or so exciting as orthodoxy. It was sanity; and to be sane is more dramatic than to be mad. It was the equilibrium of a man behind madly rushing horses." The highest happiness attainable on earth would not consist in a mere animal contentment, but in a similar precarious and adventurous balance between faith and doubt. A Utopia of sameness, Chesterton added, would be as much a nightmare as one of anarchy. The gist of the matter was that the stakes of striving must be genuine, and only orthodoxy could guarantee this: "the perils, rewards, punishments, and fulfilments of an adventure must be real, or the adventure is only a shifting and heartless nightmare. . . . For the purpose even of the wildest romance results must be real; results must be irrevocable." Consequently the modern philosophy which found no meaning to the universe was devoid of romance, and its outward emancipation and artistry concealed an inner despair, while Christian orthodoxy preserved the old pagan joy of life within the forbidding walls of its discipline and abnegations. In sum, Chesterton believed, "a man cannot expect any adventures in the land of anarchy. But a man can expect any number of adventures if he goes travelling in the land of authority."⁶

Chesterton thus turned the tables on those who, in his own time or in ours, have thoughtlessly vaunted "emancipation" or "liberation" from orthodoxy, custom, and restraint. A world without limitations, he showed, was a world without variety or romance, debilitated even in sensuality. This was all the more the case in Chesterton's day as the demand for emancipation was commonly leagued with a scientific materialist point of view. And materialism imposed a different kind of restraint, thoroughly hostile to diversity and adventure: "it abolishes the laws which could be broken, and substitutes laws that cannot. And that is the real slavery."⁷ In a larger frame, Chesterton was clearly lamenting the fading from the world of the cosmic drama of good and evil, which Carl Becker, in *The Heavenly City of the Eighteenth Century Philosophers,* conceived as creating a greater gap between the Enlightenment and the twentieth century than that between the Middle Ages and the Enlightenment. Chesterton did not deny that the older perceptions of the world had a fairy-tale quality. For the scientific determinist, he pointed out,

> the leaf on the tree is green because it could never have been anything else. Now, the fairy-tale philosopher is glad that the leaf is green precisely because it might have been scarlet. . . . Every colour has in it a bold quality as of choice; the red of garden roses is not only decisive but dramatic, like suddenly spilt blood.[8]

That increasing scientific sophistication should be accompanied by a recession of such childlike wonder was no doubt inevitable. Did that condemn the world to an existence without adventure, romance, and genuine variety, or could these values be rediscovered on a higher level? They could not be, Chesterton would have insisted, without God, without orthodoxy.

Whether such values could be recaptured at all in a modern framework was doubtful at best. Chesterton's world was romantic by modern standards, however rooted in ultimate reality. It was a world filled not only with diversity and adventure, but with the attendant qualities of gallantry and mystery. That the modern world has forsaken knightly virtues for those of commerce was a commonplace before Burke's famous lament that the age of chivalry was dead, succeeded by that of calculators, sophisters, and economists. Such qualities as gallantry, courage, and generosity are superfluous— indeed, absurd—in a world without room for variety and adventure. The nature of gallantry was to make generous acknowledgment of difference of place or role, whether a difference of inequality or of opposition. "The virtue of the splendid tradition of chivalry," Richard Weaver noted,

> was that it took formal cognizance of the right to existence not only of inferiors but also of enemies. . . . Chivalry was a most practical expression of the basic brotherhood of man. . . . [The] shortsightedness which will not grant substance to other people or other personalities is just that intolerance which finds the different less worthy.[9]

As gallantry and chivalry constituted acknowledgment of and respect for the different which was known, the sense of mystery preserved an acknowledgment of and respect for the different which was unknown. Objectively, mystery is always with us: if no other, "why does the universe exist?"—or, if a theistic position be assumed, "why God?"—is the ultimate question which one cannot imagine ever being answered by any intelligence accessible to human beings. But for the subjective sense of mystery to flourish, there must be an idea of the universe as a diverse place, a place where radical otherness is possible. Otherwise the unexplained either falls under the heading of "problems yet to be solved" or is simply dismissed as unexplainable. This is quite properly the approach of science, but what is effective as scientific method can be numbing when applied to life in general. A monistic, materialistic determinism, such as that which flourished in the nineteenth century, vitiates mystery by dogmatically reducing both the explained and the unexplained to its own terms and shoving aside any left over, ultimate questions as irrelevant or futile. The result is a smaller, which is to say a more trivial, cosmos. Whether such a man-reduced cosmos truly represents a universe which in some ways seems even objectively more mysterious than it did a hundred years ago is highly doubtful. That it better accords with human temperament and intellect, as these can be inferred from the experience of the race so far, is unlikely. "Mysticism," Chesterton thought, "keeps men sane."

> As long as you have mystery you have health; when you destroy mystery you create morbidity. The ordinary man has always been sane because the ordinary man has always been a mystic. He has always left himself free to doubt his gods; but (unlike the agnostic of to-day) free also to believe in them. He has always cared more for truth than for consistency. . . . The whole secret of mysticism is this: that man can understand everything by the help of what he does not understand. The morbid logician seeks to make everything lucid, and succeeds in making everything mysterious. The mystic allows one thing to be mysterious, and everything else becomes lucid.[10]

Life is impoverished without this obeisance to the ineradicably mysterious element of existence. To be sure, fear may often lie at the root of this kind of sensibility: one is reminded of Brooks Adams's medieval archetype of the Man of Fear, in whom martial and imaginative qualities were closely leagued. Fear of the seen, thought Adams, produced the warrior; fear of the unseen, the priest; while the artist celebrated the triumphs of both, until with the growth of wealth and capitalism the Age of Fear was succeeded by the more prosaic Age of Greed. But Adams expounded this cyclical interpretation of history within a late Victorian conceptual framework of materialistic determinism of just the sort that Chesterton regarded as monomaniacal. The eleventh-century Crusaders were for the American fairy-tale figures, dazzling paladins in a world of illusion—in reality "conscious automatons" like their fellows, passive outlets for mental energy.[11]

Chesterton would hardly have denied the association of the valorous and imaginative qualities from his own positive Christian standpoint. But for him such knightliness was of the highest reality, and fear and the courage which overcame it were not to be reduced to psychological reflexes. Whereas paganism had found virtue in balance, he pointed out, Christianity located it in conflict and nurtured an affirmative bravery in a world of hazard. It had "held up . . . above the European lances the banner of the mystery of chivalry: the Christian courage, which is a disdain of death; not the Chinese courage, which is a disdain of life." But then, for Chesterton, Christianity was a religion of valor by its very nature, the only religion which believed that omnipotence left God incomplete. "Christianity alone has felt that God, to be wholly God, must have been a rebel as well as a king. Alone of all creeds, Christianity has added courage to the virtues of the Creator." Orthodoxy's "main advantage," he added, "is that it is the most adventurous and manly of all theologies."[12]

Chesterton's paradoxes were not mere sophistry. The frame of orthodox belief did contain the large and multifarious world in which adventure was real, gallantry served as generous acknowledgment of the vagaries and varieties of existence, and the sense of mystery admitted the unknown dimensions of life. These qualities represented ideals, but the ideals influenced the ways in which people thought and lived. They have remained attractive to the conservative temperament not alone from a cultural nostalgia, or a blindness to the horror and squalor that belong also to the past, but because they appeal to a belief in the range and diversity of human possibilities. If archaic virtues need be summoned to redress the balance of the present, it would not be the first time in history, and as with the revival of classical ideals during the Renaissance, the results might be fruitful beyond the ability of those who summoned them to foresee.

NOTES

1. Gilbert K. Chesterton, *Orthodoxy* (New York: John Lane Company, 1909), 110-113.

2. Ibid., 38-42.

3. Ibid., 33, 110. "There is such a thing as a narrow universality; there is such a thing as a small and cramped eternity; you may see it in many modern religions" (p. 33).

4. Julius J. Marke, ed., *The Holmes Reader* (New York: Oceana, 1955), 100; Paul Zweig, *The Adventurer* (New York: Basic Books, 1974).

5. Chesterton, *Orthodoxy,* 19, 177-183.

6. Ibid., 185, 210, 227-228, 257, 292-293.

7. Gilbert K. Chesterton, *Heretics* (New York: John Lane Company, 1909), 227-228.

8. Chesterton, *Orthodoxy,* 105-106.

9. Richard M. Weaver, *Ideas Have Consequences* (Chicago: University of Chicago Press, 1962), 175-176.

10. Chesterton, *Orthodoxy,* 49.

11. Brooks Adams, *The Law of Civilization and Decay: An Essay on History* (New York: Alfred A. Knopf, 1951), 123 and passim.

12. Chesterton, *Orthodoxy,* 170-171, 256-257.

Part Two

British and American Patterns

4 Law, Science, Romance

There have been many efforts to find a formula to explain modern history in terms of an altered balance or relationship between the One and the Many. For Henry Adams, although he saw its paradoxical aspects, the tendency of history between the thirteenth and twentieth centuries was from Unity to Multiplicity. Herbert Spencer and John Fiske sought to explain social as well as biological evolution in terms of an inexorable progression from indefinite, incoherent homogeneity to definite, coherent heterogeneity. A host of commentators since have found the key to modernity variously in standardization, social atomism, or irresistible centrifugal tendencies—"the center cannot hold." All such formulations may contain something of the truth; certainly all testify to the widespread feeling that the aspects of experience characterized by the terms "unity" and "diversity" are askew; yet the problem remains a thicket of contradictions. If asked to identify one leading characteristic of modern Western history, many would no doubt point to the growth of personal freedom and individuality. Yet immediately this assertion comes up against the totalitarian invitation to "escape from freedom," or the perhaps more seductive invitation to take an indefinite leave of absence from it with a highly bureaucratized welfare state. Even apart from such relatively clear political questions, it is difficult if not impossible to define any simple trend in a society which seems to become more standardized, more committed to the uniformity of existence, at the same time that unity of values shrinks to the minimal, and the means of self-satisfaction available to individuals in economically advanced countries become increasingly numerous. The resulting kaleidoscopic social dance, offering itself a kind of ever-changing sameness to numbed senses, has been bewildering to conservatives as it has to others. While in general it may be said that conservatives in the Burkean tradition, at least, have wished to preserve traditional diversities and have been suspicious of new ones, especially when they seem to defy any rationale of unity in diversity, they have found no simple solution to the problem. Any effort to unravel it must consider it in its historical framework.

Conservative consciousness in the matter of diversity is rooted in a number of social, political, scientific, and aesthetic considerations. Historically, it appears to be a late-articulated corollary of the medieval "discovery of the individual" as a being apart from his community—itself a logical outgrowth of the Christian idea of the ultimate value of the individual.[1] This unique and critical development in Western civilization opened the way for an endless proliferation of peculiarly personal traits, concerns, eccentricities, and obsessions, which came in the long course of time to be positively encouraged by prevailing ideas and values. But it also worked ultimately to cut the individual off from the social and traditional sources of his individuality—a consummation which has been glimpsed fully only in our own time. The long-term disintegration of the traditional community and the tendency toward an atomized mass society may have assumed the stylized contours of a myth or the shopworn ones of a cliché, but it would be difficult altogether to deny the pattern. The point to be made here is that it became part of the conservative understanding of history, and was interpreted to mean, among other things, that the increasing isolation of the individual threatened a properly diversified social order.

This was an apprehension shaped and abetted by conservative perceptions of related historical developments during the period that modern conservatism emerged as a self-conscious body of thought. Burke's indictment of political rationalism drew upon an older British preference for experience and tradition in the law and contributed to a growing conservative suspicion of legal and political standardizing. Science, completing its early modern transition from qualitative to quantitative assumptions, seemed to put its rapidly increasing weight down on the side of uniformity. The Romantic and historicist movements, on the other hand, offered rallying points for conservative champions of diversity, although not without serious difficulties and pitfalls. While these broad and cardinal developments in Western history obviously cannot be thoroughly explored here, we must consider something of their effects on conservative attitudes.

Law and politics offered perhaps the most obvious perspective from which to regard the supplanting of the diversified traditional social order by individual isolation and mass society. From this point of view, the emergence of the absolute state in early modern Europe, and its jealousy of any competing claims to individual loyalty, were seen to have exerted strong pressures for uniformity. John Neville Figgis offered an historian's appraisal of this process, which at the same time was that of a conservative Englishman of the early twentieth century. Figgis drew a sharp contrast between medieval political diversity and modern uniformity. To Nicholas of Cusa he attributed

> a magnificent expression of the ideal of a Christendom ruled by the principle of harmony, rather than that of uniformity, in which one polity shall still embrace both civil and spiritual activities, and brotherhood, the supreme principle of Christianity, shall become the inspiration of a delicately articulated society, the source of a varied and developing activity.[2]

The failure in the fifteenth century of the conciliar movement, however, signaled the triumph of a quite different polity; the papal triumph, Figgis thought, "meant the victory of the unitary and Roman over the federalist and Teutonic conception of society. . . . [The] notion of a single omni-competent social union set over against a mass of individuals became the normal idea of the State." Modern society, he added, was correspondingly both more individualistic and more socialistic than the medieval. The effect of subsequent developments, most notably of those connected with the Protestant

Reformation, had been to strengthen the "unitary system" of the nation, weaken federalist structures, and vitiate communal and corporate autonomies. It was left to dissenting groups like the "Monarchomachi" to resist the absolute state, insisting against the manifest tendency of history that "there are spheres of life and bonds of association which do not arise from its fiat and cannot be dissolved by it."[3]

The standardizing tendency which Figgis decried in the Roman law did not go unchallenged, especially in England. J.G.A. Pocock traces the roots of Edmund Burke's philosophy to a conception of custom worked out by sixteenth-century French and seventeenth-century English thinkers, the latter seizing on the common-law tradition as an alternative to the Roman. Legal scholars like Sir John Davies, Sir Edward Coke, and Sir Matthew Hale emphasized that (as Pocock paraphrases Davies) "written laws contain no more than the wisdom of one man or one generation, whereas custom in its infinite complexity contains the wisdom of many generations, who have tested it by experience, submitting it to a multitude of demands." In Coke, this insight issued in the idea of "artificial reason": that the law which "speaks through the judge is the distilled knowledge of many generations of men." There was in this school of thought, and appearing perhaps most clearly in Hale, the image of society and experience as endlessly diverse and complex—far too much so to be governed by laws which were the product of the will or of the reason of a moment. Burke, whose own thinking was "saturated" with these ideas,[4] would make them staples of his attack on the rationalists and revolutionaries who attempted to reduce all social and political diversity to fit their own designs.

Aside from purely legal thinking, there was coming into being in England by the eighteenth century a body of political opinion which explicitly valued social diversity, associating it both with differences of rank and differences of opinion. In particular the Whig "Commonwealthmen" described by Caroline Robbins inveighed against uniformity as rather the aspect of "brute creation" than of civilized human society. Sometimes the emphasis was on the folly of "leveling" the necessary and salubrious differences of social rank; at other times, as with Joseph Priestley, diversity was identified with liberty of belief and expression. Priestley believed that differences of opinion even in religion were entirely healthy—a notable departure in his day—and was wary of any attempt by the state to assume the function of education. State control, he feared, would promote uniformity. "The chief glory of human nature, the operation of reason in a variety of ways and with diversified results would be lost."[5]

Burke and the Commonwealthmen of his day were at sharp odds, especially over the French Revolution and the question of natural rights.[6] It is notable that they shared a sense of the positive value of diversity, however, and that except for the most radical Whigs, they shared also a tendency to couple diversity of social rank with diversity of belief and opinion. Burke was not alone in perceiving in the French revolutionary attack on rank not only an attack on the social order, but an attack on liberty. To those imbued with English notions of ordered liberty, the "uniformitarianism" of continental prophets of equality smacked at best of abstraction, at worst of tyranny, but little of liberty. Thus in its genesis as a conscious tradition, English conservatism imbibed a distrust of the monistic and uniform. In resistance to the threatened absolutism of monarchy, it was impelled to articulate the wise diversities of custom and tradition. And when the vastly more thorough absolutism of a revolutionary egalitarian ideology arose as a specter and at least partial reality in the late eighteenth century, very much the same arguments served. In the political arena, it appeared, the diversity of experience must stand opposed to the uniformity of abstract reason.

Attitudes toward diversity were powerfully affected also by developments in science. The "Scientific Revolution," culminating in the seventeenth century, was manifold and pervasive in its consequences. One of its effects was to alter permanently Western notions of unity and multiplicity. On one level, the new science revealed a world of undreamt variety. The invention of the microscope, in particular, showed the diversity of creation to be extended to minute realms below the threshold of unaided vision. A world of varied life existed in a drop of water.[7] The telescope revealed no new forms of life, and might seem to have added simply to the quantity of known stars and other bodies rather than to have introduced any new element of diversity. Yet it was possible to speculate about an endless variety of populated worlds. Giordano Bruno indeed had done so before the telescope was invented, but the progressively revealed dimensions of the macrocosm gave greater plausibility to such imaginings. Scientific investigation brought to light phenomena unknown before, revealed new planets and organisms, and eventually showed even the past to be far greater and more diverse than could earlier have been imagined—not six thousand years of a biologically static creation, as traditionally supposed, but a vast span including many millions of years of strange and struggling life forms.

Yet in other ways—and as it came to appear, more profound ways—the new science depicted a world that was only superficially diverse, a world of regularity and uniformity. Whereas Aristotelian science had been a science of qualities, modern science was one of quantities. Its whole technique was to reduce the multifariousness of the physical world and of man's experience in it to a few abstractions which could be precisely measured and manipulated. It could not have succeeded as it did without recourse to this kind of reductionism. The science of qualities had shown itself to be, after two thousand years, a dead end. Diversity to the new science, except as raw material for analysis, seemed a snare and a delusion—a veil that obscured reality, and behind which it was the mission of science to penetrate. In this new metaphysical picture of the world, a true hypothesis "reveals a mathematical order and harmony where before there had been unexplained diversity," E. A Burtt pointed out. "The real world is a world of quantitative characteristics only; its differences are differences of number alone."[8]

Thus Galileo drew a sharp distinction between primary and secondary qualities. Primary qualities, including number, figure, magnitude, position, and motion, belonged to an absolute, objective, and mathematical world, the *real* world which could be truly known. Secondary qualities, including color, taste, and odor, were relative and subjective, belonging to the "realm of opinion and illusion." Suggesting that all matter could ultimately be reduced to atoms which possessed only mathematical properties,[9] Galileo pointed unmistakably toward the dispensation of nineteenth-century scientific naturalism, for which "nature was essentially a mass of uniformly evolving atoms and energy."[10] Poets made prolific use of Newton's *Opticks* to sing of the beauties of a world touched by the variegated colors displayed by the prism, as Marjorie Nicolson has shown, but at least a few were chilled by the uniform dead-ness of the "real" world which science said lay behind the illusions of the rainbow.[11]

This radical reduction of the world of experience was part of a larger development which has been described as no less than the "destruction of the cosmos," of the cosmos, that is to say, as a variegated, hierarchical structure imbued with value and purpose. Involved in this was "the replacement of the Aristotelian conception of space—a differentiated set of inner-worldly places—by that of Euclidean geometry—an essentially infinite and homogeneous extension." The effect for philosophy as well as for science was, as Alexandre Koyré put it, to demolish "the conception of the world as a finite, closed, and hierarchically ordered whole" and to install in its stead "an indefinite and even infinite universe which is bound together by the identity of its fundamental components and laws, and in which all these components are placed on the same level of being."[12]

Although essential to the development of the modern scientific method, this reductionism need not logically have impinged upon a human or divine scale of values, or the variegated cosmos which went with it. Indeed, the sundering of the world of value from the external world of atoms and motion might reasonably have guaranteed the integrity of the former as effectively as it did that of the latter. After all, Christianity itself, by drawing a relatively clear line between Creator and Creation, in contrast to the ancient animism still strong even in Aristotle, carried a latent tendency to the sort of cold dissection of nature which was the triumph of seventeenth-century science. But Christianity had long compromised with animism and had found animistic elements positively congenial even at the time that Aquinas adopted Aristotle as "The Philosopher" in the thirteenth century. The eventual reaction against the qualitative, animistic cosmos might be indeed only the final realization of the Christian logic, but the compromise with animism had in practice so entangled Creator and Creation that their final separation could only be traumatic to the religious sense and damaging to the hierarchical array of values to which it gave life.

Besides, Cartesian dualism—to cite the clearest expression of this separation—asked too much of the human ability to compartmentalize experience. Human, or at least Western, consciousness seems ineluctably sacramental, ever seeking the inward and spiritual grace in the outward and visible sign. The conception of the physical universe did in fact impinge on the world of values, eroding the sense of the world as a place of diverse qualities. Even in politics, L. Pearce Williams points out, the progress and prestige of science in the eighteenth century helped to discredit the Old Regime. "The symmetry, order, and relative simplicity of the Newtonian world stood in vivid contrast to the chaotic hodge-podge of institutions, overlapping jurisdictions, irrationalities and sheer arbitrariness of the government of pre-revolutionary France."[13] But if the assumption of simplicity and uniformity paid enormous dividends for science, Edmund Burke and others were to find these qualities utterly pernicious when superimposed on the "hodge-podge" of human custom and political experience.

The Romantic Movement was in one aspect a reaction against scientific reductionism and the determinism and attempted exclusion of values that went with it. Bacon, Newton, and Locke were villains for William Blake, in their seeming denial of the real beauty of the world, and Wordsworth and Coleridge in their own ways rejected the materialism that they found in contemporary science.[14] Thomas Carlyle glimpsed diabolism in the purely mechanistic world view. While he heeded this "Everlasting No," "the Universe was all void of Life, of Purpose, of Volition, even of Hostility; it was one huge, dead, immeasurable Steam-engine, rolling on, in its dead indifference to grind me limb from limb." But to the "Everlasting Yea," the universe became one vast and living symbol of God.[15] Romanticism was of course a much broader phenomenon than this revolt against a colorless, monistic, steam-engine universe. Most notably for present purposes, it drew upon a mutation in aesthetic sensibilities considerably older than Romanticism as a self-conscious movement of the late eighteenth and early nineteenth centuries. In her aptly titled *Mountain Gloom and Mountain Glory: The Development of the Aesthetics of the Infinite,* Marjorie Nicolson described the fundamental change of attitude toward nature which took place during the seventeenth century. In brief, ideals of regularity and uniformity were challenged by those of "diversity, variety, irregularity." This new aesthetic was manifested most dramatically in the change of attitude toward mountains. Long considered ugly evidences of the fall of nature, mountains now became "sublime" in their very vastness, irregularity, and variety. Mountains were essential, it came to be felt, to a pleasingly diverse world.[16]

Actually, this shift in sensibility was not a simple one in favor either of diversity or of uniformity. After all, the abhorrence of mountains had coexisted well enough with satisfaction in the fullness and variety of God's creation. The distinction seems to be that this variety, insofar as it was deemed felicitous, could be understood as existing within a regular and uniform scheme, such as that of the Great Chain of Being. Mountains, being irregular and discontinuous in form, were more easily viewed as evidences of a "fallen nature." The new aesthetic, on the other hand, pulled toward a freer, less restrained diversity outside the bounds of regularity and symmetry. In another perspective, the Western consciousness seems at this point to divide: part of it accepting the reductionist uniformity commanded by the new science, part embracing a new temperamental and aesthetic hyperdiversity beyond the older ordering principles.

Not that this psychic split was complete, or sharply defined—the new aesthetic indeed drew upon those aspects of the scientific revolution which seemed to reveal the teeming plenitude of the Creation and the multifarious ingenuity of the Creator.[17] But there did emerge during the Enlightenment a heightened tension between the new sense of the diversity of the world and the scientifically reinforced desire to reduce it to order. It was one of the marks of the Enlightenment itself to place the dominant emphasis on regularity and uniformity; the Romantics brought a set of opposing values to temperamental and aesthetic consummation.

The "Romantic Movement" was notoriously a hydra-headed phenomenon, and whatever is said about it, usually the opposite can be said as well. Critics have generally agreed, however, in ascribing to Romanticism a heightened sense of the variety of life, of particulars as opposed to universals, of asymmetries alike in the external world and in the human psyche.[18] Arthur Lovejoy identified "diversitarianism" as a leading tendency of the Romantic period. "One of the most revolutionary of the ideas of the 1790s," he thought, "was an assertion of the value of diversity in human opinions, characters, tastes, arts and cultures." Where before it had been assumed that only the uniform could accord with rationality, now it seemed profoundly true that diversity was natural to life.[19] While the "uniformitarianism" of eighteenth-century rationalists had made room for an individualism based on "the equality and inter-changeability of individual beings or groups," as a later historian put it, the new sensibility valued especially their singularity or peculiarity. Thinkers like Locke who seemed not to do justice to these qualities were accordingly devalued.[20]

This new appreciation of diversity did not mean that Romantics sought to break down experience into unrelated fragments; here the distinction between unity and uniformity must come into play. If Romantics were repelled by the spectacle of uniformity, much of their energy was expended in seeking the ultimate unity within the flux and multiplicity of existence—the "Multeity in Unity," as Coleridge called it.[21] But the unique concrete entity maintained its integrity; even Ralph Waldo Emerson allowed that "Nature will not be Buddhist: she resents generalizing, and insults the philosopher in every moment with a million of fresh particulars." Consequently human beings were "amphibious creatures, weaponed for two elements, having two sets of faculties, the particular and the catholic."[22]

This was not quite the older ideal, beloved of conservatives, of unity in diversity, however. Romantic diversity differed most fundamentally from earlier conceptions in being dynamic in principle rather than a static plenitude. In this aspect, Romanticism was simply one mode of expression for the characteristic nineteenth-century preoccupaton with the time process, which was manifested also in the maturation of historical studies, in historicism, in the full ripening of the idea of progress, in deterministic schemes of social development such as the Marxist, and in the Darwinian theory of biological evolution, with all the productive and dubious inferences drawn from it. Obviously not all of the manifold results of this dynamic spirit were congenial to conservatism. They could mean disavowal of tradition, the indiscriminate embracing of novelty, even revolution. But they could encourage also respect for continuity, concern with the past as forerunner of present and future, and reliance on experience as opposed to abstract reason. Burke's "partnership of generations" was a partnership of greater significance in the heightened awareness that each generation represented its own distinct possibilities of expression, different from those of any other.

Amidst all the varied emphases on process, the idea of diversity itself was historicized; it now came to be regarded as the product of time. Hegelian idealism gave the fullest philosophical expression to this view. Unity, in Hegel's interpretation, realized itself progressively through a multiplicity of expression. Of the One, the Spirit, Hegel wrote that

> we see it exerting itself in a variety of modes and directions; developing its powers and gratifying its desires in a variety which is inexhaustible; because every one of its creations, in which it has already found gratification, meets it anew as material and is a new stimulus to plastic activity. The abstract conception of mere change gives place to the thought of Spirit manifesting, developing, and perfecting its powers in every direction which its manifold nature can follow. What powers it inherently possesses we learn from the variety of products and formations which it originates.[23]

Not only was history at large a process of proliferation and differentiation, but, Hegel found, these qualities were most pronounced in the most felicitous ages of human culture. Heterogeneity, for example, was characteristic of the Greek spirit. In Athens, elements of freedom and equality had combined with local autonomy and an indwelling spirit of beauty, Hegel thought, to provide a framework within which "all diversities of character and talent, and all variety of idiosyncrasy could assert themselves in the most unrestrained manner." When the Roman power arose, on the other hand, it was in "deadly contraposition to the multiform variety of passion which Greece presents," although according to the dialectic, Roman uniformity would prepare the way in turn for the higher freedom of Christianity.[24]

In the Hegelian as well as in other nineteenth-century schemes of history, diversity of expression was balanced by unity of process. The potential existed for either element to swallow the other. In fact, as the Romantic mood gave way after mid-century to the "Age of Realism and Materialism" (in the phrase of Carleton J. H. Hayes), there was a tendency for such historical schemes to become more narrowly monistic and deterministic, a change of emphasis visible in contrasting the Marxian dialectic with the Hegelian. Even the benign formula of Herbert Spencer and John Fiske, tracing the historical process from "indefinite, incoherent homogeneity" to "definite, coherent heterogeneity," was applied so narrowly as to seem to champions of the "open universe" like William James intolerably tame and reductionist.

For all the metaphysical pitfalls, however, the new consciousness of diversity in time became ineradicably part of the Western mind. The Romantics were less likely than their predecessors to attempt a facile equation between the Roman and American republics, or, as Jefferson did, to seek in Virginia a kind of restoration of King Alfred's England, an idealized England purged of Norman feudal corruptions. They ceased to write off the Middle Ages as an epoch of "Gothic" barbarism and superstition. And this interest in the past for its own sake, in terms of its own peculiar qualities, could only suggest the positive value of at least some of the baggage of tradition which society carried.

In some, the feeling for the past combined with the Romantic disdain for abstract reason to produce a reaction against the present as less interesting, less diverse, duller, and more regimented than the past. Thomas Love Peacock understood this point of view. In his *Crotchet Castle* (1831), various allegorically named characters discourse on the state of the world. There is

> Mr. Toogood, the cooperationist, who will have neither fighting nor praying; but wants to parcel out the world into squares like a chess-board, with a community on each, raising every thing for one another, with a great steam-engine to serve them in common for tailor and hosier, kitchen and cook.

(Peacock here combines two recurring images of modern uniformity: the checkerboard and the engine or dynamo.) Quite different, however, is the vision of Mr. Chainmail, the partisan of the Middle Ages:

> I do not see any compensation for that kindly feeling which, within their own little communities, bound the several classes of society together, while full scope was left for the development of natural character, wherein individuals differed as conspicuously as in costume. Now we all wear one conventional dress, one

conventional face; we have no bond of union, but pecuniary interest . . . we have no nature, no simplicity, no picturesqueness: every thing about us is as artificial and as complicated as our steam-machinery.

The same plaint, in very much the same terms, would be echoed by romantic conservatives down to the present. Mr. Chainmail's assertion that moderns were incapable of a medieval intensity of feeling could have been delivered by Henry Adams three-quarters of a century later: "Hearts, heads, and arms have all degenerated, most sadly. We can no more feel the high impassioned love of the ages, which some people have the impudence to call dark, than we can wield King Richard's battleaxe."[25]

Part of the association of the old and traditional with the diverse lay in the Romantic attachment to place, to the immediate ties of kinship and locality, as opposed to the universal, uniform, and abstract. This feeling was strong, for example, in William Wordsworth, who after seeing the French Revolution fail to achieve fraternal community on the grand scale, sought it in local and traditional groupings: Burke's "little platoons."[26] Wordsworth, in his mature conservatism, disdained those reformers who would sacrifice the near to the remote and private obligation to public virtue, who would rule out of account "every thing intricate in motive, and mixed in quality" in favor of a uniform national allegiance.[27] Wordsworth was a patriot, but he shared the Romantic conservative sense of patriotism arising through proximate attachments. His was perhaps the most winning statement of the Burkean view which is limited in space but long in time:

> Love and admiration must push themselves out towards some quarter: otherwise the moral man is killed. Collaterally they advance with great vigour to a certain extent—and they are checked: in that direction, limits hard to pass are perpetually encountered: but upwards and downwards, to ancestry and to posterity, they meet with gladsome help and no obstacles; the tract is interminable.[28]

Similar sentiments are found in Sir Walter Scott, who remarked that "my patriotism is so much stronger than my general philanthropy that I should hear with much more composure of a general conflagration at Constantinople than of a hut being on fire at Lichfield.''[29] Scott, who has been called ''a Burke for the multitude'' during the nineteenth century, found the richness and variety of life in the accretions of time and custom. His conservative need for order and stability, Crane Brinton suggested, was complemented by a romantic need for the sorts of social contrasts and conflicts that give rise to adventure. Reform politics satisfied neither of these requirements, while the standardizing policies which often accompanied reform seemed to Scott to fly in the face of reality itself:

> The degree of national diversity between different countries is but an instance of that general variety which Nature seems to have adopted as a principle through all her works, as anxious to avoid, as modern statesmen to enforce, anything like an approach to absolute uniformity.[30]

As an artist, Scott could hew more closely to nature. The concreteness and variety with which he was able to imbue the life of the past were largely responsible for the effectiveness of his Waverley novels, while on a more philosophical plane he has been credited as a harbinger of historicism for his willingness to portray a period on its own terms.[31] To do so was to make possible for the first time a full consciousness of the diversity of human experience.

Samuel Taylor Coleridge was a more complicated case. Coleridge combined a Platonic and Neoplatonic approach to Christianity with a Burkean emphasis on social institutions, the products of history, as providing the necessary framework for rights and duties. Next to Burke, indeed, it was perhaps Coleridge who did most to establish the intellectual basis for British conservatism in the nineteenth century.[32] Coleridge was the champion of unity in life and thought, but of a unity of parts, not of a unity of uniformity or of massed social atoms. The former was truly, he believed,

> the principle of unity, and that derived from within, not from the objects of our senses, (which deprived of the interpreting power from within are but an alphabet run mad, are in reality

only a tendency like matter itself to be divided and divided *ad infinitum*) that unity in which we have to thank our better nature that though we may perish without end, we cannot utterly cease to be.[33]

But the antithesis of this kind of transcendent unity, Coleridge supposed, was to be found in what he thought of as the modern mechanical, "Atomistic" faith. The ancients, he believed, had had an organic sense of the world: of the

self-subsistence, yet interdependence, the difference yet Identity of the forms they express'd by the symbol of begetting. With the Moderns, on the contrary, nothing grows; all is made— Growth itself is but a disguised mode of being made by the superinduction of jam data upon a jam datum.

So far had the mechanical mode of thought permeated English thinking, Coleridge exclaimed, that "it is in spite of ourselves that we are not like a Herd of Americans, a people without a *History*." The allusion was unfair, but it would not be the last time that America would serve as the specter of an atomized, rootless, undifferentiated society.[34]

These qualms about the increasing standardization of culture were markedly modern in tone. It seemed to Coleridge that "now you may pass from one end of England to the other and scarcely know you are twenty miles from London, from the general uniformity of language, habit, information." That this uniformity tended to increase confidence between Englishmen and augment the physical strength of the country, he gratefully acknowledged. "But it has taught us to consider men, our fellow creatures, mere parts of the machine," he feared. "It has directed us to consider the quantity of consumable *goods* without reference to the quality of the consumer."[35] This economic man, Coleridge thought, was very little of a whole man.

Genuine wholeness, the lesson was, must encompass real diversity. Coleridge recognized that attempts to arrive at unity through abstraction, through political absolutism—whether monarchical or democratic—or through a deracinated cosmopolitanism, ignored the varying character of human existence, with its roots in locality and nationality. This, he thought, was the danger incurred by such a thinker as Jean Jacques Rousseau:

> He must admit *expedience* founded on *experience* and particular circumstances, which will vary in every different nation, and in the same nation at different times, as the maxim of all Legislation and the ground of all Legislative Power. For his universal principles, as far as they are principles and universal, necessarily suppose uniform and perfect subjects, which are to be found in the *Ideas* of pure Geometry and (I trust) in the *Realities* of Heaven, but never, never, in creatures of flesh and blood.[36]

Such unity as was attainable in this life arose from concrete particulars. Men like Plato, Luther, and Newton were universal in their significance, but they had arisen not from "the wide empires of Asia, where millions of human Beings acknowledge no other bond but that of a common slavery," but from "a circle defined by human affections," he pointed out. Patriotism, denoting devotion to a distinct and coherent social environment, was thus the link between individual genius and true universality.[37] "Let us beware of that proud philosophy which affects to inculcate philanthropy while it denounces every home-born feeling by which it is produced and nurtured," Coleridge urged in sum. "The paternal and filial duties discipline the heart and prepare it for the love of all mankind. The intensity of private attachments encourages, not prevents, universal benevolence."[38]

Although pronounced in figures like Scott and Coleridge, the Romantic affinity for conservative ideas about diversity was only partial and contingent. In some of its manifestations, of course, Romantic sensibility was profoundly antipathetic to conservatism itself. Rebelling against custom and standards, Romantics glorified the individual ego, sometimes to antinomian lengths. Faith in the loftiest of human possibilities sanctioned revolutions and perfectionist social experiments, such as those of American socialist communities. Even touching the notion of diversity, Romanticism was too protean a movement not to work in different directions. At times, contrary to the conservative assumption that unity and diversity were properly concomitants, Romantics seemed to enshrine variety merely for the sake of self-expression, sensation, variety's own sake. The Romantic delight in idiosyncrasy, Lovejoy notes, easily became a belief in its superiority. The result could be a "particularistic uniformitarianism, a tendency to seek to universalize things originally valued because they were not universal."[39] Thus Romantic appreciation of the distinctive traits of particular cultures could become a nationalism or racialism which ascribed universal validity or supremacy to one's own culture, for example. This could in the end contribute to the rise of such a uniformitarian, totalitarian movement as National Socialism, as abhorrent to conservatives as to liberals.

Certainly an ample share of the criticism of the Romantic Movement has come from conservative quarters, and partly on the grounds that it distorted or undermined a proper sense of diversity. The New Humanist critics of the early twentieth century, Paul Elmer More and Irving Babbitt, attacked the influence of Romanticism precisely on the point of its unchecked diversitarianism, which they thought led through relativism to nihilism. Neither More nor Babbitt was hostile to diversity, but both believed that Romanticism slighted or rejected the necessary balance of unity. More suggested that an unrestrained pursuit of diversity would turn back against itself and, in the absence of fixed standards, forfeit the ability to differentiate. This could lead, for example, to a noble-sounding but vague and indiscriminate humanitarianism, in which vital distinctions among human beings were lost in an abstract conception of humanity. More called for a dualism, and approvingly quoted Plato: "Show me a man able to see both the one and the many in nature, and I will follow in his footsteps as though he were a god."[40]

Babbitt, although he regarded himself as nearer to Buddha than to Plato in his treatment of the problem, also invoked the Greek philosopher. "The complete critic," he thought,

> will accept the historical method but be on guard against its excess. He will see an element in man that is set above the local and the relative; he will learn to detect this abiding element through all the flux of circumstance; in Platonic language, he will perceive the One in the Many.

But the Romantic, or "Rosseauist," lacking a sense of bounds and the discipline of an ethical center, could attain no real sense of unity, Babbitt thought; at best he could grasp unity as a kind of dream. Genuine unity must abide within the flux and diversity of reality.[41]

Other twentieth-century conservative thinkers have been equally dismayed by the relativistic tendencies of the Romantic age. Leo Strauss, in his skillful defense of natural right, subjected to particularly weighty criticism the historicism which emerged from this period. This criticism was all the more noteworthy in that it included Edmund Burke among the culprits. Burke and other conservatives, Strauss implied, had entangled themselves in one of the great ironies of intellectual history—although not without the aid of such as Jean Jacques Rousseau.

Rousseau, by suggesting that man's real humanity is a product of the historical process, had helped intellectually to arm the opponents of the French Revolution, Strauss pointed out. Perceiving the revolutionary potential in the appeal to universal principles, conservatives responded by rejecting the universal in favor of the historical.

> The only kinds of rights that were neither incompatible with social life nor uniform were "historical" rights: rights of Englishmen, for example, in contradistinction to the rights of man. Local and temporal variety seemed to supply a safe and solid middle ground between antisocial individualism and unnatural universality.[42]

In taking such ground, however, men like Burke were preparing the way for an historicism which denied eternal principles and held all human thought and culture to be simply the product of history. And this was far more revolutionary in consequence than revolutionary misuse of natural rights philosophy. It issued logically in relativism and even in nihilism, for without external standards of judgment, history itself became a meaningless procession of events. "The attempt to make man absolutely at home in this world ended in man's becoming absolutely homeless."[43] By the same path, Strauss might have added, an excess of historicism could lead finally to a recession of historical consciousness—signs of which there have been in our own time.

As Strauss acknowledged, Burke's own devotion to classical and Christian canons of virtue kept him well short of the full logic of historicism. And we might see in this simply another demonstration of the principle in intellectual history that it is unforeseeable where ideas will lead and what company they will keep. (Mussolini claimed a debt to William James.) The facile and not completely satisfactory lesson would be that of balance. Strauss himself admitted an inherent tension between the natural-rights doctrine and "respect for diversity or individuality."[44] (He seems to have equated the latter two.) Certainly there is a parallel tension between experience and principle. We seem to be led back to the proposition that standards, regarded as absolute, are needed to set the values of the diverse elements of life, and that experience may exemplify or clarify these standards, but does not beget them.

As Strauss showed the incompatibility of conservatism with a pure historicism, he suggested too the limits of its compatibility with the closely related phenomenon of Romanticism. In practice, of course, conservatism neither wholly embraced nor wholly rejected Romanticism; it was certainly tinctured by the Romantic mood. Of most concern here are the ways in which conservatism in its modern and self-conscious inception imbibed a devotion to diverse experience, not only for its intrinsic worth, but as furnishing unfriendly soil for political and intellectual absolutism. Romantic currents helped to make explicit the positive value of diversity which earlier precepts implied: among these currents were a new aesthetic going beyond canons of uniformity; appropriation of the varied world revealed by science, but rejection of scientific reductionism; and a sense of the historical past as the source of the pleasing and fertile variety of social life. An older adherence to customary law could merge easily—perhaps too easily—with the grander conceptions of time process that characterized the nineteenth century. Politically, for conservatives, Romanticism reinforced the distrust of ideology which sacrificed the concrete to the abstract, and which in attempting to universalize human experience threatened to pulverize it into individual quanta which would be trivially differentiated at best. These were lessons of some relevance for a future in which triumphant science encouraged a less inspired scientism, and in which new means of state power tempted those who would use it to politicize and regulate the whole of life—at the cost, conservatives thought, of its diverse abundance.

NOTES

1. See Colin Morris, *The Discovery of the Individual, 1050-1200* (New York: Harper & Bros., 1973).

2. John Neville Figgis, *Political Thought from Gerson to Grotius, 1414-1625* (New York: Harper & Bros., 1960), 70.

3. Ibid., 59-60, 78-80, 92, 189.

4. J.G.A. Pocock, *The Ancient Constitution and the Feudal Law* (New York: Norton, 1967), 34-36, 171-173, 242-243.

5. Caroline Robbins, *The Eighteenth Century Commonwealthman* (Cambridge: Harvard University Press, 1961), 21, 284-285, 350, and passim.

6. Ibid., 345, 380.

7. Marjorie Hope Nicolson, *Science and Imagination* (Ithaca: Cornell University Press, 1962), 208-211 and passim.

8. Edwin Arthur Burtt, *The Metaphysical Foundations of Modern Physical Science* (Garden City, N.Y.: Doubleday & Co., 1954), 65, 67. (Original italics omitted.)

9. Ibid., 83-86.

10. Frank Miller Turner, *Between Science and Religion* (New Haven: Yale University Press, 1974), 24.

11. Marjorie Hope Nicolson, *Newton Demands the Muse* (Princeton: Princeton University Press, 1946), 149-151 and passim.

12. Alexandre Koyré, *From the Closed World to the Infinite Universe* (Baltimore: The Johns Hopkins Press, 1957), viii, 2.

13. L. Pearce Williams, "The Politics of Science in the French Revolution," *Critical Problems in the History of Science,* ed. Marshall Clagett (Madison: University of Wisconsin Press, 1959), 294.

14. Nicolson, *Newton Demands the Muse,* 165-171; Hans Georg Schenk, *The Mind of the European Romantics* (London: Constable, 1966), 169.

15. Thomas Carlyle, *Sartor Resartus* (New York: Macmillan, 1927), 138, 179.

16. Marjorie Hope Nicolson, *Mountain Gloom and Mountain Glory* (Ithaca: Cornell University Press, 1959), 16, 139, 268-270 and passim.

17. Ibid., 130-137.

18. E. g. Carl Woodring, *Politics in English Romantic Poetry* (Cambridge: Harvard University Press, 1970), 327-328.

19. Arthur O. Lovejoy, "The Meaning of Romanticism for the Historian of Ideas," *Journal of the History of Ideas* 2 (June 1941): 275-277.

20. Schenk, *European Romantics,* 15. Woodring notes that Locke's psychology and political philosophy "have a common flaw for the romantic. They neglect human and social originality, growth, and variety." *Politics in English Romantic Poetry,* 34.

21. Quoted by James Engell, *The Creative Imagination* (Cambridge: Harvard University Press, 1981), 358.

22. Ralph Waldo Emerson, *The Complete Essays* (New York: Modern Library, 1950), 441, 437.

23. Georg Wilhelm Friedrich Hegel, *The Philosophy of History* (New York: Dover Productions, Inc., 1956), 73.

24. Ibid., 227, 260, 277-278.

25. Thomas Love Peacock, *Crotchet Castle* (New York: AMS Press, 1967), 61, 123-124, 145.

26. See Michael H. Friedman, *The Making of a Tory Humanist* (New York: Columbia University Press, 1979), 92; Ronald W. Harris, *Romanticism and the Social Order, 1780-1830* (London: Blandford Press, 1969), 186.

27. William Wordsworth, "To the Freeholders of Westmorland," *The Prose Works of William Wordsworth* (London: Edward Moxon, Son, and Co., 1876), I, 234.

28. William Wordsworth, "Concerning the Convention of Cintra," *Prose Works,* I, 156.

29. Walter Scott, *The Letters of Sir Walter Scott* (New York: AMS Press, 1971), I, 397 (Scott to Anna Seward, November 23, 1807).

30. Crane Brinton, *The Political Ideas of the Engish Romanticists* (Ann Arbor: University of Michigan Press, 1966), 117-119, 141.

31. David Brown, *Walter Scott and the Historical Imagination* (London, Boston, and Henley: Routledge & Kegan Paul, 1979), 190, 194, 204.

32. Harris, *Romanticism and the Social Order,* 219-221, 232.

33. Samuel Taylor Coleridge, *The Philosophical Lectures of Samuel Taylor Coleridge* (London: Pilot Press, 1949), 196 (Lecture V, January 18, 1819).

34. Samuel Taylor Coleridge, *Collected Letters of Samuel Taylor Coleridge,* ed. Earl Leslie Griggs (Oxford: Clarendon Press, 1959), IV, 761 (Coleridge to Lord Liverpool, July 28, 1817).

35. Coleridge, *Philosophical Lectures,* 287 (Lecture IX, February 22, 1819).

36. Samuel Taylor Coleridge, *The Collected Works of Samuel Taylor Coleridge* (Princeton: Princeton University Press, 1969), I, 202.

37. Ibid., I, 292-293.

38. Samuel Taylor Coleridge, *The Political Thought of Samuel Taylor Coleridge* (London: Jonathan Cape, 1938), 39.

39. Arthur O. Lovejoy, *The Great Chain of Being* (New York: Harper & Row, 1960), 313-314. See also Lovejoy, "The Meaning of Romanticism," 277.

40. Paul Elmer More, *The Drift of Romanticism* (Boston and New York: Houghton Mifflin Co., 1913), 281, 302.

41. Irving Babbitt, *Rousseau and Romanticism* (Cleveland: The World Publishing Company, 1968), 8-9, 12, 26, 150.

42. Leo Strauss, *Natural Right and History* (Chicago: The University of Chicago Press, 1953), 13-14.

43. Ibid., 316-323, 12-14, 6, 18.

44. Ibid., 5.

5 The "English Garden of Politics"

The British, unlike the Americans, have a remarkably full and articulate tradition of thought explicitly linking the idea of diversity to groups, ranks, and corporations within society. This reflects, certainly, the more clearly stratified nature of British society, the antiquity of its ranks and orders, and a constitution which expressly recognized the ancient fundamental social divisions of the country. The onset of democracy in the nineteenth century was very far from obliterating these distinctions, and among British conservatives there continued to be into the mid-twentieth century a willingness, far greater than among any counterpart group of Americans, to associate diversity with social hierarchy.

Had its own clear interests and inclinations not impelled it to recognize this association, British conservatism would still have possessed the authority of its reputed father, Edmund Burke. Burke regarded man as by nature a corporate being.[1] The individual found his proper relation to the state not as an atom in a mass, but as a member of one or more of the corporate bodies which comprised the kingdom. The natural diversity of society found expression through the diversity of orders, recognized and established by the constitution. This was, indeed, inevitable in a constitution which was the product of time and experience.

You will observe, that from Magna Carta to the Declaration of Right, it has been the uniform policy of our constitution to claim and assert our liberties, as an *entailed inheritance* derived to us from our forefathers, and to be transmitted to our posterity; as an estate specially belonging to the people of this kingdom, without any reference whatever to any other more general or prior right. By this means our constitution preserves a unity in so great a diversity of its parts. We have an inheritable crown; an inheritable peerage; and a House of Commons and a people inheriting privileges, franchises, and liberties, from a long line of ancestors.[2]

From its Burkean (and pre-Burkean) fountainheads, British conservatism developed a coherent though never systematized body of beliefs. At bottom these beliefs rested on a temperament or attitude which refused to countenance the reduction or diminution of life for the sake of ideology. "The political importance of this instinct of enjoyment, this largely thoughtless devotion to the life of here and now in all its richness and variety," as one commentator put it, "is that it puts politics in its place as something secondary or incidental." Viewing men as living ultimately under not a political but a cosmological order, Reginald J. White suggested, conservatives were not disposed to regard politics as the be-all and end-all of existence, and were, conversely, friendly to the private sphere of life. This meant not to leave at liberty a mass of isolated individuals, however, but to give free play to a diverse and "organic" society of groups and classes. To the conservative, White supposed, individuality was rather a religious than a political concept, and for the state to act on the premise that individuals were the ultimate elements in society was for it to usurp the functions of a church, and with the means, lacking to modern churches, of thorough-going tyranny.[3]

The close association of diversity with groups and classes was distinctly conservative. It drew, however, on a penchant for variety which was a broader phenomenon in British life and thought. John Stuart Mill's plea for liberty and against conformity was animated in part by diversitarian sentiments. Mill recognized, moreover, that diversity had to some extent a collective character. Europeans had been preserved from a Chinese type of stagnation, he thought, by "their remarkable diversity of character and culture. Individuals, classes, nations, have been extremely unlike one another: they have struck out a great variety of paths, each leading to something valuable."[4] Primarily, however, Mill associated diversity with individuality.

> It is not by wearing down into uniformity all that is individual in themselves, but by cultivating it and calling it forth, within the limits imposed by the rights and interests of others, that human beings become a noble and beautiful object of contemplation; and as the works partake the character of those who do them, by the same process human life also becomes rich, diversified, and animating, furnishing more abundant aliment to high thoughts and elevating feelings, and strengthening the tie which binds every individual to the race, by making the race infinitely better worth belonging to. In proportion to the development of his individuality, each person becomes more valuable to himself, and is therefore capable of being more valuable to others.[5]

Mill was a prophet of liberal ideas of diversity, emphasizing the value of individuality and nonconformity, even to the point of eccentricity, as of the essence of liberty. Eccentricity, he supposed, was apt to appear in any society in proportion to genius, strength of character, and moral courage, and he regarded it as ominous that few dared to be eccentric in his own time.[6] (Later, of course, the Victorian eccentric would become a stock character.) There was little room in this view for the conservative notion of diversity as nurtured by tradition and local and familial associations, however. Such things indeed, Mill suggested, were threats to individuality, and hence to diversity; more than once he spoke of the "despotism of custom," and argued that in the present age, "the mere example of nonconformity, the mere refusal to bend the knee to custom, is itself a service."[7] One wonders whether, had he lived a century later and been confronted with the spectacle of hordes of people conforming to a free-floating *Zeitgeist* in the name of liberation, he would have recognized in custom and tradition inexpendable supports not only for diversity but for individuality itself.

Gertrude Himmelfarb has recently argued that under the influence of his wife, Mill shifted significantly in *On Liberty* away from his more moderate earlier views to make of liberty, with its corollaries of individuality and variety, virtually an absolute—a paramount value unbalanced by considerations of authority or moral restraint. In this view, he helped to undermine the traditional and historical bases of particular liberties and to foster an assumed equation of individuality and liberty with an adversary posture toward society. Ignoring the possibility that liberty would be used to "explore the depths of depravity" as well as to elevate the human spirit, Mill must consequently share the blame for an immoderate relativism characteristic of our time: in particular the "denial of distinctions, the all-or-nothing mentality, which is one of the most prominent features of current liberalism."[8] The effect was not necessarily to promote real heterogeneity. Himmelfarb points out with regard to the feminist cause, for example, that "where Mill sought to liberate women in order to release the greatest variety of individuality, the movement today emphasizes the search for a common identity, a shared 'consciousness,' a 'sisterhood' which will promote the common cause against a common enemy."[9]

These conclusions have been disputed, on scholarly as well as ideological grounds. But the questions raised by Mill and his critics, past and present, do at least indicate with some clarity the way in which a desirable diversity is differently understood by liberals and conservatives. Mill incurred in his own time most notably the conservative strictures of James Fitzjames Stephen. Stephen attacked the "odd manner in which Mr. Mill worships mere variety, and confounds the proposition that variety is good with the proposition that goodness is various." Mill seemed to deny that any form of variety could be judged on its merits, and to suggest that any effort to discriminate was pernicious. As for Mill's praise of eccentricity, that quality seemed to Stephen more apt to be a mark of weakness than of strength, and certainly no sign of genuine originality.[10]

Stephen was not hostile to diversity, but he conceived of it as belonging to a social order which recognized inevitable inequalities of ability and attainment. Men were, he thought, fundamentally unequal, and this inequality would naturally manifest itself in social and legal distinctions.[11] From this perspective, it appeared that Mill had grossly overemphasized British conformity. "Many and many a fisherman, common sailor, workman, labourer, gamekeeper, policeman, non-commissioned officer, servant, and small clerk, have I known," Stephen recalled, "who were just as distinct from each other, just as original in their own way, just as full of character as men in a higher rank of life." (Calling attention here to a certain social myopia in Mill's dismissal of ordinary lives, Stephen fell into the same error in dismissing American "equality" as productive of "an immense multitude of commonplace, self-satisfied, and essentially slight people."[12] Diversity suffers from distance.) Indeed, Stephen implied, Mill's libertarian and egalitarian vision, while animated by the most benevolent sentiments, was not calculated to produce a truly diverse society. Rather, Mill seemed to contemplate "an enormous number of human creatures substantially equal, substantially alike, substantially animated by the same desires and impulses. Divide the materials of happiness equally between them," Stephen concluded sarcastically, "and let them do as they like."[13] For the liberal, diversity was the natural product of personal liberty and equal rights; for the conservative, it inhered in an ordered social hierarchy and in the natural variations of private life outside the political sphere altogether.

From their different points of view, Mill and Stephen pointed to one of the dispiriting tendencies of modern life. Even before the publication of Stephen's *Liberty, Equality, Fraternity* (1873), his brother Leslie Stephen had identified this tendency as "the macadamisation of society," which he characterized as the grinding down of the individual and the decline of energy and independent spirit.[14] The image proved an enduring one; F. W. Maitland spoke similarly of the "pulverizing and macadamizing tendency of modern history,"[15] and in the twentieth century the bulldozer became an updated symbol of "macadamisation." Such figures captured very well the constructive-destructive, leveling aspect of "progress."

Whereas for Mill the hope of overcoming social conformity appeared to lie in the progress of democracy, to Leslie Stephen it was obvious that the two increased together. "The individual becomes powerless in proportion as society becomes a dead level," he supposed. Given a "mass of human units," each with the same education, opportunities, and privileges as every other, the tendency was "for each man to become a mere epitome of the qualities which find favour with everybody else." Stephen agreed with Tocqueville

that democracy would work against the heights and depths of experience, that there would be fewer grievances but less heroism: "in
short a kind of spiritual roller is passed over human nature, crushing
it into dull though comfortable mediocrity." Public opinion in
such a society could be more confining than formal laws. "Place
all mankind on a dead level," Stephen feared, "and a crushing
public opinion will be generated as spontaneously as electric action
will be set up when you form a galvanic battery."[16] This could have
been a prescription for twentieth-century totalitarianism, although
no leveling tyranny to date has effected such extreme tractability in
its subjects.

Interesting in the light of present-day feminism, with its seeming
aversion not only to sexual inequality, but to sexual differences,
is Stephen's perception of this question as central to the whole
matter of social diversity. It seemed clear to him that the emancipation of women "would increase the monotony of society." Women
thought differently from men on such matters as politics and religion;
they entertained different moral standards and developed themselves from infancy on a different model altogether. Rightly or
wrongly, any change in this state of affairs, any abolition of masculine privileges, as Stephen frankly stated it, would tend strongly
toward social uniformity and homogenization. "Extinguish this
difference, if it be possible, let us all, men and women, hold opinions
of the same character," Stephen thought in sum, "and you would
have done more to destroy the influences which now diversify
society than much philosophical preaching can ever remedy."[17]
The abolition of other privileges, he acknowledged, would tend the
same way. Implicit was the conservative refusal to sacrifice diversity
on the altar of equality.

Stephen's defense of diversity was not bounded by defense of
privilege, however, and his views on the problem were not simplistic.
He associated social variety with a kind of personal vigor, and
thought it clear that this quality could not be strengthened merely
by removing external restrictions. It was the "intrinsic force" of
character which had to be nurtured, as it was, Stephen believed,
in Calvinistic societies, or in those otherwise prominent in Matthew
Arnold's "Hebraising" tendencies. At the same time, in opposition to what he took to be the position of Mill and others, Stephen

denied that variety, either of character or of opinion, was an absolute good. Certain types of personality were best allowed to become extinct, even at some cost to diversity; many opinions must give way to the progress of truth. In other ways, as Adam Smith had shown, progress required constant differentiation. It was, it seemed finally, a matter of balance: variety was desirable within limits; it should be the corollary not of chaos but of order, not of the "pulverisation" but of the organization of society, not of eccentricity but of originality. "We require, therefore, so much diversity as is compatible with, and indeed necessary to, harmony, but no more," Stephen suggested. There could be, he thought, a fruitful diversity only when there was agreement on fundamentals; without a basis of mutual understanding, monotony rather than variety was apt to be the result. Paradoxically, then, "a greater unity of opinion" was "the first condition towards greater vigour, and even towards greater originality and diversity of thought."[18]

It was characteristic of British conservative thinking to draw a connection between the kind of leveling which Leslie Stephen and others deplored and political institutions which failed to recognize the diverse orders and interests of the country. It was popular government, or democracy, which threatened to produce this result in the nineteenth century, to the detriment, conservatives feared, of both liberty and diversity. The tendency of popular governments, Sir Henry Maine apprehended, was "towards a dead level of commonplace opinion, which they are forced to adopt as the standard of legislation and policy." In consequence there arose, or rather descended, a kind of inverted monarchy, in which "the multitude" required the kind of obeisance once paid to kings. Incapable of producing aristocracy, democracy was fertile of despotism, and it seemed clear to Maine that the simplification of political institutions led to absolutism, the absolutism either of an autocrat or of an autocratic majority.[19]

By the "simplification" of political institutions Maine meant the concentration of power, the removal of what Americans called "checks and balances." This kind of governmental uniformity, he thought, the United States itself had thus far largely managed to escape. While the Civil War had reversed the tendency toward state rights and the diversity of institutions which they represented, the country across the Atlantic had retained a wise constitution which posed formidable barriers to simple popular rule. Maine believed, for example, that the provision for the equal representation of the states in the Senate, regardless of size, demonstrated the way in which a political principle with sufficient historical roots could be effectively opposed to unchecked majority will. Unlike that of some conservative critics, therefore, Maine's view of the United States remained cautiously approving. The Jacksonian historian George Bancroft used the ocean as a glowing metaphor for the restless, atomistic energy of democracy; Henry Adams later made of the course of the Rhine to the sea a parable of democratic entropy. Maine, choosing the same river for his figure, fell between the idealized optimism of the one American and the idealized pessimism of the other. In contrast even to the English river, seeming always in flood, Maine thought, constitutional restrictions had acted in the United States "like those dams and dykes which strike the eye of the traveller along the Rhine, controlling the course of a mighty river which begins amid mountain torrents and turning it into one of the most equable waterways in the world."[20]

Other conservatives emphasized the function of the British state in representing the various orders and interests of the country. Echoing Burke, Benjamin Disraeli lamented the uniformitarian course of the French revolutionaries. France could readily have found in its old local divisions, customs, institutions, and orders a variety of interests adequate to have sustained a free and stable constitution, he thought. Instead, the revolutionaries had set about destroying not only law and custom, but their very country, in its ancient provincial diversity. "They measured their land, and divided it into equal geometrical departments, without the slightest regard to difference of soil or population, variety of manners, or diversity of temperament; and in this Laputan state that great country," it seemed to Disraeli, "still remains."[21]

The British constitution, on the other hand, had continued to represent the great, permanent, and varied interests of the nation, Disraeli believed. To the "Tory Democrat," it was clear that England was all the more a democracy for recognizing classes and orders, rather than being simply "a mass of individuals governed by a metropolis." The basis of English society, he could maintain, was equality; not the kind of equality that "levels and destroys," but that which "elevates and creates. . . . The principle of the first equality, base, terrestrial, Gallic, and grovelling, is that no one should be privileged; the principle of English equality is that everyone should be privileged."[22] It was only by taking formal institutional cognizance of the diversity of society, Disraeli appeared to say, that the Englishman could truly be accorded participation in his own government.

William Lecky somewhat more thoroughly related social diversity to constitutional complexity. In the time of Burke, Lecky pointed out, statesmen had regarded the constitution as "a highly complex and delicate machine, fulfilling many different purposes and acting in many obscure and far-reaching ways." That not all of these ways were amenable to an immediately perceptible pattern of logic did not necessarily condemn them. If the House of Commons, for example, was elected by means which were entirely lacking in uniformity and symmetry, there was yet a certain method in this madness.

> The objects to be attained were very various, and they were best attained by a great variety and diversity of representation. . . . It was necessary to represent, and to represent in their due proportions, the various forms and tendencies of political opinion existing in the nation. It was necessary to represent with the same completeness and proportion the various and often conflicting class interests, so that the wants of each class might be attended to and the grievances of each class might be heard and redressed.[23]

Such means of accommodating diverse groups and interests, however, were placed in jeopardy by the ideas and practices of modern politics. Rousseau, in Lecky's view, had been the prophet of a school of thought which held absolute political equality to be the condition of freedom, to the exclusion of constitutional "diversities of power" represented by classes and interests. If applied to the British system, as by the extreme extension of the suffrage, Lecky feared, such precepts threatened to swamp "the varieties of genuine opinion by great uniform masses of ignorant and influenced voters." Democracy, he repeated the old refrain, leveled down as much as it leveled up. Perhaps most alarming, he suggested, was the increasing democratic propensity for bureaucratic regulation, with the consequent "multiplication of restrictions imposed upon the various forms of human action."[24] This was a charge which would be heard more often in the following century.

Lecky nevertheless remained hopeful that the tides of standardization and of monolithic political power could be checked. Even advanced technology, he thought, could have positive value in this regard. Although railroads had done much to centralize English life, the telegraph seemed to work in the opposite direction, making possible the growth of a vigorous provincial press and of centers of political thought beyond the metropolis. Lecky noted too, along with the rise of large political units and agglomerations, a counter-tendency toward the accentuation of "distinct national and local types," as seen in the widespread contemporary interest in regional customs and antiquities. Perhaps constitutional devices such as proportional representation could satisfy the democratic demand for equality while according a measure of representation to minority classes, interests, and opinions.[25] Lecky retained finally a conservative faith that the multifariousness of human experience and endeavor would remain incorrigible.

> The sense of right and wrong, which is the basis of the respect for property and for the obligation of contract; the feeling of family affection, on which the continuity of society depends, and out of which the system of heredity grows; the essential difference of men in aptitudes, capacities, and character, are things that can never be changed, and all schemes and policies that ignore them are doomed to ultimate failure.[26]

A similar feeling for social diversity, although strongly informed by a Roman Catholic point of view, is found in Lord Acton. Especially in his early career, when his insistence on the distribution of power led him to marked sympathy with feudalism, Austrian aristocracy, and the Confederate States of America, Acton's hostility to political or social uniformity had a strongly conservative cast. Although he was less conservative in his later years, and even rejected the appellation as applied to himself, he by no means entirely discarded his earlier views.[27]

The crux of the matter, Acton thought, was that modern political theory "swept away every authority except that of the State." It recognized liberty only in the individual for the very practical reason that only in the individual could liberty be separated from authority and thus deprived of the means of effective resistance to arbitrary power. The tendency to which Acton called attention here is one which has been felt to the full only in the twentieth century: the willingness, even the eagerness of government to encourage personal freedom—"liberation"—so long as it is perfectly divorced from any sphere of authority outside of the state, such as would give it genuine substance. Early American Protestants endorsed a political liberty largely because they thought that it would enable men to be more perfectly obedient to God; in the debased secular version, as Acton perceived, the state liberates the individual from local and traditional centers of authority in order to make him more completely its own subject.[28]

This was, at bottom, an attack on social diversity. Acton started from the cardinal principle that "liberty provokes diversity, and diversity preserves liberty by supplying the means of organisation."[29] History revealed a long struggle over the barriers posed by such diversity to centralized authority. The Roman Republic, for example (far more than the later Empire), had "laboured to crush the subjugated nations into a homogeneous and obedient mass"; medieval conditions, on the other hand, had fostered a variety of liberties and privileges, depending on status and locality. This situation was intolerable to modern absolutism, which came into its own only with the French Revolution. The paramount feature of that event, Acton was convinced, was not the limitation of the powers of government, but the curtailment of intermediate powers. And the "liberal" movement which derived from the Revolution, in his estimation, was really nationalist rather than liberal, in its intolerance of authorities independent of the state.[30]

There was, to be sure, a genuine liberalism—the liberalism, it appeared, which inhered in Burkean conservatism. Acton, like the old Whig himself, distinguished sharply between the French and English political systems. The former, he believed, made an idealized collective will supreme within the nation, overruling all partial groupings and "absorbing their divergent interests in a fictitious unity." Across the Channel, on the other hand, the spirit of nationalism was restrained by a respect for historical experience and the actual vicissitudes of life; consequently, English politics tended "to diversity and not to uniformity, to harmony and not to unity."[31]

Acton suggested an affinity of spirit between the latter, "English," system and other historical institutions. The early Christian church especially, he thought, had represented a new kind of unity in diversity. It had offered to broadly diverse nations a unity of religious belief and authority, without necessarily threatening particular laws, customs, and habits. While discouraging the isolation of nations, the Church nevertheless had perceived an interest in defending their liberty against uniformity and centralization.[32] Within the nation, the Church had served the cause of liberty and diversity in another way: by acting as a center of authority independent of the state—or more properly, as Acton put it, a "great independent authority in the State." Real liberty, in this view, depended not on the complete separation of Church and State, but on a kind of reciprocity, their "action and reaction" as different centers of authority.[33]

In a modern democracy, however, it seemed clear that no church, even if acknowledged by the state, could suffice as a check on its power. Even less, of course, did the sorts of privileges, liberties, and diversities associated with feudalism still obtain. The democratic principle of equality, which opposed "the existence of persons or groups of persons exempt from the common law, and independent of the common will," seemed to sweep all before it. Federalism had proved to be the most efficacious check on democracy, but, as Acton lamented in 1878, federalism appeared to have fallen into disrepute.[34] One reason for this, of course, was the defeat of the federal principle in the American Civil War.

Like many upper-class Englishmen, but more thoughtfully than most, Acton had taken a position in that contest strongly sympathetic to the South. He did not undertake to defend the "horrors" of slavery, although he could find no reason for its categorical prohibition on religious grounds, and observed that slavery had historically proved an essential safeguard against the tendency of democracy toward a downward-leveling homogeneity. But in the Abolitionists he found a quality of "abstract, ideal absolutism" as hostile to the English as to the Catholic spirit. "Their democratic system poisons everything it touches," he exclaimed.

All constitutional questions are referred to the one fundamental principle of popular sovereignty, without consideration of policy or expediency. . . . In claiming absolute freedom, they have created absolute powers, whilst we have inherited from the middle ages the notion that both liberty and authority must be subject to limits and conditions.[35]

Acton consequently had high praise for John C. Calhoun, whose arguments in defense of nullification in 1832 seemed to the Briton "the very perfection of political truth," combining "with the realities of modern democracy the theory and the securities of mediaeval freedom." But by 1861, it appeared to be "the spurious democracy of the French Revolution" which had triumphed, destroying the Union "by disintegrating the remnants of English traditions and institutions."[36] What was left but popular absolutism and uniformity?

The themes developed by Lord Acton in mid-nineteenth-century England (and by Tocqueville on the Continent) have remained fundamental to British conservative thought down to present times. As we look back upon the relatively quite limited British or American state of the nineteenth and early twentieth centuries, it is remarkable how early and forcefully there appeared to thoughtful minds the prospect of a new political absolutism, of what today would be denominated totalitarianism. John Neville Figgis, addressing himself before World War I to the problem of church-state relations, saw clearly the menace to social diversity of an order which refused to admit the propriety of intermediate associations between individual and state. This was a bias which Figgis, in company with Acton and others, traced especially to the ascendancy of the Roman law, which had overridden "Teutonic and feudal influences" friendlier to heterogeneity, and which ignored "the complex group-life which is to most of us more than the State."[37]

Political absolutism and social atomism were for Figgis parts of the same phenomenon, which he characterized as "a scientific monstrosity . . . the omnipotent State facing an equally unreal aggregate of unrelated individuals," and which was fatal to a varied social life. Even the personal freedom which ostensibly inhered in such a society Figgis thought illusory. "More and more it is clear," he noted in a key passage, "that the mere individual's freedom against an omnipotent State may be no better than slavery; more and more is it evident that the real question of freedom in our day is the freedom of smaller unions to live within the whole.''[38]

Even from a purely individualistic standpoint, Figgis was persuaded, the lack of a varied social context was fatal to personality. In the real world, he thought, there was no such thing as the isolated individual. No one could live without relation to society; even the very distinctiveness of individual lives was largely a social product. "Membership in a social union," he pointed out, "means a direction of personality, which interpenetrates it, and, according to your predilection, you may call either an extension or a narrowing; it is in truth both." Like Chesterton and others, Figgis found attractive the medieval custom of assigning different costumes to different callings, as emblematic of a heterogeneous society. If only a pale reflection of this practice was to be discovered in the modern world, it was to be encouraged. "Instead of an iron uniformity," he supposed, "we need more and more a reasonable distinction of groups, all of which should be honourable. There is a whole philosophy in school colours.''[39] A comment more British in spirit can hardly be imagined.

It was these smaller and largely autonomous associations, Figgis thought, which counted for most in the life of the individual, at least in England. Not merely "slices of government departments," they were in practice, even when not in theory, "infinitely diverse," and each possessed of its own character. The state itself was, in fact, a great "society of societies"—not a "sand-heap of individuals, all equal and undifferentiated, unrelated except to the State, but an ascending hierarchy of groups, family, school, town, county, union, Church, &c. &c." Figgis thus sounded the old conservative call for unity-in-diversity, to be found neither in extreme centralization nor in extreme decentralization, and certainly not in unlimited individualism, but, as he quoted an earlier writer, in an "equilibrium" of state, corporation, and individual. From this balance, Figgis agreed, the truest personal freedom arose.[40] The insight was central to the conservative tradition of British political thought.

At the metaphysical bottom of conservative tolerance of diversity, perhaps, was the feeling enunciated by Arthur Balfour that the universe was simply too big and too complex to be encapsulated by any scheme of rational uniformity—"I disbelieve because it is simple" commended itself to Balfour as an axiom.[41] Translated into political terms, this became an impatience with any "rigid, symmetrical form of doctrine," as one of Balfour's successors as Prime Minister put it. "Our own feelings and the British temperament are quite different," Winston Churchill thought in 1946.

> So are our aims. We seek a free and varied society, where there is room for many kinds of men and women to lead happy, honourable and useful lives. We are fundamentally opposed to all systems of rigid uniformity in our national life and we have grown great as a nation by indulging tolerance, rather than logic.[42]

That such a varied society entailed inequality, at least of wealth and standing, the franker conservative spokesmen have not sought to deny, although the question is less squarely faced now than it once was. Fifty years ago, Arthur Bryant was willing to acknowledge that every man should have a fair chance to rise to the highest point to which his abilities would take him, but denied that this required everyone to begin life in the same circumstances, without natural or hereditary advantage. One could not reasonably speak even of equality of opportunity, Bryant pointed out, unless all were born alike—and this was clearly precluded by nature. "The Creator of the world seems to have aimed, not at Equality, but at the widest possible diversity of creatures," he observed. "If Equality is to be achieved at all, it can only be by lowering the level of all men to that of the most savage and backward."[43] Bryant easily assumed that the inequalities and diversities rooted in nature found their normal expression through social divisions and orders.

Later British conservatives were inclined to render similar ideas in more positive and less class-bound terms. In 1947, David Clarke appeared still to entertain Figgis's vision of the nation as a community of communities. Clarke was impressed with the tremendous wealth of groups and associations which in the English-speaking countries permitted individuals not only to develop and adventure their own ideas and qualities to the full, but to add their voices to the "grand chorus of national harmony."[44] He agreed with Bryant that disparities of ability and character resulted naturally in social classes, but he was quick to invoke "an underlying unity in the brotherhood of man which over-rides classes." Altogether, the emphasis had noticeably shifted; explicitly, at least, Clarke was less apprehensive of a leveling equality as such than of a drab and sterile uniformity. In the years of Clement Atlee's Labour government, it seemed to Clarke, there were abroad basically

> two conceptions of Society. One is the conception of a living organic community resting on a rich variety of qualities and concerned to evoke the greatest variety and the highest qualities through every agency. The other is the conception of a State which casts the institutions of the country into a rigid mould at the cost of variety and quality.[45]

Clarke attached a metaphor which came naturally to an Englishman. No formal continental garden of ruthlessly clipped uniformity, he suggested,

> Conservatism is the English Garden of politics. It is a creed of unity founded on variety. It believes in the infinite capabilities of the human personality and seeks to develop them. It takes as its standard absolute moral values. It believes that Society is a living organic whole inherited from our forefathers and living in our children and their children.[46]

Perhaps the image of even an English garden is a little too neat for twentieth-century currency. Arthur Balfour, although writing in an earlier day, struck a more modern note in his discussion of the "psychological 'atmosphere' or 'climate' " engendered by the power of authority. Such a climate, he pointed out, could be diffused throughout an entire generation, epoch, or civilization, or it could be confined to a sect, family, or even a single person. Intermingling, varying greatly in force and quality, climates of authority were of an importance to individual and social life that, Balfour thought, could hardly be exaggerated.[47] It followed that local loyalties—"these various patriotisms," as he called them—need not be mutually exclusive; indeed, as civilization became more complex, it was more than ever necessary for men to learn how to combine their loyalties without weakening them, and to find a middle course between a narrow provincialism and a rootless cosmopolitanism.[48]

Variations on the same themes could be cited indefinitely. But it is clear that there persisted well into the democratic age a strong sense among British conservatives of what some of them referred to as the "corporate" nature of society and the state. They understood these entities to be composed, that is to say, not of detached individuals, but of people in groups, in corporate bodies. Only such an order could do justice to the real diversity of society. Conservatives acknowledged unity as an ideal, even perhaps as the paramount ideal, but a unity proceeding not from "a forced similarity untrue to nature," as Keith Feiling put it, but emerging as "a harmony of variations and opposites, held in equilibrium by relation to one end."[49]

In this there was, no doubt, a tincture of archaism and a nursing of old wounds in the long conservative memory. As of 1933, F.J.C. Hearnshaw had not reconciled himself to the Reform Bill of a century earlier, feeling that it had overridden the ancient and various interests and constituencies of the British state in order to impose the "monotonous uniformity of villadom."[50] Yet the conservative defense of social diversity also posed a challenge to its political adversaries in terms fully relevant to the present and future, which could not be so easily written off. "Uniformity," Feiling asserted,

> is not corporateness but sleeping sickness, and freedom to move the limbs is a condition of the body advancing at all. And so we reach bedrock. The Socialist believes that you can, and should, banish Self from man; the Conservative does not. In Self, with all its appetites and lusts and egoism, are wrapped up also vitality, quality, spontaneous affection, and when, if ever, the Fabian saints at last inherit the earth, it will be a cold and grey twilight.[51]

From the more positive standpoint, conservatives offered a criterion of national well-being which was one of "diverse quality" rather than "gross volume," in Feiling's terms. A society of "many groups, each with a life of its own as valid and rooted as the 'community's'—the lives of families, churches, localities, professions, and races, lives interpenetrated, interdependent, but yet each integral"[52]—this was the substance of the British conservative message, as it spoke to the modern world.

NOTES

1. See Peter J. Stanlis, *Edmund Burke and the Natural Law* (Ann Arbor: University of Michigan Press, 1965), 164 and passim.

2. Edmund Burke, *The Works of the Right Honourable Edmund Burke* (London: George Bell & Sons, 1892), II, 306.

3. Reginald J. White, ed., *The Conservative Tradition* (New York: New York University Press, 1957), 2-8.

4. John Stuart Mill, *On Liberty* (New York: Appleton-Century-Crofts, Inc., 1947), 72-73.

5. Ibid., 62-63.

6. Ibid., 67.

7. Ibid., 67, 70-71.

8. Gertrude Himmelfarb, *On Liberty and Liberalism* (New York: Alfred A. Knopf, 1974), 272, 302, 310-311, 320-322, 333, and passim.

9. Ibid., 174-175.

10. James Fitzjames Stephen, *Liberty, Equality, Fraternity* (Cambridge: University Press, 1967), 83-84.

11. Ibid., 191-194, 208, 211.

12. Ibid., 214, 220.

13. Ibid., 226.

14. L. S. [Leslie Stephen], "Social Macadamisation," *Fraser's Magazine,* New Series, 6 (August 1872): 150.

15. Quoted by Robert A. Nisbet, *The Quest for Community* (New York: Oxford University Press, 1953), 109.

16. Stephen, "Social Macadamisation," 151-153.

17. Ibid., 153-154.

18. Ibid., 157-164.

19. Henry Sumner Maine, *Popular Government* (New York: Henry Holt and Company, 1886), 41, 77, 169.

20. Ibid., 197, 229, 246.

21. Benjamin Disraeli, *Whigs and Whiggism* (Port Washington, N.Y.: Kennikat Press, 1971), 127.

22. Ibid., 188, 215-216, 228-229.

23. William Edward Hartpole Lecky, *Democracy and Liberty* (New York: Longmans, Green, and Co., 1899), I, 2, 5, 7.

24. Ibid., I, 12, 25, 131, 257-258.

25. Ibid., I, 254, 501-502, 269.

26. Ibid., II, 369.

27. See John Emerich Edward Dalberg-Acton, *Essays on Freedom and Power* (Glencoe, Ill.: The Free Press, 1949), lxi, lxiii.

28. Ibid., 89-90.

29. Ibid., 185.

30. Ibid., 174-176.

31. Ibid., 183-184.

32. Ibid., 186-187.

33. John Emerich Edward Dalberg-Acton, *Essays on Church and State* (London: Hollis and Carter, 1952), 441, 467.

34. Acton, *Freedom and Power,* 160, 163.

35. Ibid., 244-246.

36. Ibid., 224, 250.

37. John Neville Figgis, *Churches in the Modern State* (London: Longmans, Green, and Co., 1913), 225-226.

38. Ibid., 51-52.

39. Ibid., 88-89, 91.

40. Ibid., 47-49, 87, 111. The writer quoted was Richard Simpson, in "The Individual, the Corporation, and the State," *The Rambler* (May 1862). "Taken by itself," Simpson thought, "each of these elements characterizes a barbarous kind of existence. The absolute individual is found only in savage life; the absolute corporation in primitive patriarchal society; the absolute State in oriental despotisms."

41. Arthur James Balfour, *The Foundations of Belief* (London: Longmans, Green, and Co., 1895), 271-272.

42. Robert Lindsay Schuettinger, ed., *The Conservative Tradition in European Thought* (New York: G. P. Putnam's Sons, 1970), 375.

43. Arthur Bryant, *The Spirit of Conservatism* (London: Methuen & Co., Ltd., 1929), 7-8, 10.

44. David Clarke, *The Conservative Faith in a Modern Age* (London: Conservative Political Centre, 1947), 17.

45. Ibid., 9, 18.

46. Ibid., 38.

47. Balfour, *Foundations of Belief,* 206.

48. White, *Conservative Tradition,* 118.

49. Keith Feiling, "Principles of Conservatism," *The Political Quarterly* 24 (April-June 1953): 138.

50. F.J.C. Hearnshaw, *Conservatism in England* (London: Macmillan, 1933), 190-191. See also Clarke, *Conservative Faith,* 19-20. Hearnshaw argued that the Reform Bill "ignored the various interests and groups into which the population was divided, and recognized only the isolated individual; it conceded the vote to the individual, not as a public function to be exercised for the good of the community, but as a private right to be used for the attainment of his own ends." (*Conservatism in England,* 190-191.)

51. Keith Feiling, *What Is Conservatism?* (London: Faber & Faber, 1930), 26-27.

52. Ibid., 16, 14.

6 Federalism and Diversity in the United States

In turning from British conservatives to their counterparts in the United States, one is struck by the comparative paucity of "diversitarian" tradition in the daughter country. Until quite recently, American conservatism was far less clearly defined than the British, and, particularly for the nineteenth century, it is difficult to label many articulate and significant figures as definitively conservative; fewer still are those who would have applied that label to themselves, even after it became current during the first third of the century. Such putative founders of the "American conservative tradition" as John Adams and John C. Calhoun, however, evinced little concern with diversity for its own sake, certainly compared with foreign contemporaries like Edmund Burke or Alexis de Tocqueville. Early American political thinkers frequently acknowledged social diversity as a fact of life, but they were less disposed to treasure it as a good in itself. Diversity, in America, was an acquired taste.

In some ways, this seems odd. In certain respects the United States was a diverse country from the beginning. Even during its first century it was possessed of a remarkable ethnic—and of course racial—heterogeneity. Besides the mingled nationalities of the white population, there were black slaves scarcely removed from Africa and red Indians still in the state then denominated as savagery. A more picturesque state of contrasts, if that was what one was after, could hardly have been hoped for. Religious diversity was also spectacular. True, the great majority of church-affiliated Americans were heirs of the Protestant Reformation, but there were significant numbers of Jews by the 1840s, and a Roman Catholic population burgeoning so rapidly as to evoke a major, violent Protestant reaction against it between 1830 and 1860. Protestantism itself, moreover, was a radically manifold movement, and during the first half of the nineteenth century especially, there emerged from the Protestant background an extraordinary proliferation of sects and movements—Utopian, communitarian, postmillenarian, premillenarian, free-love, celibate, transcendentalist, and simply evangelical. America produced a largely original, and to most Christians highly eccentric, religious movement in the Church of Jesus Christ of Latter-Day Saints—the Mormons—and would later spawn the Christian Scientists and Jehovah's Witnesses. Surely this was a scene which for color ought to have appeased those romantics who bewailed the American lack of royalty, aristocracy, and ancient monuments!

In other ways too the country was, from an objective standpoint, diverse. For all that Americans denigrated social rank and class, the economic conditions in which they lived covered a range coterminous with that of civilization itself, although certainly omitting certain historical variations, such as serfdom. The gamut from poor farmer or laborer to a millionaire like John Jacob Astor, however exceptional the latter in antebellum times, or that between the enslaved field hand and the patriarch who owned him and possibly as many as a thousand of his fellows, offered nothing if not a certain variety of worldly estate. The latter case pointed also, of course, to sectional and regional variations. These were not confined to the celebrated difference marked by the Mason-Dixon Line, however, or even to the cultural peculiarities of well-defined blocs of states like New England. The relative isolation of most lives during the time made significant entities also of any number of subgroups and regions: Maryland's Eastern Shore, Virginia Tidewater, Upstate New York. But above all, one might have said, Americans were a free people, and surely freedom would result, not only in diversity, but in a high awareness and esteem of diversity.

This, however, has not entirely been the case. Although foreign commentators, even the most acute of them like Tocqueville, have rarely been sufficiently appreciative of the diversity that is encompassed in American life, their customary portrayal of a bland, conforming, middle-class society does have a root in reality. Strong pressures tended to mitigate the contrasts of American life, even before the beginning of the national history, and eventually in some ways and cases broke them down entirely. Ethnic and racial heterogeneity was sharply qualified by the fact that the overwhelmingly dominant element of the white population, especially before the Civil War, was of northern European origin and (to the extent religious) identified with one of no more than half a dozen mainstream Protestant denominations. After a generation or two, the cultural differences between English, Scottish, or Dutch background counted for little, or even German in cases where there was an active effort to assimilate. After the Great Awakening of the 1740s, moreover, differences between major Protestant denominations, which in the seventeenth century had often been regarded as matters of (eternal) life and death, came to seem of secondary importance. What was important was to "get religion," and increasingly loyalty to a denomination (if a respectable Protestant one, at least) became a matter of preference, opinion, and habit, one "persuasion" essentially as able to get you to your spiritual destination as the other, even as a Ford or Chevrolet today for more mundane journeys. Catholics and Jews were different—but they were minorities which long had little impact on the dominant culture.

A similar set of circumstances mitigated the economic and class diversity of the country, especially in its implications for social and political thought. America has always had its rich and poor, but there are reasons for the dominant impression of it as a middle-class country. Basic economic facts of early American history, summed up roughly in the formula "cheap land, dear labor," made possible a high degree of social fluidity and an entrance into the middle class that was not beyond the reach of most free white men. One corollary of this, as has been pointed out many times, was a middle-class consciousness which, although not at all universal, extended well beyond the bounds of those groups whose possessions or income entitled them to inclusion. That the word "peasant" never took root in America is certainly indicative that the relatively static, traditional way of life which it denominated in Europe was never strongly characteristic of American farmers. A similar point can be made in a later context about the enduringly alien quality of the term "proletariat" in this country. Men who hoped to succeed, whether through acquiring more acreage or by progressing from artisan to shopkeeper, were apt to think in middle-class terms of industry, thrift, and prudence. At the other end of the scale, the American rich, lacking a strong aristocratic tradition to guide them, have tended notoriously to be simply the middle class writ large—in continental terms, at best, a *haute bourgeoisie.* Tidewater plantation aristocrats and New York patroons have been exceptional—as were, far more numerously, the slaves.

The diversity of regions and sections was also often less in actuality than standard categories would suggest. Regionalism was mitigated by Americans' extraordinary horizontal mobility, even as class division was mitigated by vertical mobility. Americans, as a group, did not stay put. New Englanders moved to New York and New Jersey, Pennsylvanians to Delaware. The West was necessarily a region of migrants. To some extent, of course, those who moved adopted the ways of the region into which they moved, even at times the ways of Indians. Northerners moving south, if they sometimes injected a spirit of Yankee enterprise at their new location, sometimes also ended up as the most militant of Confederates. But regardless of qualities so culturally superficial as political loyalties, the constant mobility and mixture of population worked clearly against any enormous diversity of regional mores. Compared with the patchwork of custom and dialect that persisted in much of Europe during modern times, the difference represented by a southern drawl and a New England twang might appear almost superficial.

If diversity is nurtured by tradition, as many conservatives have believed, then America as a relatively untraditional society was not disposed on this count toward radical variety. Geographical and social mobility were far from being limited to America, although they were especially pronounced here during the early part of our history. But there was less in the United States in the way of social and institutional structure to channel and shape this horizontal and vertical movement. It was not that Americans were really a "new" people without a history, despite what they as well as Europeans liked to believe. They did not lose their memories in crossing the Atlantic; America did not efface their customs or confiscate their cultural baggage (as it did to a considerable extent that of the slaves). If America selected parts of the European heritage and rejected others, still Americans could claim as much as other Westerners to be the heirs of the Middle Ages and Antiquity. Continuity of religious belief alone would be enough to refute the once-fashionable idea that the American frontier had felicitously washed American brains clean of their European dirt. But traditional currents found new forms, or encountered more often a comparative formlessness, and when like river water they burst their weak American levees to flood the neighboring plain, they seemed shallow as well as aimless. If the point may be rescued from metaphor, a society which had its traditions, but which was weak in the structure and stability of traditional life, tended more to mixture and confusion of peoples and customs than to the maintenance of social diversity.

Where there were serious divisions in American life, furthermore, they tended to be understood in terms of sharp bifurcation rather than of any more complicated multiplicity: alternatives narrowed to either-or. Just as the dominant American racial codes ignored intermediate shades of color and classified persons as either black or white, so regional differences were compacted into the assumption of two more or less monolithic sections, North and South, with their attendant myths, as William Taylor has shown, of "Yankee" and "Cavalier." Even the West, apart from its function as a synonym for the frontier, was subordinated to the primary division represented by the Mason-Dixon line and the Ohio River. In part, of course, this represented the genuinely sharp division between free and slave states, and the consequent exigencies of politics and war, which were not hospitable to fine distinctions. To some extent too, the normal pressures of "taking sides" were reinforced by the homogenizing and nationalizing pressures within each section. If "Yankee" became a term applicable not only to New Englanders but to Ohioans and Oregonians, it was also true that New Englanders had spread their seed and creed to Ohio and Oregon. The vulgar apprehension of "the southerner" ignored the differences between the Virginian and the Texan, but the Texan might well be a transplanted Virginian. Border states like Maryland

and Missouri, incompletely assimilable to either side, were seldom permitted to remain border states, but were doomed to permanent identity crisis, alternatively classified as southern or northern. The result of these kinds of polarization was to minimize what genuine diversities were to be found in both sections.

There was also the whole pattern of uniformity in thought and behavior engendered by egalitarian and democratic standards, of which Alexis de Tocqueville remains the outstanding critic, and which will be more thoroughly discussed in another section. Suffice it to say here that the Jacksonian notion that one man was pretty much as good as another did not much encourage one man to be startlingly different from another. No doubt the rule is overstated; America had perhaps its share of eccentrics and of authentic individualists, but certain avenues of diversification were cut short. The very individualistic quality of American diversity was a severe limitation, denying it both permanence and extended influence. Concomitantly, while wealth was always a possible means of distinction, aristocracy, as an expression of local prominence and deference, was in most parts of the country after the Revolution a very restricted possibility. Freedom in America offered economic opportunities, personal liberties from oppressive laws, and the leave to obey God without undue mundane interference; but while these boons were very far from negligible, they did not necessarily make for a diverse society.

The political institutions of the country made possible a considerable diversity, at least so long as judicial proclivities to "activism" and the bureaucratic passion to standardize were held in check. Beyond the constitutional stipulation of "republican government," and apart from the rather light obligations of the constitutional compact, the great charter of 1787 might have served for thirteen or fifty little countries, joined in their dealings with foreigners, but having largely separate and distinct existences otherwise. Of course this has never really been the case, due to the homogenizing pressures already noted. Federalism, consequently, has never been an adequate expression of American diversity—or perhaps it would be more to the point to say that American federalism has never been animated by an adequate diversity. Between Indiana and Illinois, North Dakota and South Dakota, Vermont and New Hamp-

shire, the differences seem, at least to an outsider, more of sentiment than of substance. One could contrast extremes—say Mississippi
and Massachusetts—but these are more expressive of regional
variation than intrinsic to the federal system. And historically the
state-rights doctrine has been used chiefly as a weapon in struggles
more general than that of a single state.

It must be added that there was very little in early American
political thought to encourage diversity, although there was a great
deal on the side of permitting it. The founding fathers, not un-
touched by the Enlightenment preference for uniformity, acknowledged differences within the country, differences stemming partly
from the vagaries of human nature and condition, partly from the
scope and variety of the American environment. They were less
inclined to delight in this spectacle of diversity than to minimize
it, emphasizing that as Americans were "one people," they should
overcome their differences under a common government. Diversity,
as in the form of "faction," was a problem to be controlled. Government, in the stock Newtonian metaphor, was a mechanical matter
of balancing powers and interests, not an organic conciliation of
unity and multiplicity—even for John C. Calhoun, who used the
organicist terminology fashionable in his day. The machinery of
government was designed to safeguard liberty, but liberty was
almost always viewed in linear relationship to authority, at the
opposite pole from oppression. At most it was understood as the
prerequisite of a virtuous and rewarding life. There seems to have
been little disposition, even with the wafting of Romantic airs across
the Atlantic, to hail liberty as the means to diversity. The great
seal of the United States proclaimed not "let a hundred flowers
bloom," but "e pluribus unum." Aside from the important considerations that the Chinese slogan was entirely specious in its
totalitarian context and that the United States, on the other hand,
did not become conclusively one even politically until the end of the
War Between the States, it is notable that the American motto
looked from diversity toward unity, and not toward progressive
botanical differentiation.

Those Americans usually characterized as conservative do not,
prior to the Civil War, seem to have been greatly concerned with
the question of diversity, and offer little real corrective to more

general attitudes. John Adams was acutely aware, indeed, of human variation, but cited it not as a condition to be cherished, but in refutation of a misguided egalitarianism. In the nature of things, Adams pointed out, no two creatures were perfectly alike, or perfectly equal.

> Although among men, all are subject by nature to *equal laws* of morality, and in society have a right to *equal laws* for their government, yet no two men are perfectly equal in person, property, understanding, activity and virtue—or ever can be made so by any power less than that which created them; and whenever it becomes disputable between two individuals, or families, which is the superior, a fermentation commences, which disturbs the order of all things, until it is settled, and each one knows his place in the opinion of the public.[1]

Adams came to the conclusion that in view of these diversities, which for political purposes he assumed could be ranked vertically in terms of ability, virtue, and related traits, the necessary and sufficient condition of good government was a balance of orders: "a mixed government of three independent orders, of the one, the few, and the many," representing the primary factions of rich and poor, "gentlemen and common people."[2] (The executive was assumed to hold the balance between the more democratic and the more aristocratic branch, and to represent the common good.)

Although this tripartite division of powers was derived mainly from the English model (as distinguished from the English reality), Adams's application of it to America seems more rigid and mechanical than anything which a British counterpart would have been willing to embrace. There are genuine affinities between Adams and Burke, but Randall B. Ripley was correct in pointing out that Adams's search for a "true scientific balance" in government was quite different in tone and implication from Burke's reliance on tradition and usage; perhaps inevitably in a country in which tradition was shallowly rooted, the American relied on the very sort of political metaphysics that the British Whig condemned.[3]

The reduction of social variety to three orders of government, although perhaps defensible as a strictly political device, seemed in different ways to overestimate and to underestimate the actual diversity of American life. A writer in the Philadelphia *Independent Gazeteer* in 1787 doubted that such a balance of power was practicable. England, which possessed real distinctions of rank and interest, was better suited to such a scheme, he argued, although even there the three orders of government existed in name only. America, the implication was, lacked the clear diversity of rank which Adams's plan required if it were to have any chance of success. Thus, it seemed, "the only operative and efficient check upon the conduct of administration, is the sense of the people at large."[4]

If America had too great a social homogeneity to be plausibly divided into orders of government (a point which the subsequent history of the country certainly bore out), it seemed to John Taylor of Caroline, on the other hand, that Adams's tripartite division failed to do justice to the kind of variety that there was. "The magick contained in the number three," he pointed out, "is the magick of habit, not of nature. Human qualities are infinitely more divisible. . . . In India, titles and tribes are endless." Rather than rely on three orders, which Taylor thought would all too readily coalesce, why not rely on the "multitude of divisions" with which the federal system was already invested, and ultimately on that great division of power inherent in the reservation of a great portion of it by the people themselves? This would, Taylor believed, adequately guard against tyranny even while tending to unite the country in a common interest.[5] Here too there was little concern for variety for its own sake, although Taylor evinced a lively and almost Burkean sense that human diversities were beyond the ability of political metaphysics to encompass—an insight which he used to attack Adams's rationalistic contention that "mixed government" was uniformly the best.

> The traces of intellectual originality and diversity; the shades and novelties of the human character, between the philosopher and the savage; between different countries, different governments, and different eras; exhibit a complexity, which the politician and philologist have never been able to unravel. Out of this intellectual variety, arises the impossibility of contriving one form of government, suitable for every nation;

and also the fact, that human nature, instead of begetting one form constantly, demonstrates its moral capacity, in the vast variety of its political productions.[6]

Americans less tolerant than Taylor was here would often in the future be accused of thinking that one form of government was best for every country in the world.

In the controversy over ratification of the Constitution, the question of diversity was ancillary to other arguments. The authors of the *Federalist* papers argued from both the uniformity and the variety of the country, as convenient. John Jay in Federalist No. 2 observed that "Providence has been pleased to give this one connected country to one united people—a people descended from the same ancestors, speaking the same language, professing the same religion, attached to the same principles of government, very similar in their manners and customs." Since "to all general purposes we have uniformly been one people," Jay's obvious point was, there was no reason not to unite under a strong general government. James Madison, on the other hand, cited in No. 37 the difficulties of producing a government for a country with such a variety of circumstances and interests, in order to argue that, all things considered, the Convention had done remarkably well. Alexander Hamilton, perhaps disingenuously, contended that the variety of small state concerns and interests, which did not lend themselves to federal administration, was a safeguard against too great a centralization of power.[7]

The most significant application of the idea of diversity to be found in *The Federalist* was of course the argument that the greater variety of interests on the federal level made an oppressive majority faction less likely to coalesce there than on the state level. Faction, after all, was but the political manifestation of the acknowledged diversity in the abilities, virtues, interests, temperaments, and beliefs of mankind. Yet within the bounds of particular states, it appeared, this natural diversity of human nature had only limited play. "At present," noted Madison in No. 56, "some of the States are little more than a society of husbandmen. Few of them have made much progress in those branches of industry which give a variety and complexity to the affairs of a nation."[8] It was this circumstance which posed, thought Madison, the danger of majority faction: a dominant interest, economic, religious, or otherwise, might with relative ease within a single state govern against the general interest, and oppress the majority, with no effective check from the basic republican safeguard of majority rule. But the existence of a large republic, made possible by the federal system, would substantially obviate this difficulty. "Extend the sphere," was Madison's famous formula in Federalist No. 10,

> and you take in a greater variety of parties and interests; you make it less probable that a majority of the whole will have a common motive to invade the rights of other citizens; or if such a common motive exists, it will be more difficult for all who feel it to discover their own strength, and to act in unison with each other.[9]

Madison did not underestimate the diversity of interests in the country, and these would become more numerous and in some respects more widely varied as time went on. He did not adequately anticipate the degree to which political parties and coalitions could unite diverse interests into what would amount to majority factions on particular issues; nor could he well have foreseen the extent to which, as George W. Carey points out, massive government intervention and attempts "to reduce men as far as possible to the condition of sameness" in the name of equality could vitiate the checks against majority faction.[10] These weaknesses indicate the limitations of this rather mechanical eighteenth-century approach to diversity—namely, the interpretation of it as a (perhaps dismal) fact of human life, which resulted in faction and which could only be controlled, in turn, by giving diversity sufficient scope to cancel out its own bad effects. What has seemed to some twentieth-century conservatives to be required, on the other hand, is a substantive defense of diversity as a good in itself, to be balanced certainly with unity, equity, and other general goods, but not acknowledged merely as something to be controlled.

Antifederalists seem to have had no greater a concern with the effects of union on diversity. One finds the occasional comment, as that by George Clinton, that the United States was simply too diverse a country to be governed by "a consolidated republican form of government''; hence, Clinton feared, the new experiment must be wrecked by its divisions or a monarchy ensue.[11] There is sometimes the hint of anxiety that the federal government will seek to impose a kind of uniformity on the states.[12] But in general, American political debate at this time revolved around more legalistic questions such as those of local liberties and the rights of states, without much concern for the results of those liberties and rights in terms of diversity or uniformity.

The sectional controversy, which became increasingly heated after 1819, could elicit a greater positive awareness of the diversity of the country, although it could also provoke partisans on both sides to reduce regional and local differences to a double myth of a homogeneous North and a homogeneous South. George Fitzhugh drew an almost Manichean line between the social systems of the two sections, but his portrayal of the South as a combination of plantation communities, each the ''beau-ideal of communism'' in its joining of the interests of capital and labor, was not a celebration of diversity. John C. Calhoun was a different case. Although none wish now to praise his defense of slavery as such, Calhoun has been hailed as a man who ''thought in terms of diversity and not a deadly conformity, and . . . expressed his thoughts boldly in behalf of diversity without fear of consequence.''[13]

Calhoun does, certainly, evince an articulate, if sparingly expressed, awareness of the variety of human society. This society cannot be comprehended in a single community on account of its diversities of language, custom, and pursuits, he points out.[14] Gone is the cozy view of *The Federalist* that Americans comprised one people, and Calhoun's analysis of the problem of American government is framed accordingly. ''With us,'' he suggests,

> the choice lies between a national, consolidated and irresponsible government of a dominant portion, or section of the country,—and a federal, constitutional and responsible government, with all the divisions of powers indispensible to form and preserve such a government, in a country of such vast extent, and so great a diversity of interests and institutions as ours.[15]

The device of concurrent majority, Calhoun's major contribution to political science, was based on this assumption of a permanent "diversity of interests and institutions," although Calhoun supposed that a conflict of interests would arise from the "action of the government itself" even in a perfectly homogeneous society. Concurrent majority required the approval, on any measure affecting its fundamental well-being, of each of at least the most important of "the various natural interests, resulting from diversity of pursuits, condition, situation, and character of different portions of the people."[16] This was then an attempt to institutionalize diversity, in the form of basic interest groups, in a way that the federal system itself never directly purported to do, and for which purpose, as Calhoun came to realize, federalism was an inadequate means. Within limits, states could protect diverse interests, but they could be outvoted and constitutionally overridden; Calhoun, although in a way not clearly defined, would give to these diverse interests direct powers of veto.

Yet Calhoun was not engaged in a celebration of diversity for its own sake, and his invocation of the principle in defense of local rights and interests has a metallic mechanical ring more akin to Madison's *Federalist* No. 10 than to the developing British sense of traditionally nurtured, "organic" orders and groupings. And after all, of course, Calhoun's overriding concern was the sectional struggle and his central purpose to give the South sufficient constitutional protection to offset the increasing advantage of the North in population and wealth. The attempt to institutionalize diversity finally came down to the suggestion, made in the *Discourse on the Constitution and Government of the United States,* that two presidents serve at the same time, in the manner of Roman consuls, one elected from the slave states and one from the free, and each with the power of veto. Such formal schemes received no serious hearing. Yet it is true, as David Potter pointed out, that Calhoun described a certain reality in American politics that the South, despite its defeat, was usually able to take full advantage of over the next century: the power of a strong minority interest to obstruct measures fundamentally obnoxious to it.[17] Within these severe limits, Calhoun can be regarded as a realistic defender of certain kinds of diversity in American life.

A more direct defense of diversity was provided by Francis Lieber, who not coincidentally was a German immigrant, and who brought with him to the United States elements of continental liberalism and nationalism, as well as a cast of mind and set of assumptions that permit him to be ranked among the conservative thinkers of his adopted country. Lieber was a professor at South Carolina College while Calhoun served that state in Washington, but went north before the Civil War to teach at Columbia College in New York. Lieber, who was acquainted with Calhoun, rejected the concurrent-majority doctrine. To give to every major interest a veto, he thought, "would produce a multitudinous antagonism, instead of a vital organism. . . . We cannot hope for liberty in a pervading negation, but must find it in comprehensive action."[18] The distinction was vague, but it served to suggest differences of assumption and temperament between the two men, as well as, after all, the disparity between a politician looking for practical defenses for a beleaguered section and a somewhat romantic academic theorist.

Lieber was a nationalist, in a way that Calhoun had not been since his early political career, if then; and with the coming of secession and the Civil War, he made clear his wholehearted support of the Union and rejection of state-rights doctrine. "What is great, what is noble, what is patriotic, what is inspiriting to behold, in our history and public men," he proclaimed in March 1861, "is Pan-American. Provincialism has neither freed nor raised this people."[19] Lieber was never a champion of centralization or uniformity, however. While sharing the nineteenth-century liberal belief that freedom was the keynote of the age, he insisted more clearly than most that freedom "allows of variety." The too rationally ordered system risked undermining the very liberty which it sought to institute.

> Symmetry is one of the elements of humanity; systematizing is one of man's constant actions. It captivates and becomes dangerous, if other elements and activities equally important are neglected, or if it is carried into spheres in which it ought not to prevail. . . . But freedom is life, and wherever we find life it is marked, indeed, by agreement of principles and harmony of development, but also, by variety of form and phenomenon, and by a subordinate exactness of symmetry. The centralist,

> it might be said, mistakes lineal and angular exactness, formal
> symmetry and mathematical proportions, for harmonious evolu-
> tion and profuse vitality.[20]

Lieber's comment was part of an indictment of French centralism,
which he thought tended toward a dangerous concentration of
power and the obscuring of the individual. On the other hand,
he wrote, nothing so impressed the continental European, in both
England and the United States, as the "all-pervading associative
spirit in all moral and practical spheres," which served to diffuse
authority and initiative. Lieber concluded as axiomatic that "the
freer the nation, the more developed we find it in larger or smaller
spheres; and the more despotic a government is, the more actively
it suppresses all associations."[21]

Lieber was led consequently to draw a sharp distinction between
two kinds of liberty, the "Anglican" and the "Gallican." The
latter tended to absolutism in the name of equality. The "Anglicans,"
on the contrary, kept in mind that equality and democracy were no
guarantees of liberty, and that they could be, if subversive of individuality and personal responsibility, "the worst of despotisms."
In particular, without local self-government, in the Anglican view,
there was no real self-government and no real liberty. Lieber acknowledged that such division of authority and responsibility entailed
a certain "jarring" of laws and institutions, but if this horrified
"absolutists, whose beau-ideal is uncompromising and unrelieved
uniformity," it was nevertheless, he thought, both a corollary of
civil liberty and a means of social development.[22]

Finally, Lieber put his finger on a crucial distinction, one that
seemed almost always to elude native American political thinkers
in the nineteenth century. He discerned that whereas "Gallican
liberty" demanded uniformity,

> Anglican liberty consists in or produces the utmost variety,
> as all untrammelled life and unfettered individual action neces-
> sarily does. Equality (if sought in aught else than in equality
> of freedom from interference, and if believed to consist in
> uniformity alone) is monotony and becomes the opposite to
> life and action.

Carried too far, Lieber acknowledged, Anglican individualism could lead to a selfish egotism and isolation. But the idea of equality seemed to contain greater dangers. "If equality means absence of privilege, unfounded upon political equivalents," Lieber was willing to admit,

> it is comprehended within the term of liberty; if it means, however, social uniformity, it is rather the characteristic of absolutism, and not of liberty. For if liberty means unrestrainedness, it implies variety. . . . Diversity is the law of all organic life, and despotism and freedom find their parallels in nature, in inorganic matter, and organic bodies.[23]

Reminiscent in some ways of Tocqueville, these passages lack the "Gallican" lucidity of the Frenchman, losing themselves at times in a Teutonic haze. Certainly Tocqueville would not have accepted Lieber's facile distinction between Anglo-American and French forms, oblivious as it was to the evidences of social conformity in America to which Tocqueville devoted so much attention, and, for that matter, to the French individualism which survived all the follies of political rationalism because it clung to more important things. Tocqueville saw much the farther, in perceiving roots of uniformity in the political and social conditions of democracy itself, and not merely in a French perversion of it. Yet their observations did to some extent run parallel, and nowhere more so than in their perception that egalitarianism, applied to the exclusion of other values, threatened the variety essential to a civilization characterized by vitality and excellence.

Lieber, who has been described as a German liberal become American conservative, brought to bear on American political problems a European sensitivity coached by such thinkers as Burke and Kant, Alexander von Humboldt and the German Romantics.[24] An exotic perspective of some sort seems almost to have been necessary in the nineteenth century to view American politics in terms of diversity or its lack. The case of Orestes Brownson suggests that even Roman Catholicism (which seemed exotic enough to the Protestant majority) might have sufficed for such a perspective, although Brownson himself did not pursue the matter very far. Brownson was a convert, a one-time Transcendentalist and radical who had denigrated institutions as barriers to man's access to divinity, who had viewed, indeed, organized religion, marriage and the family, and private property as the major obstacles to human happiness. In a later phase, having studied such Old World conservatives as Maistre and Burke, he became a "disciple" of John C. Calhoun and an advocate of the state-sovereignty doctrine. (Unlike Calhoun, however, Brownson viewed constitutional limitations on federal authority as necessary partly to protect the poor from the rich.)[25]

Under the influence of his conversion to Catholicism (1844), and later of the Civil War, Brownson's views underwent still further transformations. With the zeal of the convert, he now argued that only the Catholic religion could truly sustain republican government. Protestantism eventually failed to do so, he thought, because it was subject to popular control and could provide neither the religious foundations of political virtue nor the moral unity that a republic required.[26] His more distinctly political ideas also changed. In his major work of political thought, *The American Republic* (1865), Brownson rejected the state-sovereignty doctrine in the usual sense of the term. He now maintained that "the sovereignty of the American Republic vests in the States, though in the States collectively, or united, not severally, and thus escape alike [sic] consolidation and disintegration."[27] While eschewing secession, then, Brownson attempted equally to avoid a centralized democracy, the tendency to which he chiefly blamed for provoking the War Between the States. If southerners had tended to deny the unity of the human race, with its attendant social obligations, Brownson argued, certain northerners had tended to the opposite extreme. The Abolitionist in particular, he charged, was "so engrossed with the unity that he loses the solidarity of the race, which supposes unity of race and multiplicity of individuals; and fails to see any thing legitimate and authoritative in geographical divisions or territorial circumscriptions."[28]

Although Brownson's phraseology was vague and idiosyncratic, he clearly sought a basis for social diversity within the frame of moral and political unity: a "real living solidarity," as he put it, "which gives to society at once unity of life and diversity of members." Applied to American federalism, this meant that "the organic American people do not exist as a consolidated people or state;

they exist only as organized into distinct but inseparable states."
How were unity and diversity to be politically reconciled? Not,
Brownson emphasized, by means of the customary "checks and balances" formula, pitting power against power. "The American method," he thought, "demands no such antagonism, no neutralizing of
one social force by another, but avails itself of all the forces of society,
organizes them dialectically, not antagonistically, and thus protects
with equal efficiency both public authority and private rights."[29]

Whatever this might mean in practice, it was to Brownson but
the political emblem of true Christianity. "Theological principles
are the basis of political principles," he was persuaded. "All has its
origin and prototype in the Triune God, and throughout expresses
unity in triplicity and triplicity in unity, without which there is no
real being and no actual or possible life." From this perspective,
which he managed to make at the same time one of old-fashioned
American patriotism, Brownson gave his own twist to the invidious
distinction between English and French forms indulged in by political
writers like Acton and Lieber. The English political system, being
based on "antagonistic" elements, strayed from the theological
model by denying the unity of God, he thought, whereas the centralizing French, by denying the existence of opposites, imitated
pantheism. Only the United States, despite its unfortunate Protestant
background, had somehow contrived to be "dialectically constituted,"
which was to say founded on true Catholic principles.[30] The eccentricity of this analysis was perhaps a measure of its rarity as an
effort to relate American diversity to American unity outside of the
usual legalistic formulas of constitutional debate.

The nature of the American federal system was being determined
even as Brownson wrote, and on a less ethereal plane. Blood and
iron made the state-sovereignty debate obsolete, and the increasingly national scale of economic life after the Civil War sealed the
result. State efforts to regulate business fell before the Due Process
clause of the Fourteenth Amendment—due, it must be added, to
the efforts of people like Justice Stephen J. Field who are now
regarded as conservatives. State initiative enjoyed a brief resurgence
with the early Progessive movement, but the Progressives placed
their last best hopes in a vigorous national government.

Although any real balance between state and national power has
been lost, federalism has survived in an attenuated form, and con-

servatives have been its not-always-consistent defenders. Diversity has continued to be a minor theme in discussion of the American federal system, not infrequently invoked, but seldom developed much beyond the invocation. Felix Morley argued in *Freedom and Federalism* (1959), for example, that "the federal form of government is adaptable to the greatest diversity of cultural and climatic conditions," and contended that in the United States "the principle of home rule has permitted union without a stultifying uniformity."[31] James Jackson Kilpatrick's *The Sovereign States* (1957), written primarily in response to court-ordered racial integration, noted that "recognition of the diversification and contrariety of interests among the States of the American Union lies at the essence of our Constitution," and accused the Supreme Court of a studied hostility to "diversity and variety." Kilpatrick somewhat narrowly defined the last phrase as "locally administered law to deal with local problems," however, and the main burden of the book was an exposition and history of the state-rights argument from a legal and constitutional point of view.[32]

Still, Kilpatrick glimpsed a deeper question. The "centralists" seemed to him to offer only a "dreary Hell" in the guise of Utopia. "Their god," he feared,

> is the brutal bulldozer, squat as a pagan idol, whose function it is to bring down the mountains and to fill up the valleys. They fear excellence as they abhor ineptitude. The diversity of the States offends their pretty sense of order, and from the comfortable living rooms of Scarsdale they weep tears for Mississippi.[33]

It was deeply unfortunate that questions of uniformity and diversity should be so entangled with those of racial equity, in the twentieth as in the nineteenth century. The conservative problem in America was to find matrices for social diversity comparable to those of class and tradition in Great Britain. A federal system animated by local patriotisms transcending old legalisms, resentments, and prejudices, and in which the legitimate rights of states help to protect a regionally diversified life from national pressures for uniformity, remains potentially one such matrix. For it to become so very far in actuality, despite present conservative interest in turning governmental responsibilities back to the states, would require a greater reversal of the tendencies of modern life than now seems likely.

A consciousness of diversity as a desirable quality of life has grown in America since the Civil War, as we shall see, and it has contributed to the stock of ideas of the present flourishing conservative movement. But this consciousness derived more from literary and philosophical sources than from political thought or practice, and federalism influenced it chiefly by its symptomatic and alarming failure.

NOTES

1. John Adams, *Discourses on Davila* (New York: Da Capo Press, 1973), 20-21.

2. John Adams, *A Defence of the Constitution of the United States of America* (New York: Da Capo Press, 1971), III, 273.

3. Randall B. Ripley, "Adams, Burke, and Eighteenth-Century Conservatism," *Political Science Quarterly* 80 (June 1965): 219-222. For the Burkean affinities of American conservatism, see Willmore Kendall and George W. Carey, "Towards a Definition of 'Conservatism'", *The Journal of Politics* 26 (May 1964): 406-422.

4. "Centinel," in the Philadelphia *Independent Gazeter*, October 5 and 24, 1787, Morton Borden, ed., *The Antifederalist Papers* (Lansing: Michigan State University Press, 1965), 133-134.

5. John Taylor, *An Inquiry into the Principles and Policy of the Government of the United States* (Indianapolis and New York: Bobbs-Merrill, 1969), 351-353, 368.

6. Ibid., 14.

7. Alexander Hamilton, John Jay, and James Madison, *The Federalist* (New York: The Modern Library, n.d.), 9, 231, 102-103.

8. Ibid., 368.

9. Ibid., 61. Similarly Hamilton, in no. 60, discounted the fear that federal elections might be rigged to favor a particular class. "There is sufficient diversity in the state of property, in the genius, manners, and habits of the people of the different parts of the Union," he argued, "to occasion a material diversity of disposition in their representatives towards the different ranks and conditions in society. And though an intimate intercourse under the same government will promote a gradual assimilation in some of these respects, yet there are causes, as well physical as moral, which may, in a greater or less degree, permanently nourish different propensities and inclinations in this respect" (ibid., 390).

10. George W. Carey, "Majority Tyranny and the Extended Republic Theory of James Madison," *Modern Age* 20 (Winter 1976): 51-52.

11. "Cato" [George Clinton] in *The New York Journal*, October 25, 1787, Borden, ed., *The Antifederalist*, 36-37.

12. E.g., "A Farmer," in the *Maryland Gazette and Baltimore Advertiser*, March 7, 1788, ibid., 7-8.

13. John C. Calhoun, *A Disquisition on Government* (New York: The Liberal Arts Press, 1953), xxx. The comment is that of the editor, C. Gordon Post.

14. Ibid., 9.

15. John C. Calhoun, *A Discourse on the Constitution and Government of the United States* (Columbia, S.C.: A. S. Johnston, 1851), 268. Almost repeating the last phrase, Calhoun later on characterized the United States as "a country of such vast extent and diversity of interests and institutions" (ibid., 381).

16. Calhoun, *Disquisition*, 14-15, 61.

17. David M. Potter, *The South and the Concurrent Majority*, ed. Don E. Fehrenbacher and Carl N. Degler (Baton Rouge: Louisiana State University Press, 1972), 8, 89, and passim.

18. Francis Lieber, *On Civil Liberty and Self-Government* (Philadelphia: J. B. Lippincott and Co., 1859), 366.

19. Francis Lieber, *The Miscellaneous Writings of Francis Lieber* (Philadelphia and London: J. B. Lippincott and Company, 1880), II, 117.

20. Lieber, *Civil Liberty*, 17, 56, 401.

21. Ibid., 379, 128-129.

22. Ibid., 286-287, 253, 346.

23. Lieber, *Miscellaneous Writings*, II, 379-380, 385.

24. Bernard Edward Brown, *American Conservatives* (New York: AMS Press, 1967), 26, 40, 89-90.

25. Hugh Marshall, *Orestes Brownson and the American Republic* (Washington, D.C.: The Catholic University of America Press, 1971), 7, 19, 30-33.

26. Orestes Augustus Brownson, *Essays and Reviews* (New York: Arno Press, 1972), 368-381.

27. Orestes Augustus Brownson, *The American Republic* (Clifton, N.J.: Augustus M. Kelley, Publishers, 1972), xi.

28. Ibid., 11, 354-355.

29. Ibid., 66, 245, 270.

30. Ibid., 401-402, 410, 423.

31. Felix Morley, *Freedom and Federalism* (Chicago: Henry Regnery Co., 1959), 220, 207.

32. James Jackson Kilpatrick, *The Sovereign States* (Chicago: Henry Regnery Co., 1957), 189, 293, and passim.

33. James Jackson Kilpatrick, "The Case for 'States Rights,' " *A Nation of States*, ed. Robert Goldwin (Chicago: Rand McNally, 1963), 100.

7 Southern Demons

To the extent that diversity can be embodied in legal and constitutional formulas, the South has had a greater stake in it than any other section of the country. From the 1820s to the 1960s, state-rights doctrines were associated primarily with the South, although earlier they had been invoked in a New England disaffected from the War of 1812, and they were invoked time and again by whatever state or region happened to feel at the moment menaced by federal authority. (It has been fashionable to assert that because the state-rights argument has served as a doctrine of convenience, it is therefore invalid, as if all legal and constitutional doctrines did not serve in precisely the same way, or as if a principle could be refuted by the motive for advancing it.) Nevertheless, the fact that the South found itself a beleaguered minority first on the slavery issue, and a century later on the segregation issue, made it preeminently the champion of the rights of states.

That the South has had historically the greatest interest in constitutional doctrines impeding the progress of centralization has not, to be sure, always made it the defender of any more broadly conceived diversity. Strong political and social pressures long made it difficult for southerners to deviate from those values regarded as sacrosanct, and the rigid black-white division obscured more complex diversities. But pressures for uniformity within the sectional and racial categories were never more than partially effective.

Wilbur J. Cash could entitle his 1941 classic of intellectual history *The Mind of the South,* but such recent historians as C. Vann Woodward and Carl N. Degler dissuade one from believing that there was ever any such entity. Intellectually as well as politically, socially, culturally, they have shown, Southerners even of the same race have varied widely.[1]

For the most part independently of this historical reexamination, some twentieth-century Southern conservative intellectuals became conscious of diversity as part of a way of life that they sought to defend. They were impelled to some extent, it seems, by the realization that state rights was a limited and narrowly legalistic defense, and one too associated with slavery and segregation to be widely persuasive outside their section. They were influenced too certainly by more general currents of twentieth-century thought, within which the idea of diversity has attained some significance. The "Southern Agrarians" of the 1920s and 1930s furnish the most conspicuous case in point. Wilbur Cash had little use for the Agrarians, in their defense of a markedly idealized rural South. While Cash's skepticism of the Agrarians' rosy picture of agrarian virtures was justified, they glimpsed qualities in that way of life that he missed, qualities which the "Twentieth-Century Mind"—to follow Cash's mode of classification—was coming to value. Cash delineated the myths of Old and New South in a bold relief which isolated them from the main currents of modernity; the Agrarians, while making ample use of myth themselves, also sought a juncture between southern tradition and modern sensibilities. In particular, they hoped through such a juncture to express their revulsion at the rule of industry and technology.

This was distinctly a modern revulsion, as modern as its object. It involved among other things a temperamental and aesthetic distaste for uniformity, the apparent end of the strongest political tendencies of modern times, but fully realizable only through the most modern technology. In their 1930 compendium, *I'll Take My Stand,* at least certain of the "Twelve Southerners" showed an awareness of such issues and attempted to show the relevance of the agrarian life to them. Southern intellectuals have always been more effective in attacking the North than in defending the South, and the Agrarians were no exceptions. The historian Frank Owsley reflected the fashionable between-the-wars theory that the Civil War had been brought on by the urge to power of American capitalism as, gazing northward, he bitterly contemplated the Yankee "doctrine of intolerance, crusading, standardizing alike in industry and in life," which had spurred the "Juggernaut" across the recalcitrant Confederacy. Stark Young more gently remarked that part of the interest which he found that many people had in the South arose "from a certain boredom at the flatness, excitement and sterility of this American life that they have made for themselves. . . . They like to think of some state of living in which there is less exhaustion, colorless repetition, imitation, and joylessness." Some, he added, were "bored at the celebrated uniformity of American life, which they may excuse sometimes on the grounds of the rapidity of our development but deplore on the grounds of entertainment, variety, and vital detail in human life."[2]

In what way did the agrarian life offer surcease from this American uniformity? Here, certainly, a caveat must be entered, for it has been all too easy to romanticize the agrarian life, especially for those who have never been farmers. It is easy to ignore the drudgery and monotony of traditional farm life and to enthuse about the farmer's harmony with nature. (As critics have pointed out, Southern exploitation and frequent exhaustion of the land indicated no better harmony than that which existed in other parts of the country.) The venerable yeoman farmer "myth," as it is customarily referred to, illustrates these propensities in American experience. On the other hand, a "myth," in the proper sense of the term, is not a lie, but a heightening, stylizing, or symbolic representation of selected aspects of reality, a "public dream," as it has been called, with the problematical and distorted relation to reality that dreams have. It is not necessarily naïve to find positive values in agrarian life, although it is to be unaware of its harsher aspects. The case can be made, at any rate, for the greater subjective diversity of agrarian existence; certainly it has been repeatedly put forward. The very limitations and simplicities of the more traditional way of life may make the diversities that there are—of the seasons, of tasks, in crops and livestock—stand out in sharper relief. The argument has gained force by the gambit of contrasting the varied tasks of the farm with the mechanical routine of the factory. "I know it is said that a man must find it monotonous to do the twenty things that are done on a farm, whereas, of course, he always finds it uproariously funny and festive to do one thing hour after hour and day after day in a factory,'' G. K. Chesterton remarked. The sarcasm was not frivolous, reflecting as it did an apprehension of growing standardization and sterility. "Just as we spread paving-stones over different soils without reference to the different crops that might grow there," it seemed, "so we spread programmes of platitudinous plutocracy over souls that God made various, and simpler societies have made free."[3]

Chesterton's American contemporaries, the Southern Agrarians, seemed to be groping toward a similar line of argument. "The day of each member of the [farmer's] family is filled with a mighty variety," noted Andrew Nelson Lytle,[4] somewhat cryptically perhaps for his nonagrarian reader. It required the abilities of John Crowe Ransom to give the point real intellectual weight, however. In his *God Without Thunder: an Unorthodox Defense of Orthodoxy* (1930), Ransom contrasted the subtle diversity of the natural environment with the basic simplicity of the artificial. The effect of the city, he argued, was "to insulate its inhabitants against observation of . . . the infinite variety of nature." This urban withdrawal from natural diversity was, on a very immediate and practical level, simply an aspect of a way of life capped by the ascendancy of science. Whereas religion encompassed nature, was indeed "the system of myths which gives a working definition to the relation of man to nature," science abstracted. It was "quite willing to lose the whole for the sake of the part," and thus amounted to "an order of experience in which we mutilate and prey upon nature," seeking practical objectives at any cost. The heart of the matter was that "the concrete thing never capitulates to the scientific enterprise. The essense of the concrete thing is its *variety*."[5]

That the scientific way of thinking should so far have prevailed indicated to Ransom a radical imbalance in Western consciousness, an imbalance symbolized by the triumph of Logos over the *daimon*. To the Greeks the *daimon,* or demon, was "the embodiment of variety and freedom who resists determination," whereas the Logos represented "the universal as a single quality presiding over an infinite realm of quantity." Since the Middle Ages, the bias of the

West had been toward Logos, and in contrast to the Orient, the world had become for it entirely "a rational and possessable world," constant and determinate. Ransom did not deny that such assumptions had been the foundation of remarkable achievements, but their slighting of the irrational and the contingent, he thought, carried a heavy cost. "Love is conditioned on respect for the object, and what it loves is to contemplate the infinite variety of the object: its demonic and invincible individuality."[6]

Whether or not this metaphysical superstructure lent verisimilitude to Ransom's portrait of the farmer on his spot of ground—"he would till it not too hurriedly and not too mechanically to observe in it the contingency and the infinitude of nature; and so his life acquires its philosophical and even its cosmic consciousness"[7]—it provided him with a vantage point from which urban cacophony seemed more monotonous than the lowing herd of more traditional life. It had, however, greater relevance to the central concerns of modern thought in tying the idea of diversity securely to the concrete as opposed to the abstract, experience as opposed to theory, authenticity as opposed to the merely derivative. That it did so in the name of a traditional way of life, even in the name of religious orthodoxy— of a God who in His fullness "is the God whom we can never familiarly nor intelligibly possess. . . . the only God we can ever really love"[8]— ought to be of great interest to conservatives.

The Agrarian consciousness embraced not only the innate variety of traditional rural life, but also the diversity of regions. As the title of *I'll Take My Stand* indicated, the Agrarians accepted, rather too easily, the equation of the South with agriculture and the North with industry; it has never been that simple. Otherwise, they seem realistic enough in judging that the preservation of the agrarian way of life depended on a healthy regional diversity. They might have applied this to the various regions within the South itself, but perceiving the pressures for standardization and conformity to be emanating from the North, they found it more natural to take their "stand" on the old sectional lines. This could lead, however, to a genuine appreciation of the regional diversity of the country, unconstrained by the old animosities and not bounded by the racial and other sectional issues which exercised a constant distortion on the state-rights argument.

In later years, Donald Davidson, among the original Agrarians, became most prominently the champion of regional diversity. The United States was in fact, he thought, a regionally diverse country, and he remained optimistic—perhaps overly optimistic, as it seems now—that it would remain so. Davidson had experienced in the nineteen-twenties the widespread intellectual—"urban," as he called it—assumption that political and cultural standardization must run its full course, and the howls of rage when a Dayton, Tennessee seemed to resist the tide. The pressures of centralization, concentration of power, and standardization, to which Davidson collectively applied the term "Leviathan," had certainly not diminished since the twenties. Nevertheless, encouraged by the regionalist movement in arts and letters, Davidson thought that there was probably less uniformity in the America of 1938 than in that of even a century before. In the constitutional abstract a federation of states, America remained in reality a nation of sections, and representative figures like Davidson's "Brother Jonathan in Vermont or Cousin Roderick in Georgia," did not seem members of endangered species. Not even with its new "mask of humanitarianism and benevolence" did Leviathan seem likely to prevail, for which Davidson rejoiced. "The diversity of regions rather enriches the national life than impoverishes it," he thought. Regions were "a national advantage, offering not only the charm of variety but the interplay of points of view that ought to give flexibility and wisdom."[9] In 1957, despite the progress of industry and the new pressures of racial integration, Davidson remained confident that regional diversities would endure.[10]

The Southern Agrarians developed a defense of a section and a way of life, but they had not, in their days as the "Vanderbilt school," been much concerned with conservative philosophy per se. In the 1920s and 1930s, there was very little in the way of a coherent conservative intellectual movement in the United States to which the Agrarians could have tied their ideas. (Even less, of course, was a conservative agrarianism calculated for political success. Its necessary hostility to industrial capitalism could not have endeared it to the Republican Party, and few Southern Democrats were interested in manning the barricades against industrial encroachments.) The heirs of the Agrarians among Southern intellectuals of the 1950s and 1960s faced a quite different situation. By then the particularist

Agrarian program for the South had clearly failed. This failure freed the defense of traditional values from the sectional strategy which almost inevitably had given it the aspect of a second lost cause, however; it also freed it from too narrow an identification with a preindustrial society no longer tenable in the United States. By the fifties, moreover, there was a concerted conservative movement within which the Southerners could find a voice and an intellectual climate in general ways more hospitable than that of the thirties to what they had to say. The integration crisis threatened to negate these positive factors, and to enlist conservative Southern intellectuals in still another Confederate defeat, but at least some of them managed to transcend the issues of the "Second Reconstruction."

Perhaps the most interesting voice from the post-Agrarian Southern conservative school was that of Richard Weaver. Weaver saw clearly the opportunity of relating Southern particularism to the fundamental elements of conservative thought, including, quite prominently, the idea of diversity. Indeed, he regarded respect for the principle of diversity as itself an historically differentiating factor between North and South.

> There are those who maintain that the true principle of history is a dynamic universalism, so that all true development is a sloughing off of particularities and individualities in an approach to the typical. There are others who believe that life consists in the richness of diversity and that conformity to a universal pattern is a kind of death. . . . On the level of everyday politics it takes the form of democratic resentment against exclusiveness, just as the second expresses itself in distaste for incorporation into something felt to be alien or inferior. The backwoods politicians of mid-nineteenth-century America were unknowingly entangled in the great debate of the Schoolmen, with the Southern separatists playing the part of Nominalists, and the Northern democrats and equalitarians that of Realists.[11]

Weaver's philosophical figure was not entirely felicitous, as nominalism can tend more to atomism than to genuine diversity, while a qualified realism may admit the principle of unity-in-diversity, as it did in the Middle Ages. It does however demonstrate Weaver's strong sense of the enduring philosophical division represented by North and South. The South, he maintained, was "*the last non-materialist civilization in the Western World.* It is this refuge of sentiments and values, of spiritual congeniality, of belief in the word, of reverence for symbolism, whose existence haunts the nation.''[12] More convincingly, in one of his last pieces, he distinguished between the two theories of liberty expressed by Hayne and Webster in their famous debate: the Northerner conceiving of liberty in universal terms and impatient with "intermediate structures and centers of authority," the Southerner understanding it as an intimate quality centered on the hearth and tied to local associations.[13]

Although he placed far less emphasis than had the Agrarians on the economic determinants of sectionalism, Weaver shared their belief that traditional and modern societies fostered sharply differing qualities of life. Endorsing Russell Kirk's affection for the "variety and mystery of traditional life," Weaver saw in it above all a given reality to which respect and piety were due. The conservative, he thought, was "prepared to tolerate diversity of life and opinion because he knows that not all things are of his making and that it is right within reason to let each follow the law of his own being.''[14] The diversity of task and occupation on the traditional plantation, he somewhat romantically suggested elsewhere, was a practical foundation for this kind of consciousness, in addition to encouraging "an intense provincialism.''[15]

As with other discerning defenders of the South, Weaver's own studied provincialism led him to see more deeply into the ills of modern life. He shared the widespread sense of modern disintegration, of a "severe fragmentation" of man's world picture, leading to "an obsession with isolated parts.''[16] But this loss of unity was also a loss of diversity, for the conservative order in which Weaver believed encompassed both. Even in narrow political terms, it seemed to him, democracy could not rest on belief in the "magic of numbers," but must instead rest "upon a belief that every individual has some special angle of vision, some particular insight into a situation which ought to be taken into account before a policy is decided on." The "very diversity and variety" of responses which it elicited gave democracy its value as a form of government.[17]

On a more general level, Weaver saw clearly that society "exists in and through its variegation and multiplicity," and that when it broke down, it was precisely through a confusion of roles and consequent loss of distinction and differentiation.[18] While it remained healthy, on the other hand,

> a culture is a means of uniting society by making provision for differences. . . . A just man finds satisfaction in the knowledge that society has various roles for various kinds of people and that they in the performance of these roles create a kind of symphony of labor, play, and social life. There arises in fact a distinct pleasure from knowing that society is structured, diversified, balanced, and complex. Blind levelers do not realize that people can enjoy seeing things above them as well as on a plane with them. Societies with differentiation afford pleasure to the moral imagination as an aesthetic design affords rest to the eye.[19]

These conditions could not obtain, Weaver suggested, in the absence of "cultural pluralism." Culture by its nature, he thought, required a certain exclusiveness, or it could not maintain its integrity, or the "particularities" which give it character. In the twentieth century, unfortunately, there was a principle at work, to which the term "technological uniformity" seemed appropriate, which by threatening all cultural differentiation, threatened the nature of culture itself.[20]

Weaver could not but feel oppressed, then, by the "massive trend toward uniformity and regimentation" which he recognized in the modern world. Part of it was a conscious radical war against the particular. The Communist, "looking upon this world with its interesting distinctions and its prolific rewards and pleasures," seemed to him the type of Satan peering maliciously into the Garden of Eden. But communism was only the most extreme and deliberate expression of a tendency which in the form of radio and television, for example, had largely destroyed the distinctive Kentucky mountain culture with the "external and hollow" uniformities of those media.[21] Whether the deliberate plan of reformers or revolutionaries, or the thoughtless product of technological ingenuity, imposed uniformity, Weaver suggested, was destructive because it distorted reality, and overrode the differences and distinctions which followed from the complexity of reality. Perhaps reality could be altered. But to replace a structured society with a shapeless mass, Weaver was convinced, would be fatal to civilization. "Because it depends upon an ordering of qualities and places, civilization is in fact a protest against this featureless condition."[22]

Believing that differences and divisions were essential to any society which rose above the egalitarian lowest common denominator of appetite, Weaver called—quixotically as it may seem now—for a restoration of the traditional distinctions of social life (for example, "the fruitful distinction between the sexes, with the recognition of respective spheres of influence"). Such differences, he thought, meant "as much to living as rules mean to a game," imparting to life a transfiguring drama far removed from the meaningless clash of forces offered by scientists and utilitarians.[23]

Weaver's perception of fragmentation and uniformity as simply different aspects of the same social malaise gave him a place in a venerable line of conservative thought. Thus it was natural for him to cite Lord Acton in reiterating that "there is a good higher than unity. Unity means oneness. The goal is harmony. Harmony is the fruitful co-existence together of things diversified."[24] Definitions of such terms vary; Acton's idea itself was ancient. But in an age still distracted by nineteenth-century ideologies which required as the price of progress both relentless conflict and the uniform organization of the conflicting units—Marxian, nationalist, and racist ideologies, especially—and lulled by newer programs which promised material satisfaction and absence of conflict at the price of standardization, it seemed not altogether stale.

Weaver left a clear imprint on Southern and on conservative thought. In fundamental respects in line with the Agrarian tradition, but not so committed to a particular economic pattern, he did much of his work at a time when there was even less intellectual sympathy with the South than in the thirties. Any Southern conservatism, especially if it showed resentment at federal efforts to impose uniform social patterns, was sure to be written off in the North as not too covert racism. Regional diversity was difficult to defend in such circumstances.[25] Weaver, however, could not so easily be dismissed. M. E. Bradford indicated something of the lasting import of Weaver's thought, as well as of that of the Agrarians, when he cited their opposition to those old enemies of the Godsweal, perfectionism and its twin, the envious and cowardly dream of uniformity: the impulse to "fix everything" and thus pretend to create it, to cover with uniforms and affix numbers. . . . Southerners like Weaver and his predecessors attempt to keep clear of this first error by "seconding God's motion," by approving the variety inside of Being, what the theologians call "plenitude." They doubt that the given world requires repairing. . . . Their uneasiness about "homogenizing" schools is notorious.[26]

Bradford elaborated subsequently on these points himself, ascribing to the millennialist strain in American history much of the impatience with differences which, he thought, amounted to a hatred of the plenitude and variety of Creation.[27]

Southern thinkers did, then, produce something of a defense of social and regional diversity in the conservative vein, more at any rate than issued from any other section of the country. In part, this was only a kind of epiphenomenon of the state-rights position, designed as a defense against specific national policies and encroachments. And certainly with racial tensions somewhat allayed, and at the same time nationalized, with the agrarian basis of Southern distinctiveness drastically reduced, with a recent Southern president whose policies seemed to conservatives indistinguishable from those of a Northern liberal, with all the internal and external signs of standardization wrought by commerce and technology which know no state or sectional lines, it is difficult in the 1980s to view the South as an especially effective bastion against cultural uniformity. Southern thinkers of this century, Weaver and the Agrarians particularly, consequently decline in significance insofar as they were leaders of another sectional lost cause. They were more than that, however, men who drew from the Southern experience insight into a fundamental question of modernity: that of unity and multiplicity, as Henry Adams termed it. In this respect, it may be that the stature of the Southerners will grow.

NOTES

1. See especially C. Vann Woodward, *The Strange Career of Jim Crow* (New York: Oxford University Press, 1966); and Carl N. Degler, *The Other South: Southern Dissenters in the Nineteenth Century* (New York:

Harper & Row, 1974). A defense of Cash's interpretation is offered by Richard H. King in *A Southern Renaissance: The Cultural Awakening of the American South, 1930-1955* (New York: Oxford University Press, 1980).

2. Twelve Southerners, *I'll Take My Stand* (New York: Harper & Row, 1962), 91, 333-334, 356. Donald Davidson, arguing that the agrarian was a more congenial environment for art than the industrial, remarked of the objects of science in art that "their role is mainly Satanic. Since their influence on humanity is to dehumanize, to emphasize utilitarian ends, to exalt abstraction over particularity and uniformity over variety, the artist tends to view them as evil" (ibid., 47).

3. Gilbert K. Chesterton, *The Outline of Sanity* (New York: Dodd, Mead & Company, 1927), 127, 188.

4. Twelve Southerners, *I'll Take My Stand,* 223.

5. John Crowe Ransom, *God Without Thunder* (Hamden, Conn.: Archon Books, 1965), 124-125, 136-137, 156, 258.

6. Ibid., 291, 296, 304-305, 315.

7. Twelve Southerners, *I'll Take My Stand,* 19-20.

8. Ransom, *God Without Thunder,* 315.

9. Donald Davidson, *The Attack on Leviathan* (Gloucester, Mass.: Peter Smith, 1962), 72, 104, 6, 191, 12, 110.

10. Donald Davidson, *Still Rebels, Still Yankees* (Baton Rouge: Louisiana State University Press, 1957), passim.

11. Richard M. Weaver, *The Southern Tradition at Bay* (New Rochelle, N.Y.: Arlington House, 1968), 197.

12. Ibid., 391.

13. Richard M. Weaver, "Two Orators," ed. George Core and M. E. Bradford, *Modern Age* 14 (Summer-Fall 1970): 235-237, 241.

14. Richard M. Weaver, *Life Without Prejudice* (Chicago: Henry Regnery Company, 1965), 143, 167, and passim.

15. Weaver, *Southern Tradition,* 52.

16. Richard M. Weaver, *Ideas Have Consequences* (Chicago: University of Chicago Press, 1962), 59.

17. Weaver, *Life Without Prejudice,* 61-62; see also Richard M. Weaver, "Illusions of Illusion," *Modern Age* 4 (Summer 1960): 318-319.

18. Weaver, *Life Without Prejudice,* 3.

19. Richard M. Weaver, "The Image of Culture," *Modern Age* 8 (Spring 1964): 195.

20. Weaver, *Life Without Prejudice,* 18, 110.

21. Ibid., 108-110, 142, 5.

22. Weaver, *Southern Tradition,* 37.

23. Ibid., 392-394.

24. Weaver, *Life Without Prejudice,* 112.

25. Let alone racial diversity. One who attempted a defense of the latter was Robert Y. Drake, who argued in 1958 that "all this stir about 'equality' is really due to a perversion of the idea of unity in diversity. For I suspect that what the Southerner is most vitally concerned about is not the preservation of unequal status, but the preservation of the characteristic racial differences, to lose which would seem, to him, disastrous." "What It Means to be a Southerner," *Modern Age* 2 (Fall 1958): 348.

26. M. E. Bradford, "The Agrarianism of Richard Weaver: Beginnings and Completions," *Modern Age* 14 (Summer-Fall 1970): 254.

27. M. E. Bradford, "A Fire Bell in the Night: The Southern Conservative View," *Modern Age* 17 (Winter 1973): 11-13. See also Bradford, "The Heresy of Equality: Bradford Replies to Jaffa," *Modern Age* 20 (Winter 1976): 62-77.

Part Three

Conservatism, Diversity, and Modernity

8 Several Turn-of-the-Century Voices

The extent to which the nineteenth century furnished the basic terms for our contemporary discourse about the world is widely appreciated. If we enlarge the chronological century to take in the years between the French Revolution and the First World War, we find in it the modern formulations of conservatism and liberalism, socialism, evolution and relativity, the strong fore-shadowing at least of fascism; the list could be extended indefinitely. During this period too the qualities of unity and diversity began to take on distinctively modern connotations. Three turn-of-the-century American figures, John Fiske, Henry Adams, and William James, seem especially to illuminate the latter polarity and its significance for modern conservatism.

To its occasional profit, and more frequent detriment, conservative thought for more than a century has drawn upon insights derived from biology, and especially from the evolutionary biology associated with Charles Darwin. At best, biology has provided a standard anchored in organic reality by which to measure the ideals and abstractions of liberal and radical reform. At worst, it has lured the unwary onto the byways of Social Darwinism, resulting in serious distortions of traditional conservative values and principles.

More than most other sciences, biology lent itself to the idea of variety. This was particularly true during the second half of the nineteenth century, when a monistic determinism still ruled physics, and it seemed possible and profitable to reduce all the complexities and mysteries of Creation to the bedrock phenomena confidently labeled matter and energy. There seemed nothing ultimately to keep organic life from inclusion in this reduction, and materialist pundits did not hesitate to attempt it. On the level of practical science, however, biologists had to reckon with an enormous diversity of plant and animal life, at a time when even the present array of subatomic particles, which lends a ghostly cast of variety to the pertinent branch of physics, was far in the future. (When Henry Adams required scientific furnishings for his allegories of modern uniformity, he had recourse to physics in preference to biology.) For evolutionists, of course, variation was essential; it was inherent in the process whereby new and more complex forms of life emerged from primal and simpler ones. And the higher the life form, it was apparent, the more versatile—the more various its capabilities and possibilities, as indicated by the greater range of variations among its individual members. To some it seemed clear that a very similar set of generalizations could be applied to the evolution of human society.

Just how evolution applied to society was very much an open question. Those who emphasized the inexorable role of struggle and competition in social progress came to be known as Social Darwinists. The term has been a mischievous one in intellectual history; as Robert C. Bannister has shown,[1] "Social Darwinism" was to a large extent a stereotype created by opponents of the line of thought that it represented, and one which obscured the complexities and refinements of much evolutionary thinking. Despite its usual association with conservatism, moreover, there were good reasons for conservatives to shy away from doctrines which allegedly preached the "law of the jungle," and which did at least severely undermine Christian or other moral absolutes. Social Darwinist rhetoric was useful against what William Graham Sumner called "the absurd effort to make the world over" in defiance of the presumably ineluctable law of natural selection, but swallowed whole it negated fundamental conservative precepts of social order and harmony. And from the standpoint of the present thesis, Social Darwinists distorted any lessons which biology may have offered, because they were more impressed with the apparent uniformity of the process than with the diversity of the results of evolution.

In fact, those of conservative bent, like most others, drew highly selective lessons from evolution, weaving in those aspects of it which suited their needs with philosophical or even religious strains of thought. A case in point is George Harris, who in an often acute little volume published in 1897, *Inequality and Progress,* combined insights drawn from evolutionary theory with Hegelian idealism and an older ideal of society as a harmony of unequal ranks. Harris took as a starting point the observation that advanced societies were more complex than primitive ones, and therefore in the most obvious sense more varied. "Variety," he thought, could only mean "inequality," and he used the terms almost interchangeably to describe the natural "unlikenesses of men" and to argue that superiority and subordination were the conditions of civilized life. Citing Herbert Spencer's master principle of evolution from homogeneity to heterogeneity, Harris contrasted the monotony of savage life with civilization's "increasing variety of functions and tastes." "Equality," he concluded, "is retrogression towards the dead uniformity and precarious life of stupid savagery, of nomadic tribes, and of serfdom. Progress is marked by private ownership, by specializing of pursuits, by organization, by unity in variety."[2]

Perhaps the most interesting part of Harris's defense of variety and inequality was his sharp distinction between unity and uniformity. Unity, he pointed out,

> depends on unlikeness. Things which are alike are in juxtaposition; things which are unlike unite to form a whole. Union of equals is a process in addition; union of unequals is a process in multiplication. The Hegelian philosopher finds the unity of society in the uniqueness of individuals. The perfect society would consist of perfect individuals, each self-centered and unique.[3]

From this perspective, the "higher unity" of society became simply a "more complex variety" and one that made possible the very goods which had been falsely associated with equality. Indeed, thought Harris, "inequality is the middle term which gives personal liberty on one side and social fraternity on the other side." For "essential equality would destroy personal freedom, and would leave as much fraternity as a man enjoys when he looks at himself in a mirror."[4]

It is notable, however, that Harris applied the terms "inequality" and "variety" almost entirely to individuals rather than to the local and traditional groupings dear to Burkeans. Although a man of his time in alluding to the "inequality" of races, he believed that the "resemblances and contrasts among civilized peoples are individual rather than national," and conversely that equality existed only among masses of men.[5] Conservative in relating a necessary inequality to a desirable diversity, Harris remained simply a nineteenth-century American in his individualism. This was a point of view which left ample scope for certain kinds of inequality—that of wealth, for example; how much support it provided for authentic diversity was open to question.

The contrast between civilized diversity and primitive uniformity contained some validity and somewhat greater plausibility; it would have to be qualified in the light of modern anthropological knowledge of the complexities of preliterate cultures. But in any event, the effort to derive from this observation a universal law of development attempted too much. Such was the endeavor of John Fiske, the prolix American disciple of Herbert Spencer. Fiske, in *The Cosmic Philosophy* and other works, spun out the scientific, social, and historical implications of the master formula of evolution: the "continuous change from indefinite, incoherent homogeneity to a definite, coherent heterogeneity of structure and function, through successive differentiations and integrations."[6] According to this formula, societies as well as organisms and galaxies tended to become more complex, better organized, more manifold. In one respect, however, social life was unique; whereas the highest forms of organic life were those in which the constituent units (such as cells) had the least freedom, the highest social life was that in which the units (individuals) had the most freedom.[7]

Fiske was thus in his own way a champion of diversity, for in it, he thought, freedom was manifested. He was, to be sure, a monist, or as he preferred to put it, a monotheist, in ultimate philosophy, and his evolutionary doctrine was deterministic with little equivocation. Yet his monism was that of a pluralizing process; men might be ultimately powerless to alter the course of history, but that course was, paradoxically, in the direction of greater freedom and diversity. The highest civilization would be that which achieved the greatest variety commensurate with order and unity. The English-speaking peoples seemed to Fiske most advanced toward this goal, as indicated by the characteristic Anglo-American balance between local and central governments.[8] But heterogeneity was more than a political balance; it was central to Fiske's vision as a "cosmic theist." Indeed, he virtually presented in new terms the ancient imagery of the plenitude of God. "The consummate product of a world of evolution," he suggested, "is the character that *creates* happiness, that is replete with dynamic possibilities of fresh life and activities in directions forever new. Such a character is the reflected image of God, and in it are contained the promise and potency of life everlasting."[9]

Such comments indicate the inadequacy of the "Social Darwinist" label sometimes applied to Fiske. To the extent that conservatives actually adopted Social Darwinist ideas, they severely distorted conservatism—in the direction of a selfish individualism, amorality, and materialism, and away from tradition, social authority, and religious sanction. Fiske showed little of this tendency; on the other hand, his "cosmic theism" was genuinely conservative in its hospitality to continuity and heterogeneity, in its espousal of gradual progress in relation to certain moral absolutes. If his devotion to variety was vitiated by his monistic determinism (his was ultimately the "block-universe" of which William James was to complain), his Anglo-American parochialism, and even his ebullient optimism, which led him to a benign and cozy vision of inevitable progress, it may still be placed within the tradition that we have been describing.

John Fiske has seemed in the twentieth century at best naïve in his faith in inevitable progress, and at worst a smug Victorian moralist at home in, if not the best of all possible worlds, at least as part of the best of all possible evolutionary processes. Nevertheless, his and Spencer's conception of progress in terms of coherent heterogeneity offers a usable standard by which to measure progress and to distinguish it from mere innovation and efficiency. Their final vision, at least, was arguably more humane than that of those who tacitly accept incoherent homogeneity as the end of social evolution.

It has been noted more than once that there is a contradiction in the modern world—and it is one which keeps it from Fiske's coherent heterogeneity: its very multiplicity seems to end in a tedious uniformity. G. K. Chesterton, with his acute sense of paradox, found an example in twentieth-century entertainment, with its wonderful technical means and plethora of choices. "But even the rich variety of method and approach unfolded before us," Chesterton perceived, "seems to cover a certain secret and subtle element of monotony."[10] (Chesterton cited the passiveness of radio listening, a pastime which would later seem positively designed to elicit the imaginative participation of the audience, in comparison with television.) "Strange," remarked a more recent observer, "that a diversified civilization, abundant in goods, rich in imaginative talents, should weary by an impression of sameness."[11]

The most significant clues had already been provided by Henry and Brooks Adams. These brothers, as intense an amalgam of conservative and radical instincts as the name of Henry's proposed party, the "Conservative Christian Anarchist," would suggest, glimpsed more clearly than anyone else of their time the mockery of the old ideal of ordered freedom by the modern specter of determined chaos. For the younger brother, this was the "Degradation of the Democratic Dogma." As Brooks interpreted the powerful mind of his grandfather, John Quincy Adams had conceived of reason, science, and democracy joining in a plan of progress that was bringing to the United States and the world ever-increasing measures of liberty and enlightenment. But the scheme was held together by the superintending hand of Providence. Democracy, for the Adamses, was a way of reconciling the one and the many, freedom and order, competition and the general welfare. Yet from the vantage point of the twentieth century, it appeared that the efficacy of democracy thus conceived had depended all too heavily upon the assumption of a God who Himself was both a unifying and diversifying principle. The fading of the sense of Providence, in the cold bath of late Victorian skepticism and materialism, left only the uniformity of rushing particles of matter and the disintegration of transcendent meaning—a determined chaos. By 1915, Brooks Adams despaired of finding "any theory by which the apparent diversity about us may be resolved into a harmonious progression from a first cause to a final effect, or from a beginning to an end."[12] And without a "theory," in the Adams view, apparent diversity was as illusory as apparent unity.

The career of Brooks Adams offers a commentary on the drift of Western thought generally over the last century or so. Adams was a liberal as a young man after the Civil War, campaigning for good government, condemning dangerous concentrations of power, and hailing in historical retrospect the "emancipation" of Massachusetts from its original Puritan constrictions. Disillusioned in the economically depressed 1890s, he perversely embraced a materialistic determinism which dismissed man as "a pure automaton, who is moved along the paths of least resistance by forces over which he has no control."[13] In his last phase he became disillusioned even with this blind monism. All that was left was chaos, as he acknowledged, and a tenuous and desperate hope that religious faith might offer a way out. Without the diversity underwritten by his early liberal views, apparently, there was no ultimately convincing unity: the result was a dead end of the rational mind.

Henry Adams explored the same themes, and with greater eventual profundity. Driven intellectually to seek a principle which would unify experience, he was too temperamentally attracted to the spontaneous and diverse to be happy with the cheap unities offered by deterministic and materialistic lines of thought—and too discerning to see them as genuine unities. Yet in the hurly-burly of modern life, he was no more able to perceive, with William James, a zestful ferment, or even an authentic diversity. It seemed rather a chaos of meaningless determinism. Adams, indeed, provided the starkest metaphors for the characteristically modern fear of sameness. The ocean, which the Jacksonian historian George Bancroft had used as a symbol of democratic energy, became for Adams precisely the opposite: a dead level of democratic mediocrity. "In a democratic ocean," he observed, "science could see something ultimate. Man could go no further. The atom might move, but the general equilibrium could not change."[14] Adams later gave the image a cosmic dimension. Invoking physics to refute biology, he stood Social Darwinism on its head. Far from evolving from indefinite incoherent homogeneity to definite coherent heterogeneity, as Herbert Spencer and John Fiske had supposed, the universe was running down like an unwound clock. Taking the decadence of modern society as an illustration of the Second Law of Thermodynamics, Adams gloomily observed the dissipation of order which would finally extinguish the world in the ultimate sameness of entropy.

Adams's counterpoise to "twentieth-century multiplicity" was, of course, "thirteenth-century unity." With the accuracy of Adams's historical interpretations, of which medieval historians have often been contemptuous, we are not here concerned. His characterization of the Middle Ages by the term "unity," however, has sometimes been misunderstood. A serious scholar of the period, he was perfectly aware that the actual life of the Middle Ages presented

> a picture of suffering, sorrow, and death; plague, pestilence, and famine; inundations, droughts, and frosts; catastrophes world-wide and accidents in corners; cruelty, perversity, stupidity, uncertainty, insanity; virtue begetting vice; vice working for good; happiness without sense, a selfishness without gain, misery without cause, and horrors undefined.[15]

This catalogue of chaos is the negative of William James's vision of strenuous diversity (which we shall see in the next section), and may be more convincing to contemporary eyes. But for Adams, the Middle Ages still possessed a principle of unity which the modern world lacked. It was symbolized by the figure of the Virgin Mary enthroned in Chartres Cathedral. As the focus of popular faith, in Adams's view, she was accessible to all sorts and conditions of men. The unity of faith which she represented thus encompassed diversity, which overflowed even the bounds of divine rationality. Adams made much of the idea that Mary was a court of last resort for the wretched sinner condemned by the strict masculine justice of God the Father. Medieval men and women, he suggested, demanded a sympathy above the law: "God could not be love. God was Justice, Order, Unity, Perfection; He could not be human and imperfect, nor could the Son or the Holy Ghost be other than the Father. The Mother alone was human, imperfect, and could love; she alone was Favour, Duality, Diversity." It was left to Mary to care for that which logic excluded. "If the Trinity was in its essence Unity, the Mother alone could represent whatever was not Unity; whatever was irregular, exceptional, outlawed; and this was the whole human race."[16]

This was almost to place the Virgin herself outside law and unity. But Adams entertained a complementary, and more distinctly conservative, vision of unity arising from the very shards of broken lives. This kind of unity was represented most eloquently by the Gothic cathedral itself. The brilliance of the stained glass put the monochrome of modern life to shame. "The windows of Chartres," Adams pointed out, "have no sequence, and their charm is in their variety, in individuality, and sometimes even in downright hostility to each other, reflecting the picturesque society that gave them!" In the presumably tradition-bound society of the Middle Ages was a vitality, even a "greed for novelty," that the frenetic modern world could not match. "Our age," Adams complained, "has lost much of its ear for poetry, as it has its eye for colour and line, and its taste for war and worship, wine and women."[17]

Henry Adams delighted in paradox, and his contrasting of the many colors of "thirteenth-century unity" with the essential drabness of "twentieth-century multiplicity" afforded him polemical satisfaction in his quarrel with his own age. But there was a serious point behind it. Although driven intellectually to seek explanations in scientific determinism, Adams temperamentally was as convinced as William James that the more reductive monisms left too much out of account. While James developed in consequence his philosophy of pluralism, Adams perceived the ultimately mutual relation of unity and multiplicity. "If a Unity exists, in which and toward which all energies centre," it seemed to him, "it must explain and include Duality, Diversity, Infinity—Sex!"[18]

Thus, to Henry Adams, unity and diversity were conditions of each other. There could be no true unity which did not encompass diversity; conversely, there could be no genuine diversity without an ordering, which is to say a differentiating, principle—unity. The Virgin Mary was a perfect symbol of "thirteenth-century unity" because she made sensible order of the chaos of life by her willingness to embrace a diversity that extended even into outlawry. Modern multiplicity differs from medieval multiplicity only in that it lacks any ordering or unifying principle. Consequently, it is a multiplicity without authentic diversity. It remains a chaos; and chaos, in Adams's metaphysics, is ultimately equivalent to uniformity. He thus reverses the formula of Spencer and Fiske; it is not coherent heterogeneity toward which the world is heading, but incoherent homogeneity. Entropy will bring the final chaotic sameness from which no unity and no diversity can arise. In more mundane terms, the comparatively limited possibilities of medieval life had the quality of diversity, contrast, even spontaneity, because they all had assigned meaning; the far more numerous possibilities of modernity quickly lapse into tedium because they have none. Thus medieval unity is fittingly represented by the brilliant colors of the stained glass of Chartres, while twentieth-century multiplicity composes a monotone.

To be sure, medieval unity remained for Adams an artificial and precarious construct like the Gothic cathedral which was its emblem. Although he found it aesthetically true in its visible representation, he could not accept any medieval synthesis as objectively valid; it remained a dream which could not be replicated in the cold light of modern science. Thus when Adams playfully dubbed himself a "Conservative Christian Anarchist," it was to proclaim that "in the last synthesis, order and anarchy were one, but that the unity was chaos."[19] Yet it was Adams's habit to conceal half his meaning in hyperbole, and Conservative Christian Anarchism was more—or less—than a prescription for futility. He described himself to John Hay in 1900 "as one who belongs wholly to the past, and whose traditional sympathies are with all the forces that resist concentration, and love what used to be called liberty but has now become anarchy, or resistance to civilisation."[20] In the context of Adams's thought as a whole, it is not far-fetched to see in the figure of the Conservative Christian Anarchist the archetype of the man who has recourse to tradition and to values embedded in the past precisely because he values liberty and diversity and resists the concentrating, standardizing drift of modern civilization. There could, in this respect, be worse models for the twentieth-century conservative than this walking oxymoron, this staid and rebellious figure.

William James is not accounted part of the conservative tradition, and for reasons which seem fundamentally persuasive. As one of the American leaders of the "revolt against formalism," he helped to usher in ways of thinking which have been far more congenial to liberals than to conservatives. His "pluralistic universe" denied the existence of the absolute, and even of an absolute God. His pragmatism appeared to negate the very notion of absolute truth and to "make everything relative." Through his pragmatism he is associated, although often carelessly and unfairly, with the social engineering projects of John Dewey and his followers. It would be difficult so far to dispel such impressions as to enlist James as a certified conservative. Yet it seems to me that in some respects he has more to contribute to conservative perspectives than the orthodox. Much of his conservative value derives from the very pluralism which makes him suspect, and on this point it is instructive to compare him with his Harvard colleague and friendly intellectual adversary, Josiah Royce.

In fundamental categories Royce was certainly far more the conservative than James.[21] He was a neo-Kantian idealist, but one in whom German philosophy mingled with a decidedly American temperament and a Christian religious impulse. His main project as a philosopher was to reconcile unity with multiplicity, to the point of making them, indeed, interdependent terms. His God was veritably a community of individual wills, through which the "Absolute" realized His manifold being. This might have implied support for an atomistic society, in which the membership of all in the divine community obviated the need for more mundane groupings. American Transcendentalists—also under German influence— had been susceptible to this conceit. But Royce perceived—with the eye of one reared in near-frontier California—that the society of weak institutions was not a society favorable to the growth of real individuality. No more was that whose institutions were all cast on a mass scale. An atomistic individualism and an undifferentiated collectivism, it seemed to him, were simply "tendencies, each of which, as our social order grows, intensifies the other."[22] The huge political and economic units characteristic of modern life, he exclaimed, were "like the forces of nature. They excite our loyalty as little as do the trade-winds or the blizzard."[23] The individual who was "liberated" from traditional ties and associations was actually at the mercy of vast impersonal forces beyond his control, with the result that "individualistic communities are almost universally, and paradoxically enough, communities that are extremely cruel to individuals."[24]

Royce's proposed solution was to nurture the life of more manageable and diverse units of living, which he called "provinces." Freedom, he thought,

dwells now in the small social group, and has its securest home
in the provincial life. The nation by itself . . . is in danger of
becoming an incomprehensible monster, in whose presence the
individual loses his right, his self-consciousness, and his dignity.
The province must save the individual.[25]

The province satisfied Royce's philosophy of community by reconciling on a practical level the unity of existence and the multifariousness of its expression. He thus offered a defense of both cosmic and
social diversity that fits comfortably within the conservative tradition
under discussion. Yet, however brilliantly, he was essentially restating hallowed conceptions of plenitude and unity-in-diversity,
and the venerable conservative devotion to institutions intermediate
between the individual and the mass. William James undertook the
more hazardous task of making a place for clear distinctions and a
generous sense of diversity in a world at once in rebellion against
old absolutes and seduced by new reductionisms.

To James, Royce's system offered only a mock-pluralism disguised as diversity. The will of an Absolute, no matter how differentiated, remained absolute. Put most simply, James espoused
a deeper pluralism out of his conception of the requirements of
authentic freedom and morality. The "block universe" of idealist
or evolutionary monists, he believed, left room neither for choice
and contingency, nor for the moral meaning that could arise only
from real uncertainty and conflict. If James's brand of pluralism
helped to open the way to innovation unanchored by conventional
absolutes, it was intended as much to leave room for certain traditional Western values which in James's day, it should be remembered,
were gravely imperiled by scientific and positivistic lines of thought
which threatened to freeze into a system of absolute and universal
determinism. Royce's gentle, sophisticated idealism, James felt,
was no adequate answer; to admit any final unity played into the
hands of the Philistines. As much as anything, perhaps, James's
philosophical preferences rested on a temperamental delight in the
struggle and variety of everyday life. Conversely, he evinced a rather
patrician contempt for the middle-class tameness and uniformity of
much of American society. The philosopher's visit to a Chautauqua
meeting prompted a longing for "the flash of a pistol, a dagger,

or a devilish eye, anything to break the unlovely level of 10,000 good people.''[26] James wanted to make the universe safe for risk, and was merciless on those systems which sought to palliate it.

Even the "synthetic" evolutionary philosophy of Herbert Spencer, which was seized upon by some American conservatives as a rationale for unlimited economic competition, seemed to James ultimately tame. His stricture upon Spencer in 1879 expressed a more profoundly conservative preference for life as it is, as opposed to Utopia:

> If now I, a defective and imperfectly evolved creature, full of the joy of battle and other survivals from a savage state, say to Mr. Spencer, "I know nothing of your highest life, or, knowing, despise it"; and if I add to my other riotous deeds the sneering at evolution and the writing of sarcasms on its eventual milk-and-water paradise, saying I prefer to go on like my ancestors and enjoy this delicious mess of fears and strivings, and agonies and exultations, of dramatic catastrophes and supernatural visions, of excesses, in short, in every direction, which make of human life the rich contradictory tissue of good and evil it now is, how shall Mr. Spencer reduce me to order or coerce me to bow the knee?[27]

James's horror of the absolute was based on the perception that it cut off the myriad possibilities of truth and experience in the name of unity. Yet despite the radical character of his antiabsolutism, his approach was designed in part to keep the universe open to traditional ways of apprehension. This was most conspicuously the case with his great and sympathetic interest in the "varieties of religious experience." No enemy of science, he nevertheless recoiled from "a vision of 'Science' in the form of abstraction, priggishness and sawdust, lording it over all,"[28] and foreclosing the diverse religious and other truths outside its bounds. And James's pluralism, although it negated a traditional conservative vision of divinely appointed harmony and unity, was really in large measure an attempt to adapt old values to a new philosophical milieu. Paradoxically, it was an effort to preserve traditional absolutes by denying the Absolute. Noting in an early letter to Oliver Wendell Holmes, Jr. the demise of traditional religion, James asked whether it might not

be possible to "conduct off upon our purposes from the old morali-
ties and theologies a beam which will invest us with some of the
proud absoluteness which made them so venerable?"[29] In a way
which he did not foresee when he wrote this letter, James did just
that. His pluralistic world was designed to make good and evil stand
forth as distinct and even, in effect, absolute qualities, which could
not be subsumed as parts of the same providential or transcendent
will. This ultimate and uncompromising distinction between the
moral poles of existence was in his view inseparable from the actual
uncertainty and variety of life.

James, then, wished to preserve the sense of life as a genuine
moral drama. He was no apostle of chaos or of any sort of pure
nominalism, and his world left room for relationship, community,
and even a kind of unity almost as much as did Royce's. In fact,
James believed that his pluralism offered a superior way of expressing
social conjunctions. As social critics from Tocqueville to Robert A.
Nisbet have complained of the erosion of "intermediate institutions," James indicted "ordinary" monistic idealism for leaving
out, in the final analysis, "everything intermediary" between the
individual and the whole. "Isn't this brave universe made on a
richer pattern, with room in it for a long hierarchy of beings?" he
asked. Because nothing in such a world was all-inclusive, James
likened it to a federal republic, in which sovereign power is nowhere completely exercised.[30] Or as Ralph Barton Perry put it,
James's universe was "not a block or an organism, but an all-navigable
sea—a great neighborhood embracing lesser neighborhoods, in
which accessibility is universal and intimacy proportional to pro-
pinquity."[31]

There is in James a temperamental delight in diversity which
sets him apart from others who have borne the banner of pragmatism.
Charles Sanders Peirce, whom James generously credited as the
founder of pragmatic thought, entertained, as Perry points out,
a quite different ethical ideal from that of James. "For Peirce the
good lies in coherence, order, coalescence, unity; for James in the
individuality, variety, and satisfaction of concrete interests."[32]
In quite another way, John Dewey, although his name has been
sufficiently linked with that of James to discredit the latter among
conservatives, seems miles apart in his sense of life. It is not just

that Dewey's pragmatism lent itself more readily to social reform, while James's main concern was for the individual life. Dewey evinced little sense of the heights and depths of human existence, or of the ultimate *variety* of it; his instinct was for the right-thinking, cooperative, democratic norm. James's instinct was for something altogether different: not, indeed, for moral chaos or aimless eccentricity, but for the disciplined particular. "The solid meaning of life is always the same eternal thing," he believed, "the marriage, namely, of some unhabitual ideal, however special, with some fidelity, courage, and endurance; with some man's or woman's pains."[33]

There is in this, as in James's thought generally, certainly an element of relativism. His essay "The Will to Believe" suggested that there might be, under certain restricted conditions, different truths for different people. Yet while acknowledging the relativistic character of pragmatism, James did not altogether dismiss the notion of absolute truth. "What is challenged by relativists," he suggested, "is the pretence on anyone's part to have found for certain at any given moment what the shape of that truth is." Consequently the only absolute truth of which we could be sure was that there was absolute truth. Absolute truth could therefore be accepted as "an ideal set of formulations towards which all opinions may in the long run of experience be expected to converge."[34] At the very least, this is a relativism far removed in tone and import from the vague, amorphous attitude which goes by that name today and which conceals its indifference and lassitude behind a "tolerant" refusal to make moral judgments—unless against those who see the world in more distinct colors.

William James was an eminently tolerant man, tolerant of the many paths which might lead to an enlargement of human experience and apprehension of the truth. But this was a tolerance leagued with a fierce moral strenuosity that required one to take sides in the never ending battle between darkness and light. James rejected the notion of God as Absolute, because the Absolute, in his view, could only be an abstraction. He preferred the Old Testament conception of God as tribal chieftain, under whose banner one could freely enlist to fight a real fight.

James's pluralism then—and pluralism was the basic philosophic position to which his pragmatism and the other aspects of his thought were ancillary—was a pluralism not of diluted experience, but of a broad and intensely perceived range of experience. If Henry Adams found in multiplicity the entropy of faith, James found in pluralism the very salvation and medium of faith—faith above all in the moral meaning of the universe. "The final purpose of our creation," James suggested, "seems most plausibly to be the greatest possible enrichment of our ethical consciousness, through the intensest play of contrasts and the widest diversity of characters."[35]

From the conservative point of view, this Jamesian combination of moral intensity with diversity of experience ought to be of abiding interest. If James still be deemed inadmissably relativistic, this aspect of his thought must be weighed against his steadfast hostility to reductionism in any of its guises. James would not let a part of experience be taken for the whole, no matter how great the part, no matter how imposing its scientific, religious, or philosophical credentials. Today relativism and reductionism are strangely leagued, as they were not in James's day. Then the obstacle to full and multifarious experience seemed the old-fashioned absolutes of theologians, scientific materialists, and Hegelian idealists. Today the enemies of a spacious and various human experience are precisely those who reduce it by pat formula to the undifferentiated landscape where "all is relative." The relativists are the reductionists, and their absolutism lies in their denial of absolutes. It seems unlikely that James, with his enormous moral strenuosity, would sympathize very far today with the endlessly permissive or the aimlessly liberating. His is a standing reproach to reductionism of any fashion, and his brand of pluralism may offer the only ground in which absolutes can now flourish. The absolute requires the perspective of a diverse experiential landscape; in the homogeneous environment it is meaningless, everything and nothing. Nor can traditional values endure without a measure of "pluralism"; in the present state of the world, any socially effective monism will grind custom and tradition and the values that they bear to a powder—including the very values that we regard as absolutes.

William James and Henry Adams, starting from opposite positions, pluralistic and monistic respectively, end up as complementary figures. James, speaking from a strongly moralistic bias, as well as with a temperamental preference for struggle, proclaims that life has no meaning without genuine diversity; Adams, out of rather different intellectual and aesthetic requirements, maintains that there is no true diversity without meaning—for him, unity. Between them they suggest the possibility of a coherent conservative principle: no matter how apparently various the phenomena with which one has to reckon, without the ascription to them of definite meaning and value, they remain the stuff of an undifferentiated chaos; authentic diversity derives, conversely, from the kind of discrimination which assigns different meanings and values according to standards regarded implicitly, if not explicitly, as absolute. To this the lesser figure of John Fiske adds that genuine progress must mean a growing diversity of positive human possibilities, and that a progress which narrows the range of these possibilities is no progress at all.

NOTES

1. Robert C. Bannister, *Social Darwinism: Science and Myth in Anglo-American Social Thought* (Philadelphia: Temple University Press, 1979).

2. George Harris, *Inequality and Progress* (New York: Arno Press, 1972), 60-77, 80.

3. Ibid., 146.

4. Ibid., 149, 153-154.

5. Ibid., 16-17, 19.

6. John Fiske, *Outlines of Cosmic Philosophy* (Boston and New York: Houghton Mifflin Co., 1899), II, 221. Original italics omitted.

7. Ibid., III, 327-328.

8. John Fiske, *Essays Historical and Literary* (New York: Macmillan Co., 1902), II, 73, 76, 81.

9. John Fiske, *Through Nature to God* (Boston and New York: Houghton Mifflin Co., 1899), 114-115.

10. Gilbert K. Chesterton, *The Outline of Sanity* (New York: Dodd, Mead & Co., 1927), 187.

11. Jacques Barzun, *Science: the Glorious Entertainment* (New York: Harper & Row, 1964), 259.

12. Brooks Adams, "Can War Be Done Away With?" *Publications of the American Sociological Society* 10 (1915): 105.

13. Henry Adams, *The Degradation of the Democratic Dogma* (New York: Peter Smith, 1949), vii-viii.

14. Henry Adams, *History of the United States of America During the Jefferson and Madison Administrations* (New York: Antiquarian Press, 1962), IX, 225.

15. Henry Adams, *Mont-Saint-Michel and Chartres* (New York: Doubleday, 1959), 408.

16. Ibid., 290, 307.

17. Ibid., 196, 153, 33.

18. Ibid., 289.

19. Henry Adams, *The Education of Henry Adams* (Boston: Houghton Mifflin Co., 1961), 406.

20. Worthington Chauncey Ford, ed., *Letters of Henry Adams* (Boston and New York: Houghton Mifflin Co., 1930-1938), II, 291. Adams to Hay, June 26, 1900.

21. I discuss Royce's conservative affinities in "Josiah Royce and American Conservatism," *Modern Age* 13 (Fall 1969): 342-352.

22. Josiah Royce, *The Problem of Christianity* (Chicago: University of Chicago Press, 1968), 116. Original italics omitted.

23. Josiah Royce, *The Philosophy of Loyalty* (New York: Macmillan Co., 1908), 242.

24. Josiah Royce, *Race Questions, Provincialism, and Other American Problems* (New York: Macmillan Co., 1908), 218.

25. Ibid., 98.

26. Henry James, ed., *The Letters of William James* (Boston: The Atlantic Monthly Press, 1920), II, 43-44. James to Rosina H. Emmet, August 2, 1896.

27. [William James], "Herbert Spencer's Data of Ethics," *The Nation* 29 (September 11, 1879): 179.

28. James, *Letters of William James,* II, 208. James to L. T. Hobhouse, August 12, 1904.

29. Ralph Barton Perry, *The Thought and Character of William James* (Boston: Little, Brown, and Co., 1935), I, 516-517. James to Holmes, May 18, 1868.

30. William James, *A Pluralistic Universe* (New York: Longmans, Green, and Co., 1958), 174-175, 321-322.

31. Perry, *Thought and Character of William James,* II, 590-591.

32. Ibid., II, 411.

33. William James, *Talks to Teachers on Psychology* (London: Longmans, Green, and Co., 1908), 299.

34. William James, *The Meaning of Truth* (New York: Longmans, Green, and Co., 1914), 265-267.

35. William James, *The Will to Believe* (Cambridge, Mass.: Longmans, Green, and Co., 1905), 169.

9 The Specter of Uniformity

James's pluralism and Adams's Conservative Christian Anarchism represented, in varying degrees of brilliance and eccentricity, highly personal responses to a kind of anxiety that is distinctly modern. Only since the Romantic period has the term "uniformity" acquired strong pejorative connotations, and only in the twentieth century, perhaps, have the full practical possibilities of the dubious ideal which it represents been glimpsed. The reasons for this would have to be sought in economic and political, as well as intellectual, history. The temperamental preference of the Romantics for diversity would, at the least, have assumed far less significance without the standardizing effects of advanced industrial and technological processes of which they had early intimations. In our own age, the reality of totalitarian political ideologies armed with the weapons of a still more advanced and efficient technology gave to the prospect of coerced uniformity a terrible new plausibility. No tyranny since the earliest civilizations appeared to possess such powers to compel sameness, and for some it was the sameness even more than the tyranny which was frightening.

Totalitarianism might be resisted; it might even in the long run prove unequal to the task of breaking down the stubborn diversities of human existence. More discouraging was the growing suspicion during the nineteenth and twentieth centuries that even those ideals and projects which were expressly intended to free men from old and arbitrary restraints might deliver them to an undifferentiated and stultifying mass society rather than to a society of unique masters of their souls. Democracy "leveled," and contrary to Jefferson's vision of every republican as a potential athlete and Aristotle, it seemed increasingly to critics like Henry Adams to level down rather than up, suggesting entropy rather than kinetic exuberance. It was obvious that equality, if pursued to the last indiscriminate bounds of logic, must demand conformity; distinctions must ever be suspect. That there was a natural tension between liberty and equality could perhaps be accepted. But modern experience suggested that even a full-bodied personal liberty, when not nurtured and supported by a matrix of local, private, and traditional authority, might fail to sustain much real diversity. Even in their most genuinely libertarian character, the personal liberation movements of the late twentieth century threatened to bring only the contentless and aimless freedom of a mass of darting atoms, undifferentiated in any but the most petty ways. The ultimate liberation, it appeared, was to be liberation from the burdensome distinctions both of individuality and of the natural and social groups to which one happened to belong.

To whatever extent the apprehension of a smothering uniformity has been justified by events, it has been a psychological and intellectual reality for close to two centuries. In Samuel Taylor Coleridge's plaints about increasing standardization and quantified consumption habits in the English society of his day[1] can be found the germs of a plethora of later specters: the lonely crowd, technocracy, organization man, the System.

With Alexis de Tocqueville the dismaying image of things to come was brought more clearly into focus. It was chiefly Tocqueville, whose analyses and prophecies are so familiar, and yet so far from being exhausted of their meaning for present and future, who impressed on the Western consciousness the melancholy implications of modern uniformity. More lucidly than anyone else, Tocqueville identified ascendant democracy, not only with tremendous social power and the achievement of decent material standards of life, but also with mediocrity and conformity to the standards of the mass. His real subject was equality and the centralization and homogenization which attended it. Equality meant sameness, for men equal in social condition were hardly likely to differ very much in their habits, tastes, or ideas.[2]

Although Tocqueville is best known in this country for the strictures upon American democracy which followed his visit to the United States during the 1830s, his larger concern was with the portents of this democracy for Western society generally. In some respects located within the European liberal tradition, he nevertheless viewed the changes of his own and the previous century much as they have been by a long line of conservatives. Conservatism emerged as a self-conscious school of political thought during a time when local and aristocratic associations—often designated as "intermediate institutions" for their interposition of authority between the individual and the national sovereignty—had come under severe attack. R. R. Palmer describes as a fundamental theme of the eighteenth century the effort of such "constituted bodies" as parliaments and local councils and assemblies "to defend their corporate liberties and their independence, against either superior authorities on the one hand or popular pressures on the other."[3] In France, aristocratic resistance to the centralizing policies of the monarchy (which would have made aristocrats pay a fairer share of taxes) led directly to the French Revolution. From this event emerged an impulse to centralization vastly strengthened by the mass character of revolutionary and postrevolutionary politics. From Burke's time on, conservatives have attributed to this new politics not only the hypertrophy of the national state in the name of personal liberty, but also a program of cultural standardization: the deliberate reduction of the deeply rooted diversities of human life in favor of "a homogeneous society, in which men live upon one exclusive plane of existence," as J. L. Talmon put it.[4]

No one depicted the social and political transformations of the age more starkly than did Alexis de Tocqueville. "In olden society," he thought, "everything was different; unity and uniformity were nowhere to be met with. In modern society everything threatens to become so much alike that the peculiar characteristics of each individual will soon be entirely lost in the general aspect of the world."[5] Tocqueville closely associated this standardization with the erosion of those immediate or intermediate ties and loyalties which had drastically qualified even "absolute" monarchy.

Religion, the affections of the people, the benevolence of the
prince, the sense of honor, family pride, provincial prejudices,
custom, and public opinion limited the power of kings and
restrained their authority within an invisible circle. The constitution of nations was despotic at that time, but their customs
were free.

Equality, on the other hand, placed "men side by side, unconnected
by any common tie,"[6] and little able to resist the weight of the
social mass.

Tocqueville was well aware that the urge to uniformity was older
than modern democracy; it was also, as his studies of the *ancien
régime* suggested, more basic. Long before the Revolution, the
monarchial government of France had sought to standardize as a
corollary of its efforts to centralize power. By 1789, he noted, local
differences between provinces had been "obliterated throughout
practically the entire kingdom; this had greatly contributed to
making Frenchmen everywhere so much like each other." Even the
penchant of the royal highway department for constructing roads
which were perfectly straight, regardless of their mutilation of
ancient estates and parklands, seemed to breathe the same spirit as
that which during Revolution carved France into a checkerboard of
departments, much to Burke's disgust. The centralizing and standardizing policies of the Old Regime thus provided a starting point
for the more efficient efforts of the revolutionaries in the same
direction.[7] Yet there remained, Tocqueville thought, far more
freedom under the Old Regime than there was in the France of his
own day, intermittent and bound to privilege though it had been.
"At the very time when the forces of centralization were deliberately
crushing out all individuality and trying to impose a drab uniformity,
a sort of dingy monochrome," he pointed out, "this spirit of independence kept alive in many individuals their sense of personality
and encouraged them to retain their color and relief."[8] Once again
we are reminded of how problematical is the relationship between
formal political liberty and the social and psychological context
which nurtures the spirit of independence and maintains diversity.

If it had not invented the spirit of uniformity, however, democracy
seemed fated to give to it unprecedented scope, and America was of

course the nineteenth-century laboratory of democracy. Tocqueville's reaction to the experiment was by no means entirely negative. He appreciated the rise in average standards of comfort and felicity which democratic equality entailed, and consoled himself with the thought that if a state of equality was less "elevated," it was nevertheless more just. Yet he was, he acknowledged, saddened and chilled by the democratic prospect of multitudes of closely similar human beings.[9] It was not that the democracy which he saw in America was lacking in opportunity or dynamism; on the contrary, it offered a spectacle of enormous ferment. But this did not make for a truly varied social landscape. Aristocratic societies, Tocqueville pointed out, were relatively static, yet people were remarkably different from one another. In democracies the fortunes of individuals rose and fell, but the drama was always the same and its actors indistinguishable.[10]

The spirit of uniformity was felt in different ways. The pressure of public opinion seemed to Tocqueville to render genuine independence of mind and freedom of discussion less in America than in any other country. Nor could he think of any European nation which offered less regional diversity. The contrast between North and South, which was beginning, in some American eyes, to make the sections appear two different civilizations, did not impress him. There was less difference between Maine and Georgia, a thousand miles apart, he thought, than between neighboring Normandy and Brittany.[11]

In prospect, if democracy were to issue in its own brand of benevolent despotism, Tocqueville glimpsed that combination of individual hedonism and bureaucratic paternalism which, a century and a half later, seems only so much closer. He envisioned

an innumerable multitude of men, all equal and alike, incessantly endeavoring to procure the petty and paltry pleasures with which they glut their lives. Each of them, living apart, is as a stranger to the fate of all the rest.

Above this race of men stands an immense and tutelary power, which takes upon itself alone to secure their gratifications and to watch over their fate. That power is absolute, minute, regular, provident, and mild.[12]

Democracy seemed to require, in any event, a great leveling of possibilities. Although Tocqueville saw considerable logic and justice in this course, he could not deny that he found social uniformity an appalling prospect. "Variety," he lamented, "is disappearing from the human race; the same ways of acting, thinking, and feeling are to be met with all over the world."[13] The judgment was an extravagant one for the first half of the nineteenth century; it seems less so today.

Although Tocqueville had seen in the United States no more than the harbingers of an egalitarian world, it was easy in the nineteenth century, and even in the twentieth, to consider social uniformity as peculiarly the product of American conditions—of the country's cultural shallowness, and of its shibboleths of democracy and equality. American self-questioning based on such perceptions was primarily literary and aesthetic, rather than political, in origin. James Fenimore Cooper, for example, voiced the increasingly familiar worry in *The American Democrat* that democracy encouraged mediocrity and conformity to the standards of public opinion. Equality of rights, Cooper argued, must never be confused with equality of condition. The latter, he thought, was "incompatible with civilization, and is found only to exist in those communities that are but slightly removed from the savage state. In practice, it can only mean a common misery."[14]

Cooper struck a note which was echoed through a long vein of American self-criticism during the later nineteenth and the early twentieth century. Some of this criticism drew upon class resentments. This was true most notably of the "patrician" critics of post-Civil War American society. These were intellectuals of upperclass background or affiliation, predominantly from New England or New York, who were typically dissatisfied with the reduced role of their class and their families in American life, as well as being temperamentally and aesthetically repelled by what they perceived as American mediocrity and uniformity. Such persons often had established liberal credentials in the antislavery or other reform movements, but struck an increasingly conservative stance in the face of the difficult social and economic problems of the later nineteenth century. They were apt to see no inconsistency between their fears of social unrest and class conflict, their anxiety over "the racial agony in which we are being strangled by invading aliens,"[15] as Barrett Wendell put it, and their boredom with the drab sameness of American life. Whatever diversion and diversity such patricians sought, it was not that either of class rivalry or of ethnic heterogeneity.

Their concern, of course, was with other levels of experience. Charles Eliot Norton was depressed by the feebleness of American intellectual life and the paucity of American artistic and literary creativity, which he thought were dwarfed by the country's material achievements. In one of the first issues of *The Nation,* published several months after the end of the Civil War, Norton characterized the United States as "The Paradise of Mediocrities,"[16] and he never saw any reason to change this assessment. One factor, as he later wrote, was the "similarity of condition and uniformity of custom" that prevailed in America, and which inhibited freedom and energy of thought. Where sameness was the rule, life was less rich and interesting, the individual himself of less worth, and the community of less importance. In such a society, public opinion exercised a tyrannical authority; it established a "despotism of custom" and promoted, Norton concluded, an "essentially servile habit of mind."[17]

Oliver Wendell Holmes, Jr., represented another kind of temperament, at once more cheerful and more skeptical than Norton's and animated by the images of warfare rather than by those of art. His apprehension of the future was therefore different in tone, but it drew upon a similar distaste for sameness, and as with Norton it reflected the more conservative side of his nature. Who of us, he asked in 1895,

> could endure a world, although cut up into five-acre lots and having no man upon it who was not well fed and well housed, without the senseless passion for knowledge out-reaching the flaming bounds of the possible, without ideals the essence of which is that they never can be achieved?[18]

In less ebullient moments, Holmes feared the advent of a more monotonous and standardized mode of life, and mourned that the scope for intellectual as well as physical adventure was narrowing.[19] He was skeptical of the efforts of social reformers. "The notion that with socialized property we should have women free and a piano for everybody," he remarked, "seems to me an empty humbug."[20] It would be difficult to say whether Holmes was more contemptuous of the unreality of Utopian expectations or of the tediousness of the final Utopian vision.

Certain voices, at least, raised the revulsion at standardization above the level of the merely cantankerous. The height of patrician acuity was reached with the Adams brothers and the James brothers, of whom we have yet to consider the novelist Henry James. Henry returned to America for a visit in 1904-1905 after long years abroad, and his impressions were published as *The American Scene*. The title aptly suggested James's approach, encompassing the social aspect of his native country as well as the landscape, architecture, and atmosphere, facets of American life which he wove together with his accustomed subtlety.

James found American democracy overwhelming and vacuous; it was a specter of "the huge democratic broom" that "one seems to see brandished in the great empty sky."[21] There was much, indeed, that appealed to him—the comparative historical richness of Boston, the mild Southern charm of Baltimore—but to the expatriate America seemed all too shallow in accumulated experience, prone to reduce all to a "common mean," nurturing too narrow a human range. There was a sameness, a "continuity" of type which James found as oppressive in people as in houses. The City of Brotherly Love offered only the vision of a "vast, firm chess-board, the immeasurable spread of little squares, covered *all* over by perfect Philadelphians."[22] (Criticism of America has had its continuity too. The Loyalist Jonathan Boucher, in the bitterness of an exile less voluntary than James's more than a century earlier, had described the same city as "disgusting from its uniformity and sameness.")[23]

The same "inordinate untempered monotony" seemed to James all too characteristic of American society. The energy and restlessness of the country were undeniable. But even the miscellaneous nature of the population did not ward off the visage of "social sameness"; even immigrants seemed quickly to lose their distinctive "colour." Diversity was minimized where superficially most in evidence.

> Individuality and variety is attributed to "types" in America, on easy terms, and the reputation for it enjoyed on terms not more difficult; so that what I was most conscious of, from sex to sex, from one presented boarder to another [at a Florida hotel], was the continuity of the fusion, the dimness of the distinctions.

Not surprisingly, it was businessmen and their "indulged ladies" who comprised the type to which James found himself ubiquitously exposed, and among whom the chief distinctions seemed those of degrees of wealth. As decent and amiable as such people typically were, the "scant diversity of type" was calculated, James feared, to draw the "storyseeker or picture-maker" up short.[24]

In a man of James's generous sensitivity, these were, needless to say, more than the reactions of an aesthete or a snob. Indeed, he put his finger on the ultimate deficiency of a society lacking in social diversity: its radical impoverishment of the individual himself.

> Wonderous always to note is this sterility of aspect and this blight of vulgarity, humanly speaking, where a single type has had the game, as one may say, all in its hands. Character is developed to visible fineness only by friction and discipline on a large scale, only by its having to reckon with a complexity of forces—a process which results, at the worst, in a certain amount of social training.
>
> No kind of person—that was the admonition—is a very good kind, and still less a very pleasing kind, when its education has not been made to some extent by contact with other kinds, and, to that degree, by a certain relation with them.

In the absence of such diverse relations, the lesson seemed clear, even the vaunted American individualism lost itself in a "large unseeing complacency" impervious to the breadth of human experience.[25]

Whereas Tocqueville saw in America the foreshadowing of a universal future, James viewed it primarily as a young civilization which had not had time to accumulate the multifarious experience of Europe (and had not made the best use of the time that it had

had). The two approaches were not mutually exclusive, but in the twentieth century, Tocqueville's seemed the more broadly applicable. And for all the European horror of "Americanization," the ills of modernity assumed proportions beyond those which were readily attributable to transatlantic vulgarity. G. K. Chesterton was no admirer of the United States, which unlike most civilized systems, he thought, threatened to decline not from heights but from "a low level and . . . a flat place" to depths yet more abysmal. But it was the larger civilization which seemed to him to have achieved the worst features of the Utopian visions of Wells and Webb: centralization, impersonality, and monotony. The modern penchant for "simplification and sameness" even cut across ideological lines; from current trends, Chesterton saw nothing in prospect but "a flat wilderness of standardization either by Bolshevism or Big Business."[26]

More pervasive than the conscious designs of Communists and capitalists, however, was the mentality that went with planning, bureaucracy, and collectivisms of all kinds—a mentality certainly not new to the twentieth century, but given new scope by the hypertrophy of technology and organization. Even the liberating impulses of reform seemed to end in a convenient standardization. Some reformers displayed a penchant for regulation which was monstrous in its very pettiness. Of this habit of mind and its protagonist, Hilaire Belloc remarked early in the century that

> it is orderly in the extreme. All that human and organic complexity which is the colour of any vital society offends him by its infinite differentiation. He is disturbed by multitudinous things; and the prospect of a vast bureaucracy wherein the whole of life shall be scheduled and appointed to certain simple schemes deriving from the co-ordinate work of public clerks and marshalled by powerful heads of departments gives his small stomach a final satisfaction.[27]

Thirty-six years later, with planning installed with a vengeance in Labourite Britain, John Jewkes commented similarly on the planner's

> predilection for tidiness in the economic system. Loose ends and lack of uniformity exasperate him and account often for

his objection to a free economy with its innumerable rivulets of enterprise taking unexpected courses, its constant urge to expand and diversify, and its endless multiplicity of activities.[28]

For conservatives like Jewkes, more was at stake than free enterprise; they recognized in the excesses of regulation a symptom of a more serious debility of personality and social relations. Diagnoses differed, but conservatives had plenty of company in their alarm, and were contributing to a sustained chorus of jeremiads by the mid-twentieth century. A series of sometimes brilliant books of widely differing political coloration—including Ortega y Gasset's *The Revolt of the Masses,* Fromm's *Escape from Freedom,* Riesman's *The Lonely Crowd,* and Whyte's *The Organization Man*—developed themes which were remarkably complementary in the images they presented of modern life. Taken together, they depicted a society cut adrift from traditional authority and tending toward an anxious aimlessness, the detached members of which conformed docilely to mass standards or to those of the large organization, at worst the potential prey of totalitarians. Such a composite, indeed, is a caricature which does little justice to the subtlety and nuance with which these themes were variously developed. But it is notable that the books had in common a strong distaste for social uniformity, whether that uniformity was regarded as egalitarian, capitalist, or totalitarian in inspiration, or merely as the consequence of modern technology and social conditions. All, in one way or another, feared the conquest of the world by a deadly sameness. The prospect seemed a mockery of the old democratic vision of a society without privilege or artificial distinction.

José Ortega y Gasset struck the keynote as early as the 1920s, albeit from a decidedly aristocratic European point of view. "The mass," he defined as "all that which sets no value on itself—good or ill—based on specific grounds, but which feels itself 'just like everybody,' and nevertheless is not concerned about it; is, in fact, quite happy to feel itself as one with everybody else." We were living, Ortega was certain, in a "levelling period" of diminishing differentiation between classes, fortunes, sexes, between cultures and nationalities. Above all, it appeared, popular intolerance of distinction was more and more triumphant. "As they say in the

United States: 'to be different is to be indecent.' The mass crushes beneath it everything that is different, everything that is excellent, individual, qualified and select." Almost everywhere the "homogeneous mass" annihilated all dissent.[29] Needless to say, this was more an eloquent *cri de coeur* than an objective documentation of social realities. Uniformity has never been quite so triumphant in the nontotalitarian West as all that, and it is doubtful that the equation of difference with indecency was ever a "they say" dogma even for the High Babbittry of the American twenties. Pressures for conformity were rather more subtle than this. As the liberal David Riesman pointed out later, "other-directedness" was not incompatible with "marginal differentiation of personality." People wanted to be interesting, to stand out to an acceptable degree, to be different without being too different.[30]

A similarly judicious tone was taken by William H. Whyte, who (like Riesman) pursued the riddle of mass man in the context of post-World War II America as Ortega had done in a different time and place. Whyte eschewed facile strictures on mass society or the "surface uniformities" of American life. The monotony of suburban ranch-type houses, he was aware, was no greater than that of the row houses of an earlier day; nor did they necessarily bespeak the uniformity of their inhabitants. Surface uniformities, he pointed out, could serve as "protective coloration" for diversities within.[31] Nevertheless, Whyte's appraisal of the "organization man," the man who permitted his life to be shaped by the big business organization to the peril of his individual autonomy, drew heavily on a feeling that the organization fostered uniformity. The suburban housing developments favored by organization man seemed, after all, to represent this uniformity. They were not without significant variations; nor were the people within them without important gradations of class and prestige. The suburbs were not really an amorphous mass, but divided into cliques and neighborhood groups. Yet for all the variations, Whyte found "an unmistakable similarity in the way of life" to be found in the suburbs. They acted, indeed, as a great melting pot for a mobile population—mobile geographically as well as socially. "The more people move about," Whyte observed, "the more similar the American environments become, and the more similar they become, the easier it is to move about."[32]

Whyte's main theme, however, was organization man's conformity to the standards and values of the group—a conformity from which it was difficult to deviate very far. He saw in this no dark conspiracy of capitalists, no compulsion by implacable technocracy or mystically conceived "System." The insidious quality of the "organization," and of the way of life to which it lent itself, derived largely from their very benignity. Conformity and belongingness, in this view, were closely related. "The group is a tyrant; so also is it a friend, and *it is both at once.*" Indeed, the greatest tyranny operated not on the deviate, but on the "accepted"; for him to fail to conform in any serious way required unusual conviction and fortitude. Most alarming, to Whyte, organization man seemed not only other-directed (in Riesman's term); he seemed also to be developing a philosophy which held this condition to be the right one: the individual must bow to the group.[33]

Whyte struck an enormously responsive chord in the 1950s. "Conformity" became as popular an object of intellectual scorn as Babbittry or the Genteel Tradition had been earlier. The new worry cut across ideological lines. To an extent, it drew upon the mildly conservative mood of the fifties, and reflected disenchantment with collectivism and a new respect for individuality. In conservative eyes it was social planners, progressive educators preaching "adjustment," and meddlesome bureaucrats who were making conformists of the American people. Liberals viewed the conservative swing as itself symptomatic of the conforming spirit. The chief villains of the liberals were big business and its complacent allies of the Eisenhower administration, as well as McCarthyites out to get the unhappy soul whose nonconformity took the form of a too little enthusiastic anticommunism or Cold War élan.

Conformity is not the same as uniformity. Diverse individuals or groups can conform to prescribed rules or standards without losing all those qualities which make them diverse. Conservatives like William F. Buckley, Jr. and L. Brent Bozell insisted that society might quite legitimately require a degree of conformity that would exclude obedience to the Communist Party, for example.[34] The result need not be to make everyone identical. But conformity realized in every aspect of life would produce uniformity, and certainly the American critics of conformity during the fifties assumed the connection. Conservatives as well as liberals believed that Americans were becoming more alike, in thought as well as in external things, and they believed that this was bad. Indeed, one feels that uniformity, rather than conformity per se, was often the primary object of their disgust. Bernard Iddings Bell found that "Crowd Culture" left little room for significant differences of class, occupation, region, or even religious and ethnic affiliation. "We have moralized, unified, equalized, standardized our country from the Atlantic to the Pacific, from Canada to Mexico," he lamented.[35] Educators, Bell thought, had to share much of the blame—"Dewey-ites" whose idea of education was to inculcate conformity to group standards; even President Conant of Harvard, who had attacked private schools "because they prevent uniform devotion of pupils to a directable uniformity throughout the nation." Bell struck a particularly conservative note in suggesting that devotion to tradition could supply a corrective. "To arouse respect and love for the great ones of the past," he thought, "is the best way to contend against the pressures of mass conformities."[36]

Alan Valentine, the title of whose book *The Age of Conformity* compressed into a cliché the concerns of the hour in the same way as had Thomas Paine's *The Age of Reason,* explicitly drew the connection between social uniformity and intellectual conformity. Standardization of taste seemed to Valentine the very emblem of standardization of mind. Social uniformity, he argued,

> threatens to create mental uniformity, for those who live in identical houses with identical furnishings, identical manners and identical clothes are in danger of adopting ideas equally identical and ready-made. To progress, free society must encourage variety, and those who take nonconformist positions should not be put on the defensive.[37]

One of the most prominent avowed conservatives to enter the lists against the dragon of conformity was Peter Viereck. Viereck, to be sure, occupied a precarious position on the right. A strong critic of McCarthyite tendencies, which he attributed to a kind of right-wing populism, he incurred conservative wrath by shying away from the Republican Party, professing to believe it often less authentically conservative than the Democratic. That he found a prime example of conservatism in Adlai Stevenson's "extremely important insistence on reversing America's centralizing trend, on nurturing local patterns, traditional diversities"[38] was not calculated to endear him to admirers of Robert Taft, although it well illustrates the bent of Viereck's thought. Some conservatives saw in Viereck's *The Unadjusted Man* a plea for unadjustment at any price, a sort of atomistic nonconformity. This Viereck had explicitly denied in the work in question. "A mere anarchic individualism, a mere bohemian nonconformity, means isolation *from* society," he granted; "the conservative individualism of the Unadjusted Man means more elbow-room *within* a more organic belongingness."[39] Indeed, Viereck was attempting to address current concerns by restating old conservative truths. With Burke he emphasized that reality is "unsymmetrical, ungeometrical, imprecise," and expressed a preference for concrete traditions over abstract programs. "Intolerable," he thought, "is the very concept of some busybody benevolence, whether economic, moral, or psychiatric, 'curing' all diversity by making it average."[40] The problem, he suggested, was to adapt the basically aristocratic idea of liberty, sheltering as it did the concrete and intimate and eccentric, to a democratic age without succumbing to the egalitarian "bed-of-Procrustes 'liberty' of joining the team."[41]

Although Viereck approached the matter thoughtfully enough, much of the hue and cry of the fifties about "conformity" seems now confused or exaggerated. It is at least an open question as to what extent those critics were justified who viewed Americans—or moderns generally—as marching in lock step. Intellectual gloom over the passivity of the masses—from whatever political vantage point—has usually proved myopic, at least in America. People are more stubbornly idiosyncratic and resilient than those who purvey the specters of power elites, one-dimensional man, and mass conformity have ever realized. As the more astute critics perceived, too, there was a tendency to confuse outward with inner conformity. That people wore crew cuts and blue button-down shirts no more branded them as intellectual sheep than did wigs and knee breeches so brand those who obeyed the dictates of Dame Fashion two centuries earlier. Finally, the fear that Senator Joseph R. McCarthy had reduced the American populace to a cowering mass ought to have been allayed by the enormous controversy over McCarthy himself, ending in his effective destruction.

From the vantage point of the turbulent sixties, the "conformity" of the Eisenhower years appeared an interim phenomenon, its passing to be viewed with relief or with condescending nostalgia. Such backward glances did justice neither to the considerable real contentiousness of the fifties nor to the emotional surges, intellectual fashions, and tribal conventions of the later decade, which elicited their own massive conformities within an influential segment of the American population. Certainly they failed to do justice to the deeper issues. Conformity to what?—the question was too seldom asked. To liberals as well as conservatives, the "conformity" of the fifties was especially obnoxious because it seemed to consist in obeisance to the shallowly rooted attitudes of a society too prosperous and complacent to recognize the actual looming conflicts of the day—whether these were associated with class and race or with the Cold War. But from an historically conservative point of view, conformity in itself was no bad thing; if it meant a reasoned acceptance of valid enduring principles and traditions, indeed, it made not for a uniform but for a naturally diverse society. In recent years, conservatives of various stripe have come to this perception.

NOTES

1. Samuel Taylor Coleridge, *The Philosophical Lectures of Samuel Taylor Coleridge* (London: Pilot Press, 1949), 287 (Lecture IX, February 22, 1819).

2. Alexis de Tocqueville, *Democracy in America* (New York: Vintage Books, 1959), II, 272.

3. R. R. Palmer, *The Age of the Democratic Revolution* (Princeton: Princeton University Press, 1959), I, 23.

4. J. L. Talmon, *The Origins of Totalitarian Democracy* (New York: W. W. Norton & Co., 1970), 4.

5. Tocqueville, *Democracy in America*, II, 347.

6. Ibid., I, 338-339; II, 109.

7. Alexis de Tocqueville, *The Old Regime and the French Revolution* (New York: Doubleday, 1955), 77, 189, 60.

8. Ibid., 119-120.

9. Tocqueville, *Democracy in America,* II, 350-351.

10. Ibid., II, 239.

11. Ibid., I, 273-275, 176.

12. Ibid., II, 336.

13. Ibid., II, 240.

14. James Fenimore Cooper, *The American Democrat* (New York: Alfred A. Knopf, 1931), 36.

15. Mark Antony DeWolfe Howe, ed., *Barrett Wendell and His Letters* (Boston: The Atlantic Monthly Press, 1924), 162. Wendell to F. J. Stimson, December 18, 1904.

16. [Charles Eliot Norton], "The Paradise of Mediocrities," *The Nation* 1 (September 28, 1865): 43-44.

17. Charles Eliot Norton, "The Intellectual Life of America," *New Princeton Review* 6 (November 1888): 316-320.

18. Julius J. Marke, ed., *The Holmes Reader* (New York: Oceana, 1955), 150 ("The Soldier's Faith").

19. Mark Antony DeWolfe Howe, ed., *Holmes-Laski Letters: the Correspondence of Mr. Justice Holmes and Harold J. Laski, 1916-1935* (Cambridge: Harvard University Press, 1935), I, 51 (Holmes to Laski, January 8, 1917); Marke, *Holmes Reader,* 100-101 ("The Profession of the Law").

20. Max Lerner, ed., *The Mind and Faith of Justice Holmes: His Speeches, Essays, Letters and Judicial Opinions* (Boston: Little, Brown, 1943), 393 ("Ideals and Doubts").

21. Henry James, *The American Scene* (Bloomington: Indiana University Press, 1968), 55.

22. Ibid., 282.

23. Jonathan Boucher, *Reminiscences of an American Loyalist, 1738-1789* (Boston and New York: Houghton Mifflin Co., 1925), 99.

24. James, *American Scene,* 104, 454-455.

25. Ibid., 427-428, 432.

26. Gilbert K. Chesterton, *The Outline of Sanity* (New York: Dodd, Mead & Co., 1927), 244, 61-64, 22.

27. Hilaire Belloc, *The Servile State* (London: Constable and Co., Ltd., 1912), 127-128.

28. John Jewkes, *Ordeal by Planning* (London: Macmillan and Co., 1948), 109.

29. José Ortega y Gasset, *The Revolt of the Masses* (New York: W. W. Norton & Co., 1932), 15, 18, 26, 77, 180.

30. David Riesman, *Individualism Reconsidered* (Glencoe, Ill.: The Free Press, 1954), 156, 267.

31. William H. Whyte, *The Organization Man* (Garden City, N.Y.:

Doubleday, 1956), 11-12, 441.

32. Ibid., 305, 310, 331, 365.

33. Ibid., 397-400, 439.

34. See William F. Buckley, Jr. and L. Brent Bozell, *McCarthy and His Enemies* (Chicago: Henry Regnery Company, 1954), 308-335.

35. Bernard Iddings Bell, *Crowd Culture* (New York: Harper & Brothers, 1952), 21-23.

36. Ibid., 131-132, 148.

37. Alan Valentine, *The Age of Conformity* (Chicago: Henry Regnery Company, 1954), 103.

38. Peter Viereck, *The Unadjusted Man* (New York: Capricorn Books, 1962), 247.

39. Ibid., 21.

40. Ibid., 298, 301, 19.

41. Ibid., v, 28, 30, and passim.

10 Modern Multiplicity and Diverse Conservatism

Long a coherent tradition in Great Britain, conservatism emerged as an effective intellectual movement in the United States only after World War II.[1] Alarm at the growing menace to the West of the Communist powers, dismay at the apparent decay of moral values and social cohesion, and resentment arising from the failures and encroachments on the private and local spheres of activity of liberal government were among the more obvious factors that moved some thoughtful men and women to a conservative stance. The appearance in the nineteen-fifties of William F. Buckley, Jr.'s *National Review* and of books like Russell Kirk's *The Conservative Mind* were signs of the accompanying intellectual ferment. This in turn contributed to the most significant development in national politics of the last twenty years: their shift to the right, marked by the capture of the Republican Party by its conservative wing, and latterly by the election to the presidency of Ronald Reagan.

Postwar American conservatism was enriched by sympathetic thinkers in disciplines which transcended the everyday world of political commentary, including sociology, economics, history, and literature. It was enriched also by the influence of European thinkers, some of whom took up residence in the United States, and many of whom helped to provide a needed depth of perspective to the callow American movement. At the same time, American conservatism was too intellectually vital a phenomenon, and sprang from too many different sources, not to be divided by sharp philosophical disputes—but these too could be enriching.

One motif in these many-sided developments was the persistence of the conservative preference for a diverse society and a diverse world. Indeed, this theme has become more self-conscious and articulate during the last several decades.

Robert A. Nisbet furnishes an example of the sympathetic scholarly chords that could emanate even from sociology, a discipline of which conservatives have generally been wary. Over a quarter of a century, Nisbet has elaborated a defense of social pluralism and diversity which stands in worthy succession to that of the long line of diversitarian thinkers (liberal as well as conservative) with which his work treats. Nisbet is particularly noteworthy for restating for the second half of the twentieth century the deep connection between the quality of diversity and the intermediate association or institution.

In *The Quest for Community* (1953), Nisbet established his major theme. "The real significance of the modern State," he wrote, "is inseparable from its successive penetrations of man's economic, religious, kinship, and local allegiances, and its revolutionary dislocations of established centers of function and authority." These dislocations weakened society, Nisbet believed, because it was the small and intermediate "areas of association" within which the larger values and purposes of society could "take on clear meaning in personal life and become the vital roots of the large culture."[2]

The urge to uniformity which diminished the role of intermediate associations had intellectual roots that were old and deep, Nisbet pointed out. Plato, after all, had taken care to eliminate all partial allegiances from his Republic, even to the extent of abolishing the family. Roman law gave a consummate practical extension to the ideal. Medieval diversity and particularism had for a time overridden the ancient legacy, but with the dawn of modernity the strongest currents were flowing once again in the direction of uniformity. Nisbet noted of Bodin, Hobbes, and Rousseau that the thought of each was successively and symptomatically more hostile to intermediate authorities, and more hospitable to centralized political power combined with cultural and social leveling.[3] Those who seized control of the French Revolution were spurred by a militant rationalism impatient alike of diversity and of intermediate associations: "the passion for geometrical symmetry, inherited from Cartesian philosophy, drove them beyond a reform of the currency system, beyond a standardization of weights and measures, to a rational standardization of the very units of men's social and political life." Neither Bentham nor Marx imparted to the schools of thought associated with their names any greater respect for social pluralism.[4]

In the twentieth century, Nisbet suggested, this engrained bias in Western political thought was perpetuated largely by a misguided solicitude for individual well-being. There is, he noted, a

> widespread belief that the termination of individual insecurity and moral disquietude can come about through a sterilization of social diversity and through an increased political and economic standardization. The undoubted necessity of unity *within* the individual leads too often to the supposition that this may be achieved only through uniformity of the culture and institutions which lie *outside* the individual. And external power, especially political power, comes to reveal itself to many minds as a fortress of security against not only institutional conflicts but conflicts of belief and value that are internal to the individual. A peculiar form of political mysticism is often the result.[5]

"Sterilization" was an apt word, and one that Nisbet repeated; thus the conception of "unitary democracy," spreading from the European continent to Great Britain and the United States, required the "sterilization" of traditional loyalties and group differences. Sterilization meant, obviously, the destruction of the conditions necessary for fertility and creativity—in art, in religion, in all aspects of life. And it was an illusion to suppose that any real individuality could flourish in the absence of vigorous intermediate associations. "It is," Nisbet pointed out, "the intimacy and security of each of these groups that provide the psychological context of individuality and the reinforcement of personal integrity. And it is the *diversity* of such groups that creates the possibility of the numerous cultural alternatives in a society."[6]

Freedom itself counted for little where social and political uniformity was the rule, Nisbet emphasized. It could thrive only insofar as the diversification and decentralization of authority provided barriers against overweening government and positive support to authentic individuality. Thus it seemed to Nisbet in 1953 that the paramount internal problem of liberal democracy was to find ways of nurturing a culture rich in clear alternatives. What was needed, he suggested, was a new kind of laissez faire—a laissez faire of groups rather than of individuals, which would at least maintain the conditions in which autonomous groups and intermediate associations, and consequently genuine individuality and diversity, might flourish.[7]

Nisbet pursued the same themes in his *Twilight of Authority* (1975), but with a greater emphasis on tradition as the conservator of diversity, and with a heightened suspicion of humanitarian and egalitarian professions or programs as hostile to it. As his title made explicit, Nisbet now viewed the twentieth century as a "twilight age" marked by the erosion and decline of the "natural hierarchies" of social institutions, under the leveling pressure of centralized power.[8] In the nineteenth century, as he pointed out, much liberal and even radical thought had been directed toward pluralism and decentralization. But radicals in the twentieth century were compromised by totalitarianism or by the flight from objectivity and politics which seemed characteristic of the New Left, while liberals had embraced a kind of bureaucracy which represented the transfer of authority from people in their "natural communities" to a "class of professional technicians."[9] This left it to conservatives, with whom Nisbet himself now seemed definitely aligned, to resist that perversion of the humanitarian impulse which drew upon the affinity between egalitarianism and the centralization of power.

Nisbet directed his fire especially at the "New Equalitarians," who aimed not merely at equality of opportunity or equality before the law, but at equality of condition. Tacitly adopting this goal, governmental bureaucracy had become increasingly a means of regimentation and decreasingly one of genuine personal liberty and felicity. Bureaucratic preference for uniformity was nothing new, but egalitarian ideology gave it new force; we had now to face, Nisbet feared, "the existence of a bureaucratized welfare state that prizes uniformity above all other things and that, as a large number of recent instances suggest, will stop at nothing to enforce this uniformity."[10]

Nisbet confronted with uncommon frankness the incompatibility between this kind of egalitarianism and "the kind of liberty that goes with differentiation, variety, individuality." Beyond the principle of equal rights, he argued, inequality was the very "essence of the social bond. The vast range of temperaments, minds, motivations, strengths, and desires that exists in any population is nothing if not the stuff of hierarchy."[11] The nonpejorative use of terms like "inequality" and "hierarchy" was scandalous in an age devoted to personal "liberation." But Nisbet's message was not one of repression. Authority, he contended, must reside somewhere; if it is weakened in the family, in tradition, custom, and the local association, then it must swell on the level of nationally applicable law and administrative fiat, the uniformities of which are far more constrictive of life in its civilized complexity of loyalties and liberties.

The American conservatism of the last generation would have been a far thinner brew without the influence of sympathetic European and European-born thinkers (two of whom, F. A. Hayek and Wilhelm Röpke, will be discussed in the next section). Often, indeed, European conservatives have simply pursued lines of thought parallel to those of their transatlantic counterparts. In both Alexander Rüstow's "Subsidiaritätsprinzip"—a principle proposing the complete autonomy of every center of authority within its own sphere of competence—and in Werner Kägi's "federal order" based on "corps intermédiaires" can be found clear affinities with Robert Nisbet's work, for example.[12]

Although a venerable part of the conservative tradition, this defense of diverse intermediate bodies has been given new urgency by the ascendancy of the great ideological systems of regimentation. This has been felt most keenly perhaps in Europe, where totalitarian uniformity and the diversity of traditional patterns of life have often existed in sharp juxtaposition. Writing in the 1960s, Hans Buchheim was painfully aware that totalitarianism appealed to one of the most deeply rooted of human yearnings, that for a closed intellectual system to explain the world and prescribe action. Very much in the Burkean vein, Buchheim indicted the totalitarians for attempting to produce an "artificial, synthetic society" in place of the actual and natural diversity of life. He could only hope that society would remain obdurate in its complexity, and that efforts to make it over would finally degenerate into "a chaos of paralysis and excess organization."[13]

Another European conservative, far better known in the United States, has even more directly addressed himself to the problem. For Erik von Kuehnelt-Leddihn, the distinction between Right and Left in modern politics—the Left being defined to include totalitarianism of the fascist and National Socialist as well as Communist varieties—offered a clear index to one's attitude toward diversity. "Leftism" was radically "Identitarian," hostile to social variety as inefficient, unequal, and difficult to control—offensive even, it appears, to a perverse aesthetic of sameness, and an equally perverse psychological urge to level. Thus Procrustes was the true hero of modern tyranny. Hitler, for example, "wanted to see Germany in complete monotony, with local traditions eliminated, regional self-government destroyed, the flags of the Länder strictly outlawed, the differences between the Christian faiths eradicated, the Churches desiccated and forcibly amalgamated." Hitler even wanted to make the Germans more uniform physically, Kuehnelt-Leddihn pointed out, through such methods as eugenics, sterilization, deportation, and, of course, mass extermination. Communist despots might differ in important ways from the Nazis, but not in the fundamental identitarian urge.[14] (The Nazi case, one might interject, was a little more complicated. The Nazis adopted their absurd racial categories in order to launch a massive assault on the actual variety of human life and culture: they conjured up a false and invidious diversity in order to destroy a real and healthy diversity.)

It is perhaps easier to define the passion for sameness than the opposite quality which Kuehnelt-Leddihn attributed to the Right: "joy in the diversity and in the richness of all forms of creation." One can discern, however, an element of romantic sentiment, a pervasive human curiosity about the different, even a certain itch for novelty not necessarily incompatible with conservative sensibilities. Even the higher religions, Kuehnelt-Leddihn pointed out, rested on a yearning for otherness. There was thus in conservative "diversitarianism'' a principle of life, of reverence for people and things as they are in themselves, which was foreign to the standardizing programs of the Left. At the opposite pole from Hitler was such a figure as St. Stephen, King of Hungary, "who wrote in his will to his heir presumptive, St. Emmeric: 'A Kingdom of only one language and one custom is a fragile and stupid thing.' " Unfortunately, it appeared to Kuehnelt-Leddihn, the modern drift was still in the direction of larger and more inclusive uniformities.[15]

Such sentiments appeared in a variety of contexts sufficient to mark them as still fundamental to the conservative temperament. The distinguished political philosopher, Michael Oakeshott, believed with his British predecessors that the conservative disposition was to be found in

> the propensity to make our own choices and to find happiness in doing so, the variety of enterprises each pursued with passion, the diversity of beliefs each held with the conviction of its exclusive truth; the inventiveness, the changefulness and the absence of any large design; the excess, the over-activity and the informal compromise.[16]

Opposed to this conservative comfort with the diversity of experience, Oakeshott believed, was the rationalist habit of mind in politics. The thorough rationalist was always quick to reduce "the tangle and variety of experience to a set of principles which he will then attack or defend only upon rational grounds." His mind had "no atmosphere, no changes of season and temperature; his intellectual processes, so far as possible, are insulated from all external influence and go on in the void." Rationalist politics was consequently a politics of uniformity, for "a scheme which does not recognize circumstances can have no place for variety." In such a scheme there was room only for rational preferences, and rational preferences are assumed to coincide. Political activity was thus "recognized as the imposition of a uniform condition of perfection upon human conduct."[17]

Oakeshott found the secret of freedom to lie in the diffusion of power—its diffusion in both space (signifying present concerns) and in time. Rather than in the "preconceived purpose" of the rationalist, he thought, a free society would "find its guide in a principle of *continuity* (which is a diffusion of power between past, present and future) and in a principle of *consensus* (which is a diffusion of power between the different legitimate interests of the present)."[18] This was not a plea for a static social order. Tradition and custom, Oakeshott pointed out, lent themselves not only to local variation but, contrary to widespread opinion, to innovation: not, indeed, to discontinuous change, but to evolving variations on traditional forms. "Diversity" was thus a nexus in which conservative devotion to private choice and social continuity were joined, and to which the rationalist temperament was alien.

> In short, if the man of . . . [conservative] disposition is asked: Why ought governments to accept the current diversity of opinion and activity in preference to imposing upon their subjects a dream of their own? it is enough for him to reply: Why not? . . . We tolerate monomaniacs, it is our habit to do so; but why should we be *ruled* by them?[19]

With Eric Voegelin's *Order and History* (1956), diversification (in a highly specialized sense) was postulated as the engine of historical process. Voegelin's monumental work, much admired among American conservative intellectuals, lies largely beyond the scope of this study. In certain aspects, however, it impinges significantly on our theme.

Voegelin offered a scheme of history in which the articulation of the perceived "order of being" is accomplished through a graduation from experience understood and expressed in relatively homogeneous, "compact" ways, to more "differentiated" modes of comprehension and symbolization. The contribution to this process of every creative civilization was to draw previously undrawn distinctions which provided deeper insight into the constitution of the universe. Such a "leap in being," for example, was the Mosaic experience, in which "the meaning of existence in the present under God was differentiated from the rhythmic attunement to divine-cosmic order through the cult of the empire." More simply, as a commentator put it, Israel "differentiated righteousness from fertility and security."[20] Thus, as it seems fair to state it, diversified conceptions emerged from an original monolithic faith.

Voegelin regarded every authentic humanly articulated order as having its part to play in the search for truth. Did he tread here too close to relativism? The point seemed a touchy one; although he criticized Karl Jaspers and Arnold Toynbee for failing adequately to rank civilizations, he himself has been taxed with seeming, for example, to put Christianity on a level with Greek philosophy.[21] He made it sufficiently clear, however, that he intended respect for the diversity of cultures to be coupled with an unmuddled sense of their hierarchical relationship. He argued that "the manifold of authorities must be critically measured, and their relative rank can be determined, by the degrees of approximation to the clarity of historical consciousness and of penetration to the order of the psyche and the world." At the same time, Voegelin warned against "the fallacy of transforming the consciousness of an unfolding mystery into the gnosis of a progress in time." The object of historical study was not to show up past benightedness, but to discover "men of the same nature as ours, wrestling with the same problems as ours, under the conditions of more compact experiences of reality and correspondingly less differentiated instruments of symbolization."[22]

Voeglin offered an appraisal of history which was at once essentially conservative and distinctly of the twentieth century. The diversities of human understanding found their honorable, unequal places in relation to the transcendent order of being toward which they strove. Avoiding the progressivist, deterministic faith in secular progress of nineteenth-century thinkers like Herbert Spencer and John Fiske, Voegelin proposed a different version of the Victorians' law of tendency from incoherent homogeneity to coherent heterogeneity, and one more plausible in our time. History was neither meaningless nor a railroad trip to Utopia, but a drama in which the human ability to differentiate the tangled threads of experience made possible the clearer perception of the "order of being."

Critics of conservatism have delighted in pointing out the disparity between its traditionalist, European and Burkean varieties, emphasizing authority, social cohesion, and continuity, and the brand which emerged in the nineteenth-century United States, based on political liberty, individualism, and laissez faire, and devoted to an industrial progress that was to leave little to the sphere of tradition.

While outdated in its original terms—neither Charles X nor Andrew Carnegie is a major hero of contemporary conservatives—the antithesis between "traditionalists" and "libertarians" has remained. It has therefore been of interest to find ground on which common cause can be made against political opponents. Frank S. Meyer and others have pointed out that most traditionalists and libertarians can join in their rejection of totalitarian or collectivist state power in favor of decentralized and largely private exercise of authority (as in the family), their general support of private property and economic liberties, and in their endorsement of an objective moral order within which respect for the rights and duties of the person should have a paramount place. Remaining disagreements on the relative claims of individual freedom and social authority then need not negate the complementary qualities of these two poles of contemporary conservative thought.[23]

The idea of diversity offers another common denominator. Diversity, as conservatives have long suggested, is nurtured by a due respect both for tradition and authority and for private and individual liberties. Yet each approach needs the tempering effect of the other. Without the rich accretions of tradition and the measuring rod of authority, no society can sustain much sense of authentic diversity; yet by themselves they may become overly constrictive of the new modes of expression which continuing responsiveness to the diversity of experience requires. Conversely, without a sacrosanct sphere of individual liberty, no social diversity—pronounced as it may be between groups—can have much ultimate meaning, while an individualism unbalanced by social cohesion and traditional forms is unlikely to encourage much real individuality. The sense of diversity is maintained by an equilibrium of freedom and contraint, continuity and change. Without a "principle of unity in things with which to measure the manifoldness and change," Irving Babbitt noted, "the individual is left without standards and so falls necessarily into an anarchical impressionism."[24]

Among American conservatives of the post-World War II period, there has been a widespread recognition of the value of diversity, an inverse reflection perhaps of the actual drift toward uniformity in so many aspects of the national life. This has been not merely a matter of sentiment or aesthetic sensibility; it has arisen also from the feeling that diversity was essential to any genuine freedom, justice, or creativity. "Variety," one conservative writer thought,

> is not only the spice of life, that is, not simply a matter of amusement and pleasure, but the condition for biological and cultural evolution, the reason for the strongest social bonds as well as the basis for the organization of society, and the incentive for future progress and well-being.[25]

Significant individual freedom, another added, required a variety of social organizations providing "a range of truly diverse social alternatives from which the individual may select."[26] Grimmest was the fear that "behind the cult of equality" lay "an even more sinister power, the uniformitarian hatred of providential distinctions"—a nihilistic impulse, M. E. Bradford believed.[27] Nihilism seemed readily to suggest itself as the end of uniformity. Only death and the void are perfectly uniform; vitality is inseparable from differentiation.

Whatever their exact approach, conservatives were obliged to reconcile their preference for diversity with other and more prescriptive values. They had little patience with diversity for diversity's sake. Sensitive on this point, Russell Kirk somewhat harshly chided Peter Viereck for falling "into the deep pit of sentimental Romanticism," by commending "spontaneity, originality, and eccentricity as positive merits" without proper attention to norms. The true conservative, Kirk believed, neither indiscriminately denounced convention nor embraced every popular fashion. Norms were not antagonistic, but complementary, to the "proliferating variety" of life—a favorite phrase of Kirk's. "Lacking an apprehension of norms, there is no living in society or out of it. Lacking sound conventions, the civil social order dissolves. And lacking variety of life and diversity of institutions, normality succumbs to the tyranny of standardization without standards."[28]

It was not enough, in Kirk's view, to preach to the individual the virtues of nonconformity. Liberals who wished to avoid social uniformity while denigrating authority and tradition seemed to Kirk to jettison the very substance of social diversity and its attendant goods. The result, he thought, was an unexciting concept of man, [that of] a being who finds his whole duty in the triumph of self in this world, and whose highest hope is to be "autonomous"—somehow different from dull conformists, though severed from tradition, from duty, from hope of much attainment in this world, and from expectation of reward in another realm than this.

Traditional life at least had offered distinct ideals and categories of experience, as well as a range of condition and class which provided fitting objects for aspiration and a vivid differentiation of personality. Under modern conditions, unfortunately, this interesting social topography had been "eroded to the dry plain of egalitarian uniformity."[29]

A different perspective was offered by Frank S. Meyer. Meyer wrote from the individualist and libertarian end of the conservative spectrum, but he was also the leading advocate and explicator of a "fusionism" within which traditionalists and libertarians could find common ground. And although Meyer suspected writers like Kirk of subordinating the individual to tradition and community in ways that undermined conservative opposition to collectivism,[30] his own remarks on social diversity exemplified the possibilities of a fusionist approach. Like Kirk, Meyer was aware of the limits of a usable diversity. It seemed to him fatuous to suggest, as President Kennedy did in a speech in 1963, that the West and the Communist bloc, if they could not compose their other differences, might at least join to make the world safe for diversity; diversity, Meyer pointed out, was just what the Communists wished to eradicate.[31]

But if diversity was misapplied to incompatible systems, one of which rejected the very principle, it was nonetheless to be cherished as one of the qualities of life for which the West stood. Meyer regretted the increasing homogenization of American life, which in reducing regional, occupational, and other differences seemed to be leading to a bland uniformity of culture and attitude. The prevailing social and political ideology exacerbated the tendency. "The bigotry with which Liberalism systematically attempts to destroy any person or idea or attitude that asserts the existence of a many-chambered universe, outside the arid and sterile cell in which the

Liberal mind would confine the human imagination, becomes,''
Meyer exclaimed, "day by day more and more obvious."[32]

Diversity was a quality, in fact, which lay close to the libertarian
conservative core of Meyer's thought. He perceived that it was
radically threatened by the spirit of reductionism common to otherwise disparate phenomena of modern life and thought. He criticized
Marshall McLuhan for proposing to submerge the "discrimination
and differentiation that constitute civilization" under "an inter-
personal, electronically linked collective of 'cool' togetherness."
In a different way, Meyer believed, Teilhard de Chardin sang "a
paean to that force proceeding impersonally and irresistibly to the
'Omega' point where God, man, and the whole of existence are
fused in a featureless unity much more akin to Brahma or Nirvana
than to anything in classical, Hebrew, or Western Christian thought."
Even the drug LSD, in its erosion of the clear differentiation of
experience, seemed but a narcotic analogue to the intellectual dissolution of distinctions preached by such seers as McLuhan, Teilhard,
and Norman O. Brown, the prophet of polymorphous perversity.
The reductionist approaches of all such thinkers, Meyer concluded,
shared a common goal: "all of them try to suck life and meaning
out of the rich and multiple spectacle of creation, reducing the
whole of being to nothing more than a pale reflection of the chosen
ideological force."[33]

Others of even stronger individualist and libertarian bent have
emphasized the proper diversity of society. Murray N. Rothbard
pointed out the drastically standardizing implications of the modern
shibboleth of "equality." The egalitarian ideal, he thought, could
be attained only if all men were "precisely uniform, precisely identical with respect to all of their attributes. The egalitarian world would
necessarily be a world of horror fiction: a world of faceless and
identical creatures, devoid of all individuality, variety or special
creativity." In a truly free society, Rothbard argued, all would be
equal only in the possession of their liberty, while retaining in all
other respects their natural inequality and diversity.[34]

Champions of the free market have found a cogent argument
in the desirability of a life of varied possibilities. "The test of an
economic system lies in the choices it offers, the alternatives that
are open to the people living under it," according to John Chamber-

lain. "The virtue of a free system—i.e. competitive capitalism—is that it allows energy to flow uncoerced into a thousand-and-one different forms, expanding goods, services, and jobs in a myriad, unpredictable ways."[35] In similar spirit, Milton Friedman remarked that "government can never duplicate the variety and diversity of individual action." By imposing uniform standards, Friedman believed, government "would substitute uniform mediocrity for the variety essential for that experimentation which can bring tomorrow's laggards above today's mean." In sum, the great advantage of the free market was that "it permits wide diversity."[36]

The diversity of the market is not necessarily the diversity favored by traditionalists like Russell Kirk, and is even likely to work against it in some respects. However, certain of the most thoughtful advocates of the market—notably of European background—have suggested a significant area of common ground. In particular, F. A. Hayek and Wilhelm Röpke, both old-fashioned European liberals whose studious opposition to collectivism has aligned them with contemporary conservatives, have shown clear appreciation of the role of tradition. To Hayek, the "boundless variety of human nature" doomed attempts to bring about equality of condition through equal treatment; only unequal treatment could make people alike in condition. Further, he thought it a profound mistake on the part of the advocates of "social justice" to try to eliminate the effect of accident; the growth of civilization depended largely on individuals "making the best use of whatever accidents they encounter." And tradition, Hayek implied, has this much in common with accident: it provides an undesigned, not externally controlled, variety of circumstance which gives substance to formal freedom. "Paradoxical as it may appear," he concluded, "it is probably true that a successful free society will always in large measure be a tradition-bound society."[37]

Wilhelm Röpke appeared to concur. Certainly Röpke rejected the nineteenth-century error of supposing individual freedom and laissez faire to be sufficient for the good society. The market economy, he knew, required a proper social setting. It was one thing "where atomization, mass, proletarianization, and concentration rule"; it was quite another where *"corps intermédiaires"* secured individual interest and guarded against the overweening power of the national state.[38] Conformity and uniformity there were in plenty in modern society, he acknowledged, but they consisted far less in adherence to tradition than in the truculent insistence on the new and the discontinuous. Mass man was a conformist precisely in his nonconformism. "His conformism," Röpke thought, "manifests itself in the break with tradition and continuity, in rootlessness, anti-conservatism, revolutionary romanticism."[39]

Röpke distinguished between two main types of social thought. The representatives of one sought the good society in "the subordination of the individual and the small group to a deliberately and strictly organized community," constructed ostensibly without reference to the past; their opposites sought felicity in "the independence and autonomy of the individual and the small group," spontaneous rather than contrived, and tested by time. These positions, he thought, could be denominated "centrism" and decentrism"; equality and uniformity were the properties of centrism, while decentrism was characterized by "inequality, diversity, multiformity, and social articulation." Yet this was not, Röpke made clear, a plea for a narrow provincialism or nationalism; the decentrist must be also a universalist, with an allegiance to "a larger community which is all the more genuine for being structured and articulated." Because the proper center of the decentrist was God Himself, Röpke suggested, he refused to accept collectivizing human centers which debased the universal even as they crushed the particular.[40]

Hayek and, even more clearly, Röpke, suggested that through a common devotion to social diversity, traditionalist and libertarian or free market varieties of conservatism might become, if not fully reconciled, at least complementary. No doubt this was an insight which came easier to old-fashioned European liberals than it did to native Americans of any political stripe. In the United States, the diversity fostered by groups and institutions rooted in custom and tradition seemed alien to the more familiar diversity of competitive individualism and the marketplace.

At the extremes, certainly, the two are alien, except to the extent that they arrive at social uniformity by opposite routes: that of tradition unleavened by due scope for individual initiative, and that of rootless individuals vibrating to the impulses of the mass. Yet there is some common ground less ironically shared. The negative side of it is the easier to grasp, or to defend; it consists in a shared resistance to the concentration of authority in centralized governmental bodies. Traditionalist and libertarian or free market conservatives may disagree on how best to foster diversity, but they agree that it is not the product of central planning, and this in the twentieth century is a far from negligible consensus. It is the special interest of thinkers like Hayek and Röpke, however, that they perceive a more positive nexus. They find it natural to believe that custom gives form and substance to individuality, and that free individuals in the matrix of traditional ways and institutions elicit a truly diversified social order.

Is the traditionalist conception of social harmony at hopeless odds with the libertarian free market exaltation of competition? Not necessarily: Adam Smith's "invisible hand" supposed a natural harmony of competing interests, and not even "Social Darwinists" truly saw in economic life unmitigated jungle law. The business corporation, fitting no ideal category, reflects a modern paradox: it has done much to standardize our lives even while turning out products to meet an immense variety of needs and wants.[41] It has grown by supplanting traditional life, while frequently shying from the full rigors of competition. But competition, when it works best, bends toward harmony. And conversely, harmony arises not from interests in complete agreement, but from the sufficient reconciliation of disparate and even competing elements. There is nothing strange in the notion that traditionalist sensibilities and free competitiveness can achieve effective accommodation. If they do, it is apt to be less the product of design than a fortuity of history. But the juncture will be more likely if different kinds of conservatives remember their common devotion to a world of plenitude and diversity.

NOTES

1. The most complete study of the subject is George H. Nash, *The Conservative Intellectual Movement in America* (New York: Basic Books, 1976).

2. Robert A. Nisbet, *The Quest for Community* (New York: Oxford University Press, 1953), viii, 70.

3. Ibid., 115-116, 111, 121. On the influence of the Roman law, see

Robert A. Nisbet, *Twilight of Authority* (New York: Oxford University Press, 1975), 164-176.

4. Nisbet, *Quest for Community,* 160, 176-186.

5. Ibid., 32.

6. Ibid., 252-255, 236-244, 246-247. "The great cultural ages of the past were, almost invariably, ages of social diversity, of small, independent communities and towns, of distinct regions, of small associations which jealously guarded their unique identities and roles," Nisbet pointed out (ibid., 267).

7. Ibid., 265-270, 256, 278-279. Nisbet reiterated his suggestion for a laissez faire of groups in *Twilight of Authority,* 276.

8. Nisbet, *Twilight of Authority,* v-vii.

9. Ibid., 51-57.

10. Ibid., 198-199, 201, 221.

11. Ibid., 222, 217.

12. Albert Hunold, ed., *Freedom and Serfdom* (Dordrecht, Holland: D. Reidel Publishing Co., 1961), 174, 227.

13. Hans Buchheim, *Totalitarian Rule* (Middletown, Conn.: Wesleyan University Press, 1968), 14, 20, 106.

14. Erik von Kuehnelt-Leddihn, *Leftism* (New Rochelle, N.Y.: Arlington House, 1974), 20, 167, and passim. See also Kuehnelt-Leddihn, "Utopias and Ideologies: Another Chapter in the Conservative Demonology," *Modern Age* 21 (Summer 1977): 263-275.

15. Kuehnelt-Leddihn, *Leftism,* 430, 16, 19.

16. Michael Oakeshott, *Rationalism in Politics* (New York: Basic Books, 1962), 186.

17. Ibid., 2-3, 6.

18. Ibid., 44-48.

19. Ibid., 64-65, 187.

20. Eric Voegelin, *Order and History* (Baton Rouge: Louisiana State University Press, 1956), I, 501, and passim; Gerhart Niemeyer, "Eric Voegelin's Philosophy and the Drama of Mankind," *Modern Age* 20 (Winter 1976): 29.

21. Voegelin, *Order and History,* II, 21; Niemeyer, "Eric Voegelin's Philosophy," 34-35.

22. Voegelin, *Order and History,* II, 5-6.

23. See Frank S. Meyer, ed., *What is Conservatism?* (New York: Holt, Rinehart and Winston, 1964), 7-20; Nash, *Conservative Intellectual Movement,* 82, 173-178.

24. Irving Babbitt, *Democracy and Leadership* (Boston and New York: Houghton Mifflin Co., 1924), 170.

25. Gustavo R. Velasco, "On Equality and Egalitarianism," *Modern Age* 18 (Winter 1974): 23.

26. David J. Gray, "Individualism in an Organized America," *Modern Age* 8 (Summer 1964): 268-269.

27. M. E. Bradford, "The Heresy of Equality: Bradford Replies to Jaffa," *Modern Age* 20 (Winter 1976): 63.

28. Russell Kirk, *Enemies of the Permanent Things* (New Rochelle, N.Y.: Arlington House, 1974), 23, 26-27.

29. Ibid., 195, 95-96.

30. See John P. East, "The Conservatism of Frank Straus Meyer," *Modern Age* 18 (Summer 1974): 241.

31. Frank S. Meyer, *The Conservative Mainstream* (New Rochelle, N.Y.: Arlington House, 1969), 377-378.

32. Ibid., 296, 455, 106.

33. Ibid., 476-480, 467-468.

34. Murray N. Rothbard, "Egalitarianism as a Revolt Against Nature," *Modern Age* 17 (Fall 1973): 350-351; see also Rothbard, "Freedom, Inequality, Primitivism, and the Division of Labor," *Modern Age* 15 (Summer 1971): 242.

35. John Chamberlain, *The Roots of Capitalism* (Princeton, N.J.: D. Van Nostrand Company, 1959), 165.

36. Milton Friedman, *Capitalism and Freedom* (Chicago: University of Chicago Press, 1962), 4, 15. In Milton and Rose Friedman's more recent *Free to Choose* (New York and London: Harcourt Brace Jovanovich, 1980), the authors noted that "voluntary exchange can produce uniformity in some respects combined with diversity in others" (p. 27). The emphasis continued to be on the free market's affinity with social diversity, however.

37. F. A. Hayek, *The Constitution of Liberty* (Chicago: University of Chicago Press, 1960), 86-87, 385, 61.

38. Wilhelm Röpke, *A Humane Economy* (Chicago: Henry Regnery Co., 1960), 35, 143-153.

39. Ibid., 63-64.

40. Ibid., 227-234.

41. Theodore Levitt noted uniformitarian tendencies on the part of business in "Business and the Plural Society," *Modern Age* 4 (Spring 1960): 173-179.

11 Conservatives and Others

As devotion to diversity serves as a uniting factor among different schools of conservative thought, it also offers a measure of common ground with nonconservative ideas and attitudes. Diversity is so elementary as a conception and a condition, indeed, that it could hardly be otherwise. And although much in modern culture has tended to a blurring of the distinctions on which a sense of diversity rests, this has been too dismaying a development not to have aroused protests from a wide range of sources. Conservatives will find increasingly that they need to define their own ideas about diversity against those of other political or philosophical bent.

The standard liberal-conservative dichotomy is an obvious starting point. Although these perennial parties share a sustained concern for a diversified society, there is sufficient historical warrant to call attention to a crucial difference of emphasis. Liberals have characteristically viewed diversity as the boon of individual freedom, while conservatives have insisted that individual must be sustained by group diversities. The difference in approach between John Stuart Mill and James Fitzjames Stephen, or that between George Bancroft and Orestes Brownson, illustrates the distinction for the nineteenth century. The situation has somewhat altered in our own age. The traditionalist and libertarian poles of contemporary conservatism to a degree reconstitute the older conservative-liberal division. Modern liberals, on the other hand, have worked to limit individual freedom and diversity in the economic sphere, while at the same time accentuating their distrust of local and traditional groupings which they view as a threat to personal freedoms of a noneconomic character—regarding censorship, sexual expression, abortion, and other "social issues."

With such major qualifications, and focusing resolutely on the respective centers of gravity of the two schools, we may still find Robert A. Nisbet's distinction useful. Conservatives and liberals share a fundamental concern with "freedom of individual thought and action as against the claims of the total social order," Nisbet thought, "but the conservative ideologists have for the most part seen this individual freedom as an inextricable aspect of a kind of social pluralism, one rich in autonomous or semi-autonomous groups, communities, and institutions."[1]

Using this criterion, we can cite David Riesman as a sophisticated example of the liberal view of social diversity. Riesman's *The Lonely Crowd* (1950), although more academic in tone, was in a way a liberal counterpart to Ortega y Gasset's *The Revolt of the Masses.* Both presented a picture of an ascendant human type concerned above all to fit in with the crowd, governed not by tradition or by values instilled in youth, but by peer norms and standards. Riesman found positive qualities in "other-direction" that do not appear in Ortega's jeremiad—chiefly greater sensitivity and tolerance toward others. But a similar image of uniformity obtained. As Riesman elsewhere remarked of life in the suburbs, "while all the appurtenances of variety are present, life is monotonous in the sense that it is steadily gregarious, focused on others, and on the self in relation to others."[2]

Although troubled by this tendency to social monotone, Riesman remained confident of "the enormous potentialities for diversity in nature's bounty," and hoped that "men's capacity to differentiate their experience" might come more to be valued by the individual. "The idea that men are created free and equal is both true and misleading: men are created different; they lose their social freedom and their individual autonomy in seeking to become like each other."[3] In this concluding statement of *The Lonely Crowd,* the phrase "individual autonomy" was the key. Riesman could contemplate with equanimity the fading of local and group differences. Reconsidering the question in 1961, he thought it possible that "the cast of national characters is finished"; the circumstances of life were becoming too similar for such diversity to flourish, and what differences remained in an age of rapid communication offered too great a choice for the individual easily to remain an uncomplicated national type. But Riesman believed that the growing homogeneity of national cultures, like the removal of fixed boundaries of class and caste, need trouble only tourists and the nostalgic—"provided that the differences that once arose among men due to their geographic location can be replaced by differences arising from the still unexplored potentialities of human temperament, interest, and curiosity." This development depended on the emergence of the "autonomous individual," psychologically free to choose a personal style of life whether in conformity to prevailing fashions or not.[4]

The prescription of individual autonomy was clearly in keeping with the liberal tradition. There are difficulties with it. How were autonomous men and women to relate to each other? Noting the common fears of anomie and rootlessness, Riesman suggested hopefully that "ties based on conscious relatedness may some day replace those of blood and soil." It is of course a hallmark of modern life that people do in large measure choose their friends, associates, and spouses. But there may be more serious losses than Riesman realized in casting off "the provinciality of being born to a particular family in a particular place."[5] One thinks of G. K. Chesterton's comment on the narrowness of the clique of chosen associates, as opposed to the inevitable diversity of types in the unchosen family or clan. One thinks too of Henry James's perception that individuality suffered in America from the sparcity of social types. A defensible conservative position, I think, would be that to the extent that human beings can become "autonomous," autonomy draws on both the distinctive qualities of family, locality, and class, and on the fortuitous acquaintance with different characters and personalities within each group. Whether autonomy can well be nurtured without distinctive cultural substance within which and against which to define itself, seems doubtful at best. Perhaps the autonomous person can construct a "life-style" from models external to his own experience, but as national and other types fade, his choices will become progressively less vivid and immediate.

Elsewhere, within a range of thought which is neither conservative nor properly liberal, a greater degree of affinity with conservative conceptions can sometimes be found. Even radical and counter-cultural thought, although frequently inclined to erase distinctions or moon toward some species of ersatz Nirvana, offers points of contact. A genuine revulsion against the monolithic tendencies of contemporary technology and bureaucracy was obscured by the simplistic demagoguery of the nineteen-sixties. The "Small is Beautiful" movement was a call to diversity by fostering the small group in place of mass organization. However practical or impractical the prescriptions of E. F. Schumacher, the title of whose book provided the watchcry, he sounded at times positively conservative. The truest Burkean, for example, could hardly quarrel with Schumacher's comment that "while the nineteenth-century ideas deny or obliterate the hierarchy of levels in the universe, the notion of an hierarchical order is an indispensable instrument of understanding." To view the world as such a "ladder," he added, was essential to the recognition in human life of a significant undertaking.[6] In their own ways, such critics of the "myth of the objective consciousness" as Theodore Roszak, and existentialist defenders of the undetermined and nonrational aspects of human life, struck similarly sympathetic chords.[7] Questionable bedfellows though they might be for conservatives in other respects, they all rejected arbitrarily imposed uniformities in favor of the diversity which arises from the unique value of the particular.

Lewis Mumford furnishes a particularly pertinent example of a nonconservative capable of addressing conservative concerns in a conservative vein. In books like *The Pentagon of Power* (1970), Mumford drew a sharp contrast between the mechanical uniformities that have gained the ascendancy in Western civilization and "the immense cultural variety of mankind: the rich compost of human history, which almost matches the original abundance and variety of nature." This was not a simplistic summons to "return to nature"; Mumford emphasized specifically *cultural* diversity, accumulating, mingling, striking out in new directions down through the ages.

Nor was his a Luddite voice against all advanced technology, but rather one calling for a more varied and versatile technology—in his terms a "polytechnics" rather than a "monotechnics"—capable of responding to all valid human needs and purposes.[8]

Mumford invoked themes particularly familiar to conservative thought in his comments on the rise of modern political absolutism. The "baroque absolutism" represented intellectually by Descartes, he complained, had decomposed society into a whirl of atoms. "This stripping away of the constituent groups that compose any real community—the family, the village, the farm, the workshop, the guild, the church—cleared the way for the uniformities and standardizations imposed by the machine." Mumford found it significant that almost all Utopian projects entailed the imposition of a totalitarian uniformity;[9] however short modern political ideologies fall of achieving Utopian expectations, one infers, the emphasis on uniformity is invariably retained.

The gist of the matter was, in Mumford's view, that any attempt to organize human life which sought to foreclose diverse possibilities of trial and selection operated "to arrest human cultural evolution." The only effective approach was nature's own: "to provide the possibility of an endless variety of biological and cultural types, since no single one, however rich and rewarding, is capable of encompassing all the latent potentialities of man." Mumford thus returned to an old idea, once a favorite of conservatives: the sense of plenitude, as formerly expressed in the concept of the Chain of Being. "Plenitude," he noted, "indicated more than abundance: it was the condition for organic variety, diversification, selectivity, in a word, freedom, which reached its climax in man." Mumford called for a renewal of this sense of plenitude in the context of modern life, as a standard and end, by which and to which "technics" might be directed.[10]

The weightier theories of the good society to be propounded in recent years encourage one to believe that the old monistic visions of Utopia or of historical process may at last—intellectually—be consigned to the past. A case in point is John Rawls's deservedly acclaimed *A Theory of Justice* (1971). Reduced to conventional political terms, Rawls's theory was adaptable either to welfare liberalism or social democracy, a society's capitalist or socialist orientation to depend on local circumstances and traditions. Rawls defined justice as fairness, and designated as fair those principles of association which free and rational persons in an original state of equality, ignorant of any innate advantage or disadvantage with respect to others, would choose in their own interest. Such persons, he thought, would choose two principles:

> The first requires equality in the assignment of basic rights and duties, while the second holds that social and economic inequalities, for example inequalities of wealth and authority, are just only if they result in compensating benefits for everyone, and in particular for the least advantaged members of society.

No one was to benefit from the contingencies of "natural accident and social circumstance" except in ways that helped these others.[11]

To make inequalities of condition contingent on compensating benefits to others was, from a conservative or libertarian standpoint, to negate what should be indefeasible individual rights or "entitlements." Whether such canons would give sufficient scope to social diversity, furthermore, is open to question. But it is notable that within the bounds of his theory, Rawls did make diversity a major consideration. The good of some people was not simply to be weighed against the good of others or of the aggregate; Rawls rejected utilitarianism because it did not "take seriously the distinction between persons."[12] Human good, he emphasized, was "heterogeneous." It was natural and desirable that individuals should entertain different conceptions of their own good—although not of fundamental right. From the *Nicomachean Ethics* Rawls drew what he called the "Aristotelian Principle": human beings obtain most satisfaction, other things being equal, from complex and varied activities, especially those requiring the largest "repertoire" of skills and the finest ability to distinguish and discriminate. Good social institutions, Rawls suggested, must give scope to this deep truth of human psychology.[13]

In the tenor of Rawls's insistence on the diversity of the well-ordered society, one is struck by the degree to which Burkean and nineteenth-century conservative doctrines have come to be accepted outside the conservative fold, in contradistinction to the individualistic approach of nineteenth-century liberals like John Stuart Mill. Society, Rawls thought, should contain an unlimited "variety of communities and associations," matched to diverse abilities and aspirations. His repeated description of the healthy society as "a social union of social unions" was, as far as it went, indistinguishable from a host of British Tory pronouncements on the subject. One can read into Rawls's sense of the complementary nature of these unions and associations a conservative acknowledgment of human limitations: "we must look to others to attain the excellences that we must leave aside, or lack altogether."[14] There is even finally a version of Burke's partnership of generations. The "Aristotelian Principle," Rawls argued, held for institutional forms as well as for individuals.

> Seen in this light, a just constitutional order, when adjoined to the smaller social unions of everyday life, provides a framework for these many associations and sets up the most complex and diverse society of all. In a well-ordered society each person understands the first principles that govern the whole scheme as it is to be carried out over many generations; and all have a settled intention to adhere to these principles in their plan of life. Thus the plan of each person is given a more ample and rich structure than it would otherwise have. . . . Everyone's more private life is so to speak a plan within a plan, this superordinate plan being realized in the public institutions of society.

Rawls made it clear, however, that the larger plan could not establish any dominant or transcendent end.[15]

As alive to human differences as it was, from a strictly libertarian point of view, Rawls's theory of justice violated the most fundamental of principles. Robert Nozick, in *Anarchy, State, and Utopia* (1974), offered perhaps the most cogent critique of Rawls, as well as an interesting alternative scheme for society. For Nozick the minimal state, but only the minimal state, could be justified; any more extensive state by its nature violated individual rights. In particular, the state might not legitimately "use its coercive apparatus for the purpose of getting some citizens to aid others, or in order to prohibit activities to people for their *own* good or protection."[16] The trouble with Rawls's version of contract theory, basing justice on the distribution of goods in society, was that it could not be realized without "continuous interference in people's lives," Nozick thought. He proposed instead an "entitlement" theory, historical in nature, and according to which the justice of a given distribution of goods "depends upon how it came about." Thus the robber is not entitled to his wealth, but the honest worker or enterpriser may be. The "past circumstances or actions of people can create differential entitlements or differential deserts to things." Nozick indeed was critical of writers like Rawls for suggesting that differences among persons were arbitrary and needed to be justified at all.[17]

Nozick had as keen an awareness of human diversity as Rawls, although he proposed a different way to provide for it. Self-esteem, he pointed out, was based on differentiating characteristics—"that's why it's *self*-esteem." One troubling thing about a society in which "differentiating dimensions" were diminished was the reduced opportunity for the individual to find anything at which he could excel; increasing envy would be the logical consequence.[18] Nozick's own proposals were designed to avoid such damage to the sense of self-worth.

Like Rawls, Nozick contemplated a society containing a wide range of diverse communities. He boldly shifted into a Utopian mode here, but his departure from the monistic patterns of traditional Utopias was striking. People, he emphasized, were different, and the chances of framing a social order to satisfy all were nil. Therefore, a genuine Utopia would have to consist in a variety of utopias, which is to say of a range of communities organized voluntarily according to mutually held principles. (Nozick suggested however that the more successful communities would not be those of the merely like-minded, but would contain "a diversity of persons, with a diversity of excellences.") Contrary to Rawls's conception of the just society, the framework of such a system would be that of the minimal state, but nothing would prevent the existence of a traditionalist or authoritarian community, within limits compatible with the whole and without violating the principle of individual consent. "Many communities," Nozick supposed, "will achieve many different characters," with the prospects correspondingly good that the individual could find a way to live as he wished.[19]

From a conservative point of view, Nozick's scheme had considerable appeal. He suggested a way in which libertarian and traditionalist precepts might be reconciled. It had, as he noted, certain of the advantages of the libertarian vision without the corresponding defects; in particular, individual communities might impose restrictions on their members which would be unacceptable if enforced by government. A traditionalist conservatism might flourish on such a communal basis which under modern conditions would otherwise be difficult or impossible to sustain. And it was certainly in keeping with the conservative sense of history that this Utopia of Utopias was not expected to appear overnight: "It is what grows spontaneously from the individual choices of many people over a long period of time that will be worth speaking eloquently about."[20]

Doubts inevitably arise: in practice might this not simply replicate in a more sophisticated way the pattern of individual hedonism combined with bureaucratic supervision? Despite hopes to the contrary, would not like group with like, at the cost of the individual's acquaintance with those truly different from himself? Is more than a superficial diversity compatible with the transience of membership that would be permitted among the various communities? Historically, social diversity has been a matter largely of strain and rivalry, inertia and haphazard interaction, not merely of a variety of life-styles maintained in equilibrium by a self-effacing government. Still, Nozick weaves together the themes of limited government, private initiative, and unforced evolutionary development with sufficient persuasiveness to produce a rare model of the future which is at once "inspiring" and Utopian, and at the same time attractive to conservative sensibilities.

Given so much common ground with nonconservative and marginally conservative points of view, in what ways does the tradition of Burke still offer a distinctive vision of the diversity of the world? Fundamentally, I think, in its linked conceptions of order, hierarchy, and above all perhaps of the timeless. These notions retain their vitality in conservative convictions despite the enormous need to reinterpret and adapt them in the intellectual and practical light of modernity.

As conservatives have been saying for at least two hundred years, order and diversity are true concomitants; anarchy and uniformity are their conjoined antithesis. This means a more than man-made order, an order existing in the constitution of the universe. It is necessarily a hierarchical order, moreover, as there are assumed to be in the world conditions, stations, and values of higher and lesser worth. As much a matter of common sense as this appears when applied, say, to the animal kingdom, it runs deeply counter to twentieth-century sensibilities. (Indeed, the eagerness to discover linguistic ability in chimpanzees and a sensitive intelligence in dolphins, as well as the calls for "animal liberation," seem to reflect an uneasiness even with unequal rank among species.) If hierarchy is a paradigm rooted in the Middle Ages, the modern world has moved toward a quite different one, composed of equality, relativism, and a neutral pluralism.

It would be as foolish to assert that liberals and radicals have altogether abandoned hierarchical ways of thinking as it would be to hold contemporary conservatives to the canons of the "Great Chain of Being." Yet the conservative horror of relativism bespeaks a crucial difference of emphasis. Conservatives are more likely than their opponents to rank societies, "life-styles," religions, fields of study at universities—sometimes more narrowly than they should. But relativism in the conservative view vitiates the sense of diversity by breaking down the valid distinctions that hierarchy maintains. If any one thing were to keep conservatives from embracing Nozick's Utopia of Utopias, it would most likely be, not the Utopian aspect itself, but the appearance of writing relativism into the very structure of society, the banishment altogether from the public sphere of the hierarchical principle.

Hierarchy means properly far more than inequality, of course; it denotes a coherent structure of ranks or orders. In the largest sense it means a "constitution of being" timeless in its indwelling spirit. Whatever the private convictions of thoughtful modern conservatives, their insistence of the timeless does not usually demand any particular theological orthodoxy. Some are agnostics or atheists. Not to go beyond the aspect of conservatism under present discussion, however, faith in a Creator remains the natural and highest expression of the perception of the Cosmos as a diverse and abundant place. Science can show that mass/energy assumes the most varied forms; it is preeminently religious sensibility which sets the stamp of ultimate significance on these differentiations.

However expressed, the conservative sense of the timeless is leagued to an equally essential sense of time. It is in this conjunction, I think, that conservatives find their proper and distinctive—if not entirely exclusive—point of vantage. Conservatism of the main tradition insists that serious personal freedom and self-expression must have play beyond the sphere of the individual isolated in space and time. With this many nonconservatives would no doubt agree. Certainly such a thinker as John Rawls appears to concur with the conservative belief that to be deliberately a part of a web of associations and generations is not only a source of comfort; it is to gain stature as a moral and thinking being in the frame of the world.

Conservatism as a serious school of thought in Britain and America has involved the somewhat more complicated conviction, however, that the values and truths of highest worth transcend the passing of generation and epoch, while only time and experience can render effective and authoritative their realization in human institutions. With Friedrich Nietzsche, who perceived a sterile sameness equally in the life lived without reference to the past and in unrestrained historicism, conservatives have believed that "history, so far as it serves life, serves an unhistorical power."[21] The purely temporal view of life, whether it issues in the historian's reduction of the variety of human experience to one monistic version or another of historical process, or in the reactionary's unqualified reverence for the past, must almost inevitably end in monotony. (The latter, indeed, may draw on a romantic vision of the diversity of bygone societies, but the nullity of present hopes reduces this to an ornament, extracted from life as a continuing adventure.) To the more complete Burkean, time serves the timeless. Experience points to the enduring, and in so doing assigns to the qualities of life their place and value, gives weight to distinctions and differences, and by showing the limits of realizable human aspirations, helps to define human possibilities.

This chafes against the modern cry for freedom, which means above all freedom from the past. But freedom without the substance furnished by experience is mere abstraction. Chesterton sought to economize the unknowable; allow with the orthodox one fathomless mystery, he argued, and everything else falls into place. Similarly, by accepting with open eyes the ineluctable burden of the past, one is equipped to resolve the amorphous stuff of everyday encounter into events of discrete meaning, which are the more freely apprehensible and manageable in consequence. This requires, prior to any practical result, an exercise of imagination. It is a cardinal conservative principle that the diversity of life is not so much planned as honored. Both time and the timeless have a fortuitous quality in their impact on the present. The inherited and the universal are both "givens," accidental to the individual on whom they impinge. They both bump against the bland fluidity of the present moment, offering the possibility of direction to its subjective freedom and the ordered meaning of authentic diversity to its environing multiplicity.

NOTES

1. Robert A. Nisbet, *Twilight of Authority* (New York: Oxford University Press, 1975), 48.

2. David Riesman, *Individualism Reconsidered* (Glencoe, Ill.: The Free Press, 1954), 210-211.

3. David Riesman, *The Lonely Crowd* (New Haven and London: Yale University Press, 1969), 307.

4. Ibid., xl, lix-lx.

5. Ibid., lx.

6. E. F. Schumacher, *Small is Beautiful: Economics as if People Mattered* (New York: Harper & Row, 1973), 89.

7. See e.g. Theodore Roszak, *The Making of a Counter Culture: Reflections on the Technocratic Society and its Youthful Opposition* (New York: Doubleday, 1969); and William Barrett, *Irrational Man: A Study in Existentialist Philosophy* (New York: Doubleday, 1962).

8. Lewis Mumford, *The Pentagon of Power* (New York: Harcourt Brace Jovanovich, 1970), 12, 153, 298.

9. Ibid., 81, 211, and passim.

10. Ibid., 159, 289, 395-396.

11. John Rawls, *A Theory of Justice* (Cambridge: Harvard University Press, 1971), 11, 15, 100.

12. Ibid., 15, 27.

13. Ibid., 554, 447, 426-429, 433.

14. Ibid., 441, 527, 571, 529.

15. Ibid., 528.

16. Robert Nozick, *Anarchy, State, and Utopia* (New York: Basic Books, 1974), ix, 149.

17. Ibid., 163, 153, 155, 223.

18. Ibid., 243-246.

19. Ibid., 306-310, 320, 332.

20. Ibid., 320, 332.

21. Friedrich Nietzsche, *The Use and Abuse of History,* trans. Adrian Collins (Indianapolis: Bobbs-Merrill, 1957), 12.

Conclusion

Although conservatism is commonly regarded as backward-looking, to be effective it must be forward-looking as well. For if conservatives seek to husband the experience of the past, it is after all for the advantage of the future that that practical and reverential duty is performed. The question then naturally arises: does the body of thought treated in the preceding pages offer a usable idea of diversity for the world of the late twentieth century?

Such are the complexities, instabilities, and rate of change of this world that the range of plausible futures is wide. Those that are totalitarian in nature need little comment here. Although a totalitarian state may institute an official elite, or recognize by proscription hated ethnic or other minorities, its end is a uniformity of thought and allegiance which precludes any true diversity. Those archetypal anti-Utopias which build upon totalitarian reality, Aldous Huxley's *Brave New World* and George Orwell's *Nineteen Eighty-Four,* explore alternative paths to a uniform social order; the cruelty of the one is perhaps no more convincing than the benignity of the other. Nightmare can play not only with Orwell's two-way television surveillance and Huxley's pleasure-inducing drugs, but with the possibilities of "conditioning" and behavior modification techniques if directed consciously toward producing docile populations. Beyond that, we shade more clearly into science fiction—which sometimes ceases to be fictional.

A more credible possibility, at least for the West, emerges from the extrapolation of certain recent tendencies. From this we should find a kind of synthesis of totalitarianism with personal "libera-tion"—a pervasive system of bureaucratic regulation and control combined with free play for individual idiosyncrasy and hedonism. One would be able freely enough to pursue one's happiness as a social atom; what one would not be able to do would be to extend this pursuit significantly beyond the sphere of the individual isolated in space and time. With family, community, and economic rela-tionships closely supervised by central government—in the name, of course, of social justice—the perpetuation of the diverse traditions that autonomous institutions nourish would become difficult or impossible. The cultural particularities which render personal differences more than superficial, ephemeral, and socially inconse-quential would fade. Man would be as a mayfly, without yesterday, tomorrow, or significant present.

Evidence can be found to support all except perhaps the most morbid of prognostications. Certainly contemporary experience tends to show that a weakening of traditional centers of social authority and a high degree of permissiveness are perfectly compati-ble with cultural homogenization. It is highly doubtful that even individual diversities have increased as personal liberties have broadened. Historical experience testifies, moreover, to the strong positive attraction of uniformity. It appeals to the impulse to ration-alize and to order, and quite often to the will to power. It seems to offer an end to tension and conflict. In its most heightened form it bespeaks a yearning to cast off the burdens of the separate con-sciousness. No careful student of human thought is likely to under-estimate the perennial attraction of Nirvana, which reaches far beyond Buddhists, Hindus, and New England Transcendentalists. The desire to melt into the universe with the mystic, or to recon-stitute the amorphous unity of the womb—at root, perhaps, the same thing—lies very deep in human nature. In his 1953 classic of science fiction, *Childhood's End,* Arthur C. Clarke created a strik-ingly modern and resonant image of this urge. The end of the world, in Clarke's story, is consummated by a generation of young which advances beyond individual consciousness in order that the resulting apotheosis of mankind may be absorbed into the being of a cosmic "Overmind."[1]

Clarke's description of the children of the last generation, depicted as naked and filthy, with matted hair and engaged in an endless dance, may have struck some readers of the recent past as an apocalyptic premonition of the tribalistic, drug and rock-besotted "flower children" of the sixties. If so, the gap between the prophetic and the actual is instructive. The mystical melting into unity, the transcendental moment, are themselves among the varieties of human experience, and no doubt among the highest, stretching toward the ultimate oneness of God or of the universe. But this kind of intuited unity belongs to the alpha and omega of life—its source and destiny—rather than to life itself in its mundane course. (For Christians, even this must be qualified, for the traditional heaven is itself eternally diverse: a company of souls, and of angels and archangels in the presence of God.) Efforts to approximate transcendental unity on earth by breaking down the actual distinctions and differences of life can only be disastrous for the human spirit; by presuming upon the superhuman, they achieve merely the subhuman.

This seems particularly true of civilized man. The primitive man seems indeed to live largely within a collective consciousness. His mental life is relatively little that of an individual, and very much that of a member of a group. In this sense diversity is a product of human advancement, and we may well be wary of social policies or developments which offer a regression toward savage collectivity. Yet we are told that the "savage mind," looking outward from its collective vantage point, also perceives the world in terms of a certain vivid diversity, imbued with all the rich distinctions and complexities which myth and totemism can provide. Mythical thought, as Claude Lévi-Strauss notes, has a heterogeneous repertoire.[2] Where civilized society is twisted toward collective patterns of thought and behavior, however, as in totalitarian or advanced welfare systems,[3] it is not observable that a similar keenness of sensibility is nurtured. Civilized man cannot, it seems, make himself over into a true savage. He may conform to society's ideas and standards, but he seems unable so to lose himself in the group as to shed distinctly civilized pangs of individual anxiety, loneliness, and alienation. Nor does the collectivized civilized man seem inspired to view the world in terms of any richly diversified mythology. The attendant reductionist ideologies do not encourage it, and even if attained, the womb-to-tomb comfort which they promise does not lend itself to the appreciation of a varied and dramatic world.

Disillusionment with the monistic utopias is hardly likely to destroy the perennial appeal of social uniformity. Popular visions of the future, when not apocalyptic, still run heavily to the expectation of a comfortable, uniform, technologically managed material paradise. If there are increasing laments for diversity, is this simply the phenomenon, familiar to intellectual history, of a value being most fully articulated as it begins to lose its base in reality? Maybe—but perhaps as good a case can be made that uniformitarian habits of mind are simply the dregs of late nineteenth-century determinism and materialism. The twentieth century ostentatiously and indiscriminately rejected the more superficially stifling aspects of the Victorian world—its narrow moral rigor and official prudery; perhaps the twenty-first will get around to rejecting finally the truly oppressive elements in Victorian thought: those reductionist strains which lent new force and sanction to the old dream of uniformity.

It is often maintained, of course, that advanced technology, requiring standardization, makes inexorably for a uniform society. But this seems no more persuasive than any other variety of historical determinism. It is unnecessary to suppose that assembly lines, or uniform electronic parts, or standardized IBM cards, require a similarly standardized and uniform population. Advanced technology in fact makes possible more varied experiences, more diverse ways of living, than there have ever been before. Insofar as this technology has indeed standardized life, this may be more the effect of its crude early stages than the wave of the future.

The obvious question is whether the immense external possibilities now open to us are to be reflected in subjective life. If technicians make it possible for us to live comfortably at the South Pole or on a Saturnian moon, will these loci become encapsulated adjuncts of caricatured suburbia, or will they enlarge our sense of the plenitude of Creation? Do the modern novelties and artificialities even of normal terrestrial habitats permit that sense of the familiar through which the quanta of experience acquire distinct and weighty meanings?

It is not easy to answer such questions, but it is possible to do so in ways which admit to the future those qualities of life commended by the conservative tradition. Our study of this tradition has suggested that the conservative idea of diversity depends, first, on a complementary, ordering principle of unity; and second, on a lively sense of the continuity of human experience in time. As discouraging as the last century has been to these prerequisites, it need not be assumed that they are intrinsically incompatible with modernity.

In countries like the United States and Great Britain, there are still extended areas of life governed by moral, political, and cultural consensus, as there are still great differences among groups and individuals. And despite the conspicuous novelties of modern life, our habits, customs, and ideas remain often more traditional than we realize. What conservatives need to cultivate more than anything else is precisely the *realization:* the sense that our lives are more than momentary sparks in the darkness because, on the secular plane, they conjoin with each other and with the lives of other generations in patterns which at once differentiate and unify. And although this realization can plumb the depths of philosophy, it may be that conservatives have their most reliable ally in the stubborn, often inchoate insistence of people of no extraordinary intellectual pretension on living their lives as they see fit. Although it might seem odd for a supposedly elitist school to summon popular wisdom to its rescue, conservatives rely at bottom on common experience. And this experience shows historically a quality, made up partly of inertia, partly of an affection for liberty, partly of a proprietorial instinct to enjoy the familiar and accustomed, which is often docile to change but in the end resistant to the uniformities which policy or technical convenience seek to impose.

The conservatives under present consideration have sought a more articulate sense of society, however. They are in one way handicapped by the very nature of conservatism, which is too reliant on experience and too distrustful of abstract reason to lend itself easily to systematic formulation. By way of compensation, its opponents go amiss when they try to reduce it to formula. Thus conservatism has been identified with the ideal of a static and perfectly harmonious society, a tack which makes it easy to dismiss the entire school of thought as an exercise in futility.[4] To say nothing more, this line of attack disregards the whole experiential side of the conservative tradition. From Burke's time on, conservatives have regarded social and political institutions as being properly the products of experience, which accumulates, evolves, and suggests the necessary adaptations to change. If conservatives have also shared in the old and much more general ideal of society as a harmony of orders and interests, the more consistent among them have remembered the fundamental conservative tenet that no social ideal is ever fully attainable.

It is no doubt true that no simple call to social harmony will be widely persuasive in the late twentieth century. Philosophical account must be taken of the stark discontinuities which are part of modern life and sensibility, as practical account must be taken of those modern varieties of conservatism in which risk and competition loom large. Any effective conservative vision now must draw fully upon a post-Romantic, dynamic sense of life. It must wholeheartedly accept the element of hazard in the universe. Chesterton's image of orthodoxy as the "equilibrium of a mind behind madly rushing horses"—in contrast to the closed symmetry of paganism—comes to mind, as does Henry Adams's delicately balanced Gothic cathedral, the sum not only of different, but even of clashing, elements, and William James's characterization of a whole life as one lived on the "precarious edge." Such metaphors point to ways of counterpoising the perennial unities and diversities, congruities and conflicts of existence which are in keeping with the tenor of modernity. They suggest, in lieu of a harmony existing objectively in this life, that the mind, or spirit, must often impose its own order on a world full of accidents.

Although there is in this a very modern note of introspection, there can be in it too a certain largeness of outlook with which conservatives are not usually associated, and with which they too often do not associate themselves. Conservatism is defensible in the present world precisely when it offers a more generous understanding of human life than its radical or liberal adversaries now do. It is characteristic of certain modern shibboleths that they conceal a truncation of experience beneath expansive rhetoric. "Humanism," as that term is now commonly used, excludes the religious ways by which human beings have sought to connect themselves to the universe, and thereby trivializes humanity. The exaltation of the present accentuated by contemporary disdain for history robs the present of meaning by taking it out of the course of time. Personal "liberation" is apt to jettison the fixed rules and values which render free choice a matter of genuine weight and commitment. "Pluralism" unalloyed by the presence of orthodoxy ends in monotony. Conservatives begin by recognizing limits—the limits of flawed human nature, the limits of future possibilities constrained by the burden of the past, the limits of morally permissible conduct. They accord real honor to their own tradition, however, only when their setting of bounds to man's estate serves to cultivate the diversity and plenitude which it contains.

NOTES

1. Arthur C. Clarke, *Childhood's End* (New York: Ballantine Books, 1953), 198-214.

2. Claude Lévi-Strauss, *The Savage Mind* (Chicago: University of Chicago Press, 1962), passim.

3. For a scathing view of a modern welfare society which, according to the author, systematically denigrates individual and group diversities, see Roland Huntford's account of contemporary Sweden, *The New Totalitarians* (New York: Stein and Day, 1972).

4. See W. Morton Auerbach, *The Conservative Illusion* (New York: Columbia University Press, 1959). In the face of the actual intellectual history of conservatism, Auerbach also denies it any affinity with diversity or pluralism (p. 146). Even on the basis of his own identification of conservatism with the ideal of harmony, how can there be a harmony except of elements or qualities in some respect dissimilar?

Selected Bibliography

PRIMARY SOURCES

Adams, John. *A Defense of the Constitution of the United States of America.* 3 vols. New York: Da Capo Press, 1971.

———. *The Education of Henry Adams: An Autobiography.* Boston: Houghton Mifflin Company, 1961.

———. *Mont-Saint-Michel and Chartres.* New York: Doubleday, 1959.

Adams, John. *A Defense of the Constitutions of Government of the United States of America.* 3 vols. New York: Da Capo Press, 1971.

———. *Discourses on Davila: A Series of Papers on Political History.* New York: Da Capo Press, 1973.

Babbitt, Irving. *Democracy and Leadership.* Boston and New York: Houghton Mifflin Co., 1924.

———. *Rousseau and Romanticism.* Cleveland: The World Publishing Company, 1968.

Balfour, Arthur James. *The Foundations of Belief: Being Notes Introductory to the Study of Theology.* 2nd ed. London: Longmans, Green, and Co., 1895.

Bell, Bernard Iddings. *Crowd Culture: An Examination of the American Way of Life.* New York: Harper & Brothers, 1952.

Belloc, Hilaire. *The Servile State.* London: Constable and Co., Ltd., 1912.

Borden, Morton, ed. *The Antifederalist Papers.* Lansing: Michigan State University Press, 1965.

Brownson, Orestes Augustus. *The American Republic: Its Constitution, Tendencies and Destiny.* Clifton, N.J.: Augustus M. Kelley, Publishers, 1972.

————. *Essays and Reviews: Chiefly on Theology, Politics, and Socialism.* New York: Arno Press, 1972.

Bryant, Arthur. *The Spirit of Conservatism.* London: Methuen & Co., Ltd., 1929.

Buchheim, Hans. *Totalitarian Rule: Its Nature and Characteristics.* Trans. Ruth Hein. Middletown, Conn.: Wesleyan University Press, 1968.

Buckley, William F., Jr., and L. Brent Bozell. *McCarthy and His Enemies: The Record and its Meaning.* Chicago: Henry Regnery Company, 1954.

Burke, Edmund. *The Works of the Right Honourable Edmund Burke.* 6 vols. London: George Bell & Sons, 1884-1892.

Calhoun, John C. *A Disquisition on Government and a Discourse on the Constitution and Government of the United States.* Columbia, S.C.: A. S. Johnston, 1851.

————. *A Disquisition on Government: and Selections from the Discourse.* Ed. C. Gordon Post. New York: The Liberal Arts Press, 1953.

Carlyle, Thomas. *Sartor Resartus.* Ed. Frederick William Roe. New York: The Macmillan Co., 1927.

Chamberlain, John. *The Roots of Capitalism.* Princeton, N.J.: D. Van Nostrand Company, 1959.

Chesterton, Gilbert K. *Heretics.* New York: John Lane Company, 1909.

————. *Orthodoxy.* New York: John Lane Company, 1909.

————. *The Outline of Sanity.* New York: Dodd, Mead & Company, 1927.

————. *The Uses of Diversity.* London: The Library Press Ltd., n.d. [1920].

Clarke, David. *The Conservative Faith in a Modern Age.* London: Conservative Political Centre, 1947.

Coleridge, Samuel Taylor. *The Collected Works of Samuel Taylor Coleridge: The Friend.* 2 vols. Ed. Barbara E. Rooke. Princeton: Princeton University Press, 1969.

————. *On the Constitution of the Church and State According to the Idea of Each.* London: William Pickering, 1839.

————. *The Philosophical Lectures of Samuel Taylor Coleridge.* Ed. Kathleen Coburn. London: Pilot Press, 1949.

————. *The Political Thought of Samuel Taylor Coleridge.* Ed. R. J. White. London: Jonathan Cape, 1938.

Cooper, James Fenimore. *The American Democrat.* New York: Alfred A. Knopf, 1931.

Dalberg-Acton, John Emerich Edward. *Essays on Church and State.* Ed. Douglas Woodruff. London: Hollis and Carter, 1952.

————. *Essays on Freedom and Power.* Ed. Gertrude Himmelfarb. Glencoe, Ill.: The Free Press, 1949.

Davidson, Donald. *The Attack on Leviathan: Regionalism and Nationalism in the United States.* Gloucester, Mass.: Peter Smith, 1962.

————. *Still Rebels, Still Yankees: and Other Essays.* Baton Rouge: Louisiana State University Press, 1957.

Disraeli, Benjamin. *Whigs and Whiggism: Political Writings.* Ed. William Hutcheon. Port Washington, N.Y.: Kennikat Press, 1971.

Edwards, Jonathan. *The Works of President Edwards.* 4 vols. 8th ed. New York: Leavitt and Company, 1851.

————. *Images or Shadows of Divine Things.* Ed. Perry Miller. New Haven: Yale University Press, 1948.

Emerson, Ralph Waldo. *The Complete Essays and Other Writings of Ralph Waldo Emerson.* Ed. Brooks Atkinson. New York: Modern Library, 1950.

Feiling, Keith. *What Is Conservatism?* London: Faber & Faber, 1930.

Figgis, John Neville. *Churches in the Modern State.* London: Longmans, Green and Co., 1913.

————. *Political Thought from Gerson to Grotius 1414-1625.* New York: Harper & Bros., 1960.

Fiske, John. *Essays Historical and Literary.* 2 vols. New York: The Macmillan Company, 1902.

————. *Outlines of Cosmic Philosophy: Based on the Doctrine of Evolution, with Criticisms on the Positive Philosophy.* 4 vols. Boston and New York: Houghton Mifflin Co., 1902.

————. *Through Nature to God.* Boston and New York: Houghton Mifflin Co., 1899.

Friedman, Milton. *Capitalism and Freedom.* Chicago: University of Chicago Press, 1962.

————, and Rose Friedman. *Free to Choose: A Personal Statement.* New York and London: Harcourt Brace Jovanovich, 1980.

Goldwin, Robert, ed. *A Nation of States: Essays on the American Federal System.* Chicago: Rand McNally, 1963.

Hamilton, Alexander, John Jay, and James Madison. *The Federalist: A Commentary on The Constitution of the United States.* New York: The Modern Library, n.d.

Harris, George. *Inequality and Progress.* New York: Arno Press, 1972.

Hayek, F. A. *The Constitution of Liberty.* Chicago: The University of Chicago Press, 1960.

Hearnshaw, F.J.C. *Conservatism in England: An Analytical, Historical, and Political Survey.* London: Macmillan, 1933.

Hegel, Georg Wilhelm Friedrich. *The Philosophy of History.* Trans. J. Sibree. New York: Dover Productions, Inc., 1956.

Hooker, Richard. *Of the Laws of Ecclesiastical Polity.* 2 vols. London: J. M. Dent & Sons Ltd., 1954.

Hunold, Albert, ed. *Freedom and Serfdom: An Anthology of Western Thought.* Dordrecht, Holland: D. Reidel Publishing Co., 1961.

James, Henry. *The American Scene.* Ed. Leon Edel. Bloomington: Indiana University Press, 1968.

James, William. *The Meaning of Truth: A Sequel to 'Pragmatism.'* New York: Longmans, Green, and Co., 1914.

———. *A Pluralistic Universe.* New York: Longmans, Green, and Co., 1958.

———. *Talks to Teachers on Psychology: and to Students on Some of Life's Ideals.* London: Longmans, Green, and Co., 1908.

———. *The Will to Believe and Other Essays in Popular Philosophy.* Cambridge, Mass.: Longmans, Green, and Co., 1905.

Jewkes, John. *Ordeal by Planning.* London: Macmillan & Co., 1948.

Kilpatrick, James Jackson. *The Sovereign States: Notes of a Citizen of Virginia.* Chicago: Henry Regnery Company, 1957.

Kirk, Russell. *Enemies of the Permanent Things: Observations of Abnormity in Literature and Politics.* New Rochelle, N.Y.: Arlington House, 1969.

Kuehnelt-Leddihn, Erik von. *Leftism: From de Sade and Marx to Hitler and Marcuse.* New Rochelle, N.Y.: Arlington House, 1974.

Lecky, William Edward Hartpole. *Democracy and Liberty.* 2 vols. New York: Longmans, Green, and Co., 1899.

Leibniz, G. W. *Theodicy: Essays on the Goodness of God the Freedom of Man and the Origin of Evil.* London: Routledge & Kegan Paul, Ltd., 1951.

Lieber, Francis. *The Miscellaneous Writings of Francis Lieber.* 2 vols. Philadelphia and London: J. B. Lippincott Company, 1880.

———. *On Civil Liberty and Self-Government.* Philadelphia: J. B. Lippincott and Co., 1859.

Maine, Sir Henry Sumner. *Popular Government: Four Essays.* New York: Henry Holt and Company, 1886.

Maistre, Joseph de. *The Works of Joseph de Maistre.* Ed. Jack Lively. New York: Macmillan, 1965.

Meyer, Frank S. *The Conservative Mainstream.* New Rochelle, N.Y.: Arlington House, 1969.

———, ed. *What Is Conservatism?* New York: Holt, Rinehart and Winston, 1964.

Mill, John Stuart. *On Liberty.* New York: Appleton-Century-Crofts, Inc., 1947.

More, Paul Elmer. *The Drift of Romanticism.* Boston and New York: Houghton Mifflin Co., 1913.

Morley, Felix. *Freedom and Federalism.* Chicago: Henry Regnery Co., 1959.

Mumford, Lewis. *The Myth of the Machine: The Pentagon of Power.* New York: Harcourt Brace Jovanovich, Inc., 1970.

Nisbet, Robert A. *The Quest for Community: A Study in the Ethics of*

Order and Freedom. New York: Oxford University Press, 1953.

——. *Twilight of Authority.* New York: Oxford University Press, 1975.

Nozick, Robert. *Anarchy, State, and Utopia.* New York: Basic Books, 1974.

Oakeshott, Michael. *On Human Conduct.* Oxford: Clarendon Press, 1975.

——. *Rationalism in Politics: and Other Essays.* New York: Basic Books, 1962.

Ortega y Gasset, José. *The Revolt of the Masses.* New York: W. W. Norton & Co., 1932.

Peacock, Thomas Love. *Crotchet Castle.* New York: AMS Press, 1967.

Ransom, John Crowe. *God Without Thunder: an Unorthodox Defense of Orthodoxy.* Hamden, Conn.: Archon Books, 1965.

Rawls, John. *A Theory of Justice.* Cambridge: Harvard University Press, 1971.

Ray, John. *The Wisdom of God Manifested in the Works of the Creation.* London: Samuel Smith, 1691.

Riesman, David. *Individualism Reconsidered and Other Essays.* Glencoe, Ill.: The Free Press, 1954.

——, with Nathan Glazer and Reuel Denney. *The Lonely Crowd: A Study of the Changing American Character.* New Haven and London: Yale University Press, 1969.

Röpke, Wilhelm. *A Humane Economy: The Social Framework of the Free Market.* Trans. Elizabeth Henderson. Chicago: Henry Regnery Co., 1960.

Royce, Josiah. *The Philosophy of Loyalty.* New York: Macmillan Co., 1908.

——. *The Problem of Christianity.* Chicago: University of Chicago Press, 1968.

——. *Race Questions, Provincialism, and Other American Problems.* New York: Macmillan Co., 1908.

Saint-John, Henry, 1st Viscount Bolingbroke. *Historical Writings.* Ed. Isaac Kramnick. Chicago: University of Chicago Press, 1972.

Schuettinger, Robert Lindsay, ed. *The Conservative Tradition in European Thought.* New York: G. P. Putnam's Sons, 1970.

Scott, Walter. *The Letters of Sir Walter Scott.* Ed. H.J.C. Grierson. New York: AMS Press, 1971.

Stephen, James Fitzjames. *Liberty, Equality, Fraternity.* Ed. R. J. White. Cambridge: University Press, 1967.

Taylor, John. *An Inquiry into the Principles and Policy of the Government of the United States.* Ed. Loren Baritz. Indianapolis and New York: Bobbs-Merrill, 1969.

Tocqueville, Alexis de. *Democracy in America.* 2 vols. Ed. Phillips Bradley. New York: Vintage Books, 1959.

——. *The Old Regime and the French Revolution*. Trans. Stuart Gilbert. New York: Doubleday, 1955.

Twelve Southerners. *I'll Take My Stand: The South and the Agrarian Tradition*. New York: Harper & Row, 1962.

Valentine, Alan. *The Age of Conformity*. Chicago: Henry Regnery Company, 1954.

Viereck, Peter. *The Unadjusted Man: A New Hero for Americans*. New York: Capricorn Books: 1962.

Voegelin, Eric. *Order and History*. 6 vols. Baton Rouge: Louisiana State University Press, 1956.

Weaver, Richard M. *Ideas Have Consequences*. Chicago: University of Chicago Press, 1962.

——. *Life Without Prejudice and Other Essays*. Chicago: Henry Regnery Company, 1965.

——. *The Southern Tradition at Bay: A History of Postbellum Thought*. New Rochelle, N.Y.: Arlington House, 1968.

White, Reginald J., ed. *The Conservative Tradition*. New York: New York University Press, 1957.

Whyte, William H. *The Organization Man*. Garden City, N.Y.: Doubleday, 1956.

Wordsworth, William. *The Prose Works of William Wordsworth*. 3 vols. Ed. Alexander B. Grosard. London: Edward Moxon, Son, and Co., 1876.

SECONDARY SOURCES

Brinton, Crane. *The Political Ideas of the English Romanticists*. Ann Arbor: University of Michigan Press, 1966.

Brown, Bernard Edward. *American Conservatives: The Political Thought of Francis Lieber and John W. Burgess*. New York: AMS Press, 1967.

Brown, David. *Walter Scott and the Historical Imagination*. London, Boston, and Henley: Routledge & Kegan Paul, 1979.

Burtt, Edwin Arthur. *The Metaphysical Foundations of Modern Physical Science*. Revised ed. Garden City, N.Y.: Doubleday & Co., 1954.

Cobban, Alfred. *Edmund Burke and the Revolt Against the Eighteenth Century: A Study of the Political and Social Thinking of Burke, Wordsworth, Coleridge and Southey*. London: George Allen & Unwin, Ltd., 1960.

Courtney, C. P. *Montesquieu and Burke*. Oxford: Basil Blackwell, 1963.

Engell, James. *The Creative Imagination: Enlightenment to Romanticism*. Cambridge: Harvard University Press, 1981.

Friedman, Michael H. *The Making of a Tory Humanist: William Words-worth and the Idea of Community.* New York: Columbia University Press, 1979.

Harris, Ronald W. *Romanticism and the Social Order, 1780-1830.* London: Blandford Press, 1969.

Himmelfarb, Gertrude. *On Liberty and Liberalism: The Case of John Stuart Mill.* New York: Alfred A. Knopf, 1974.

Kirk, Russell. *The Conservative Mind: From Burke to Eliot.* Revised ed. Chicago: Henry Regnery, 1960.

Koyré, Alexandre. *From the Closed World to the Infinite Universe.* Baltimore: The Johns Hopkins Press, 1957.

Lovejoy, Arthur O. *The Great Chain of Being: A Study of the History of an Idea.* New York: Harper & Row, 1960.

Marshall, Hugh. *Orestes Brownson and the American Republic: An Historical Perspective.* Washington, D.C.: The Catholic University of America Press, 1971.

Nash, George H. *The Conservative Intellectual Movement in America: Since 1945.* New York: Basic Books, 1976.

Nicolson, Marjorie Hope. *Mountain Gloom and Mountain Glory: The Development of the Aesthetics of the Infinite.* Ithaca: Cornell University Press, 1959.

———. *Newton Demands the Muse: Newton's Opticks and the Eighteenth Century Poets.* Princeton: Princeton University Press, 1946.

———. *Science and Imagination.* Ithaca: Cornell University Press, 1962.

Palmer, R. R. *The Age of the Democratic Revolution: A Political History of Europe and America, 1760-1800.* 2 vols. Princeton: Princeton University Press, 1959.

Perry, Ralph Barton. *The Thought and Character of William James.* 2 vols. Boston: Little, Brown, and Company, 1935.

Pocock, J.G.A. *The Ancient Constitution and the Feudal Law: A Study of English Historical Thought in the Seventeenth Century.* New York: Norton, 1967.

Robbins, Caroline. *The Eighteenth-Century Commonwealthman: Studies in the Transmission, Development and Circumstance of English Liberal Thought from the Restoration of Charles II until the War with the Thirteen Colonies.* Cambridge: Harvard University Press, 1961.

Schenk, H. G. *The Mind of the European Romantics: an Essay in Cultural History.* London: Constable, 1966.

Strauss, Leo. *Natural Right and History.* Chicago: The University of Chicago Press, 1953.

Talmon, J. L. *The Origins of Totalitarian Democracy.* New York: W. W. Norton & Co., 1970.

Turner, Frank Miller. *Between Science and Religion: The Reaction to Scientific Naturalism in Late Victorian England.* New Haven: Yale University Press, 1974.

Willey, Basil. *The Eighteenth Century Background: Studies on the Idea of Nature in the Thought of the Period.* New York: Columbia University Press, 1940.

Woodring, Carl. *Politics in English Romantic Poetry.* Cambridge: Harvard University Press, 1970.

Index

Acton, Lord, 16, 22, 94–97, 121, 134
Adams, Brooks, 58, 146–47, 166
Adams, Henry, 4, 7, 63, 135, 141–42, 166, 213; as "Conservative Christian Anarchist," 146, 150, 159; on democracy, 92, 160; on the Middle Ages, 38, 75, 148–50; scientific determinism of, 147, 149–50; and William James, 147–49, 156–57
Adams, John, 28, 104, 111–12
Adams, John Quincy, 146
Agrarians, Southern, 126–32, 134–35; *I'll Take My Stand*, 126–27, 129
Antifederalists, 114–15
Aquinas, Thomas, 69
Ariès, Philippe, 43
Aristotle, 69, 160; "Aristotelian Principle," 200–201. *See also* Science, Aristotelian
Arnold, Matthew, 90
Astor, John Jacob, 105
Atlee, Clement, 100
Auerbach, W. Morton, 214 n. 4
Augustine, Saint, 24

Babbitt, Irving, 79–80, 186
Bacon, Francis, 70
Balfour, Arthur, 98–100
Bancroft, George, 22, 92, 147, 195
Bannister, Robert C., 142
Becker, Carl, 55–56
Bell, Bernard Iddings, 172
Belloc, Hilaire, 168
Bentham, Jeremy, 179
Blake, William, 70
Bodin, Jean, 178
Bolingbroke, Lord, 44–45
Boucher, Jonathan, 166
Bozell, L. Brent, 171
Bradford, M. E., 134–35, 187
Brinton, Crane, 76
Brown, Norman O., 189
Brownson, Orestes, 119–21, 195
Bruno, Giordano, 67
Bryant, Arthur, 99
Buchheim, Hans, 181–82
Buckley, William F., Jr., 171, 177
Burke, Edmund, 15, 44–49, 52, 64, 70, 104, 161; on the British constitution, 40, 45–46, 49, 85–86, 93; on chivalry, 56; compared to John Adams, 111; conservative

tradition of, 15, 64, 95, 182, 185–86, 198, 203, 205; and Disraeli, 92; on the French Revolution, 3, 7, 47, 49, 67, 162; as historicist, 80–81; influence of on American conservatives, 119–20, 173, 185–86; influence of legal tradition on, 66–67; and John Rawls, 200–201; on man as corporate being, 85, 144; and Romanticism, 45, 48, 72, 75–76; and social hierarchy, 47–48

Burtt, E. A., 68

Calhoun, John C., 97, 104, 110, 115–17, 124 nn. 13–16; concurrent majority theory of, 115–17; influence on Orestes Brownson, 120

Calvinism, 22, 26, 48, 90

Carey, George W., 114

Carlyle, Thomas, 70

Carnegie, Andrew, 186

Cartesianism. *See* Descartes, René

Cash, Wilbur J., 126

Catholicism: in thought of Orestes Brownson, 119–21; in U.S., 105; and use of opposites, 54

Chamberlain, John, 189–90

Charles X (king of France), 186

Chesterton, G. K., 14, 39, 42–43, 98, 168; on adventure, 42–43, 54–56; in Brownson's politics, 121; and centralization, 96; on chivalry, 58; on Christianity, 7, 12, 21–34; for Coleridge, 76; and courage, 58; on entertainment, 146; on the family, 42–43, 197; on farming, 128; in Hegelian idealism, 73; and individuality, 64; in Josiah Royce, 24, 151; on mysticism, 57; in Nazi Germany, 182; and science, 69; on scien-

tific materialism, 53–54, 57; sense of human possibilities in, 52–55; and Social Darwinism, 142; on the Trinity, 14, 23–24; on value of limitation, 42, 54–55, 59 n. 3; on value of orthodoxy, 54–56, 58, 206, 213; in Voeglin's philosophy, 185

Christian Scientists, 105

Churchill, Winston, 99

Civil War, U.S., 91, 96, 110, 117, 121; Frank Owsley on, 126–27; influence on Orestes Brownson, 120

Clarke, Arthur C., 209–10

Clarke, David, 99–100

Clinton, George, 114

Coke, Sir Edward, 66

Cold War, 171, 174, 177

Coleridge, Samuel Taylor, 49, 70, 72, 76–78, 160

Commonwealthmen, Whig, 66–67

Communism, 133, 168, 171, 182, 188

Conant, James B., 172

Constitution, U.S., 109, 122; ratification of, 113–15

Cooper, James Fenimore, 164

Corporate bodies. *See* Institutions

Darwin, Charles, 141. *See also* Evolution; Social Darwinism

Davidson, Donald, 130, 136 nn. 2, 9, 10

Davies, Sir John, 66

Degler, Carl N., 126

Descartes, René, 199; philosophy of, 69, 179

Dewey, John, 151, 154–55; followers of, 151, 172

Disraeli, Benjamin, 92–93

Drake, Robert Y., 137 n. 25

Durkheim, Emile, 5

Edwards, Jonathan, 26–27, 34–35 nn. 10–13
Eisenhower, Dwight D.: administration of, 171, 174
Emerson, Ralph Waldo, 72; Oversoul of, 23
Emmeric, Saint, 183
Enlightenment, 31, 56, 71, 110
Equality, 10–11, 34, 48, 99; and absolutism, 96; for J. F. Cooper, 164; of opportunity, 10, 14; opposed to variety, 10–11, 143–44; for Robert Nisbet, 180–81; for Tocqueville, 160–64; for Wilhelm Röpke, 190–91
Ethnicity, 104, 106
Evolution, 31, 72, 141–45. *See also* Social Darwinism
Existentialism, 52, 198

Federalist, The, 113–16
Feiling, Keith, 101
Field, Stephen J., 121
Figgis, John Neville, 65–66, 97–98
Fiske, John, 3, 63, 74, 141, 144–47, 149, 185
Fitzhugh, George, 115
Free Market: advocates of, 15, 189–92
French Revolution, 3, 7, 67, 92, 95, 97; centralizing effects of, 161–62, 179
Friedman, Milton, 190, 194 n. 36
Friedman, Rose, 194 n. 36
Fromm, Erich, 169

Galileo, 12, 68
Glasgow, Ellen, 41
Great Awakening, 106
Great Chain of Being, 12, 14, 27–32, 34, 42, 71, 199, 204

Hale, Sir Matthew, 66

Hamilton, Alexander, 113, 123 nn. 7–9
Harris, George, 143–44
Hay, John, 150
Hayek, F. A., 181, 190–92
Hayes, Carleton J. H., 73
Hayne, Robert Y., 132
Hearnshaw, F.J.C., 101, 103 n. 50
Hegel, Georg Wilhelm Friedrich, 73; idealism of, 73, 143, 156
Himmelfarb, Gertrude: on J. S. Mill, 87–88
Historicism, 65, 80–81; condemned by Nietzsche, 205; in Walter Scott, 76
Hitler, Adolf, 182–83
Hobbes, Thomas, 178
Holmes, Oliver Wendell, Jr., 54, 153, 165–66
Hooker, Richard, 24
Huizinga, Johan, 6, 13, 17 n. 6
Humboldt, Alexander von, 119
Humboldt, Wilhelm von, 14
Huxley, Aldous, 208

Individualism, 8–10, 64, 72, 86; American, 8, 167; in George Harris, 144; J. S. Mill on, 87–88; and liberal idea of diversity, 9, 87, 195–97
Institutions, 191; as corporate bodies, 101; intermediate, 161, 178–81

James, Henry, 166–67, 197
James, William, 11, 31–32, 81, 141, 145, 166, 213; and conservatism, 17, 150, 156–57; and Henry Adams, 147–49, 156–57; and Josiah Royce, 151–52; pluralism of, 150–57, 159; as pragmatist, 150–51, 154–55; relativism in, 155–56; and scientific determinism, 152–53; on Spencer, 153

Jaspers, Karl, 185
Jay, John, 113
Jefferson, Thomas, 74, 160
Jehovah's Witnesses, 105
Jesus Christ of Latter Day Saints, Church of, 105
Jewkes, John, 168-69

Kägi, Werner, 181
Kant, Immanuel, 119; influence of on Royce, 151
Kennedy, John F., 188
Kilpatrick, James Jackson, 122
Kirk, Russell, 7, 45, 132, 187-88, 190; *The Conservative Mind*, 177
Koyré, Alexandre, 69
Kuehnelt-Leddihn, Erik von, 182-83

Lecky, William, 93-94
Leibniz, Gottfried Wilhelm, 29-30
Lévi-Strauss, Claude, 210
Liberalism: and conformity, 171; and definition of diversity, 8-10, 87, 195-97; distinguished from conservatism, 15-16
Libertarianism, 14-16, 186, 188-89, 191-92, 195; opposed to John Rawls, 200-201; of Robert Nozick, 201-4
Lieber, Francis, 116-19, 121
Livingston, William, 29
Locke, John, 26, 70, 72, 83 n. 20; psychology of, 26
Lovejoy, Arthur O., 27-29, 31, 71, 79
Luther, Martin, 78
Lytle, Andrew Nelson, 128

McCarthy, Joseph R., 173-74; followers of, 171-72
McLuhan, Marshall, 189
Madison, James, 113-14
Maine, Sir Henry, 91

Maistre, Joseph de, 14, 32-33, 120
Maitland, F. W., 89
Marx, Karl, 179; Marxism, 72-73, 134
Meyer, Frank S., 186, 188-89
Middle Ages, 4, 38-39, 43, 56, 108; discovery of individual in, 64; hierarchical assumptions of, 53, 204; particularism in, 178; realist philosophy of, 131-32; in Romantic view, 74-75
Mill, John Stuart, 86-89, 195, 201
Monarchomachi, 66
Montesquieu, Baron de, 14, 18 n. 10
More, Paul Elmer, 79
Morley, Felix, 122
Mormons. *See* Jesus Christ of Latter-Day Saints, Church of
Mumford, Lewis, 198-99
Mussolini, Benito, 81

National Review, 177
National Socialism, 79, 182
Natural theology, 24-25
New Humanism, 79-80
New Left, 180
Newton, Isaac, 70, 78, 34-35 nn. 12, 13; science of, 26-27, 68, 70; theory of applied to government, 110
Nicholas of Cusa, 65
Nicolson, Marjorie, 68, 70
Nietzsche, Friedrich, 205
Nisbet, Robert A., 154, 178-81, 196; *Quest for Community*, 178-80, 193 nn. 4-7; *Twilight of Authority*, 180-81, 193 nn. 3, 7-11
Norton, Charles Eliot, 165
Nozick, Robert, 14, 201-4; criticizes John Rawls, 201-2

Oakeshott, Michael, 183-84

Ortega y Gasset, José, 169–70, 196
Orwell, George, 208
Owsley, Frank, 126–27

Paine, Thomas, 15–16, 52, 172
Paley, William, 25
Palmer, R. R., 161
Peacock, Thomas Love, 74–75
Peirce, Charles Sanders, 154
Perry, Ralph Barton, 154
Plato, 78–79, 178
Pocock, J.G.A., 66
Pope, Alexander, 28, 30
Potter, David, 116
Priestley, Joseph, 66–67

Ransom, John Crowe, 43, 128–29
Rawls, John, 199–202, 205
Ray, John, 25–27
Reagan, Ronald, 177
Reform Bill (1832), 101, 103 n. 50
Regionalism, 4, 10, 39, 41, 47–48,
    94; in Southern thought, 129–30,
    134–35; of U.S., 105, 107–10,
    115, 163
Renaissance, 59
Riesman, David, 169–71, 196–97
Ripley, Randall B., 111
Robbins, Caroline, 66
Rölvaag, O. E., 41
Romantic Movement, 4, 12, 65,
    70–82, 159; and American poli-
    tics, 110; and contemporary con-
    servatism, 213; influence of on
    Francis Lieber, 119
Röpke, Wilhelm, 181, 190–92
Roszak, Theodore, 198
Rothbard, Murray N., 189
Rousseau, Jean Jacques, 78, 80, 93,
    178
Royce, Josiah, 24, 151–52
Rüstow, Alexander, 181

Schuettinger, Robert, 15

Schumacher, E. F., 198
Science, 24–27, 205; Aristotelian,
    12, 68–69; and art, 136 n. 2; for
    H. and B. Adams, 146–47,
    149–50; for J. C. Ransom,
    128–29; materialistic, 53–57, 65,
    68–70, 142; and scientism, 81–82;
    seventeenth century "revolu-
    tion" of, 67–70
Scott, Sir Walter, 75–76, 78
Simpson, Richard, 98, 103 n. 40
Smith, Adam, 91, 192
Social Darwinism, 30, 141–47, 192
Spencer, Herbert, 53, 143, 153; and
    John Fiske, 3, 63, 74, 144–45,
    147, 149, 185
State rights, 91, 115, 122–23,
    125–26, 129, 135; in Brownson's
    thought, 120–21; Lieber's rejec-
    tion of, 117
Stephen, James Fitzjames, 88–89,
    195
Stephen, Leslie, 89–91
Stephen, Saint (king of Hungary),
    183
Stevenson, Adlai, 173
Strauss, Leo, 80–81
Sumner, William Graham, 142

Taft, Robert, 173
Talmon, J. L., 40, 161
Taylor, John, of Caroline, 112–13
Teilhard de Chardin, Pierre, 189
Tocqueville, Alexis de, 14, 16, 22,
    89, 97, 104–5, 109, 154; on Amer-
    ican democracy, 3, 32, 162–64;
    compared to Henry James, 167–
    68; on complexity of God's ways,
    32–33; on equality, 160–64; and
    Francis Lieber, 119; on Old Re-
    gime, 161–62
Totalitarianism, 49, 63, 79, 90, 159,
    186, 210; early fears of, 97; as
    future prospect, 208–9; opposed

to cultural diversity, 40, 181–83; and Utopianism, 199; in welfare society, 214 n. 3. *See also* Communism; National Socialism
Toynbee, Arnold, 185
Tradition, 8, 36–49; in America, 107–8; as conservator of diversity, 67, 180, 184, 186, 188; in modern life, 212; reconciled with libertarianism, 202–3; and sense of scale, 52; in thought of Hayek and Röpke, 190–91; traditional society, 4, 64–65, 106, 127, 132; traditionalists, 15–16, 192
Transcendentalists, 151, 209

Valentine, Alan, 172
Vanderbilt school. *See* Agrarians, Southern

Viereck, Peter, 172–73, 187
Voegelin, Eric, 184–85

Weaver, Richard, 131–35; on chivalry, 56
Webb, Sidney, 168
Webster, Daniel, 132
Wells, H. G., 168
Wendell, Barrett, 165
White, Reginald J., 23, 86
Whyte, William H., 169–71
Willey, Basil, 30
Williams, L. Pearce, 70
Woodward, C. Vann, 126
Wordsworth, William, 13, 70; sense of place in, 75

Young, Stark, 127

Zweig, Paul, 54

About the Author

MICHAEL D. CLARK is Professor of History at the University of New Orleans. He is the author of *Worldly Theologians: The Persistence of Religion in Nineteenth Century American Thought*, and has published articles in *Huntington Library Quarterly*, *Maryland Historical Magazine*, *Modern Age*, and *Midcontinent American Studies Journal*.